Code X128

The story of the M.G. sports car

'History would be an excellent thing if only it were true.'
Tolstoy

The story of
the M.G. sports car

by F. Wilson McComb

with 100 illustrations

J. M. Dent & Sons Ltd London

First published in Great Britain in 1972
© F. Wilson McComb 1972

Made in Great Britain at the Aldine Press · Letchworth · Herts
for
J. M. DENT & SONS LTD · Aldine House · Bedford Street · London
ISBN 0 460 03982 2

Contents

List of Illustrations

Plates 9 and 57 are reproduced by permission of *Motor*; plate 69, Central Press Photos Ltd; plate 77, by permission of Tony Bugbird.

Introduction

To the more sober-minded beings of this world the motor-car is merely a means of transport, and if votive offerings of fog-lamps, wing-mirrors or seat-covers are occasionally laid before it, such worship is essentially undiscriminating. The notion that any particular car should arouse lifelong devotion is dismissed as absurd. Yet it is so, and many an otherwise normal individual is thus afflicted.

Sometimes it is one model that inspires such an emotion; less frequently it is the marque itself that is revered, suggesting a personality so distinctive that it may be recognized to varying degree in all the products of that manufacturer. Two classic examples of this are, of course, Bugatti and Rolls-Royce. But it is one of the more abiding mysteries of automobilism that the M.G., an inexpensive sports car built in quantity for such *hoi polloi* as us, also lays claim to this select category. The present general manager of the M.G. factory, Les Lambourne, recalls an American TD owner who arrived at Abingdon one day in the early 'fifties and asked to be shown around: 'I reckoned I ought to see the place while I'm here,' he remarked. 'You're staying in this part of England?' asked Les. 'Nope. I just flew over from Geneva.' The M.G. charisma is no illusion. The management of BMC may have been delighted when they discovered that they could charge more for an Austin-Healey Sprite if it were disguised as an M.G. Midget, but I cannot believe that they understood the full flavour of the jest—that the higher price was gladly paid by many who *knew* the two cars were identical, as a sort of defiant gesture of loyalty to the marque.

This book is an attempt to solve the mystery by presenting the M.G. story as comprehensively as possible without surfeit, and as accurately as the vagaries of history will allow. I have tried to provide a balanced assessment of the impact that the marque has made in the widest sense: commercially, on the design of sports cars in general, and in the field of motor sport. I do feel that, in the past, many published comments on M.G.s have either displayed a contempt for such cars matched only by the writer's total ignorance of the subject, or revealed an intensity of adoration that permitted no criticism whatsoever.

Neither attitude encourages sweet reason, and the fanatical M.G. enthusiast damages the reputation of the marque quite as much as those whose scorn is ill-founded. On the one hand I know of several M.G. models that have been successively condemned on their announcement as a slur on a famous name, accepted as quite a good motor-car, and tearfully recalled as the very last of the 'real M.G.s'—which is really rather absurd. On the other, I can remember a Porsche owner who subjected me to an astonishingly bitter attack on Abingdon and all its works because he noticed that I drove an M.G.—and as I had offered no comment on either car, it was difficult to understand what all the heavy breathing was about. Perhaps it is a back-handed compliment to the marque that it has so often been compared unfavourably with others costing twice as much.

The reader is entitled to query my impartiality. Certainly I have always been unashamedly a sports car enthusiast, but there has been no lifelong adherence to the Octagon, and it was only childish curiosity that led me—many years ago—to ask my grandfather's chauffeur the meaning of the famous initials ('They stand for Maurice Gordon, the designer,' he replied, and I accepted that piece of misinformation without question). Later I did own several M.G.s which, being old and in appalling condition, gave extremely bad service, and I carried no particular torch for the marque when eventually I joined the M.G. Car Company; this after some fifteen years of motoring and ten of motoring journalism, which itself discourages one-make enthusiasm. At Abingdon, however, I could not help but admire the men who built M.G.s, for they so clearly believed in what they were doing, and 'Safety Fast' took on a new significance for me when I saw that it was not just a publicity slogan; it was a watchword.

Reference is occasionally made in this book to the 'Abingdon atmosphere'. This may puzzle readers who have not experienced it at first hand—and perhaps may never do so, since in the opinion of many it no longer exists. I find it tantalizingly difficult to convey, although it was so tangible, for it combined the spirit of the men themselves with a host of inanimate things: Cecil Kimber's favourite cream-and-brown paintwork that lingered on in odd corners, shabby and chipped, twenty years after he had gone; the octagonal napkin-rings on the long table at which we lunched, seated between two portraits only—one of Kimber, one of Lord

Nuffield; the motor-racing pictures that could be found on the walls of almost every foreman's office, or some souvenir of Brooklands days. I count myself fortunate to have lived in that atmosphere for ten years, and if the experience has occasionally clouded my judgment a little, so be it. I cannot write of my former colleagues without affection.

In almost half-a-century there have been many M.G.s, some of them remarkably good cars, some of them really rather bad. The vast majority of models have been honest in design and execution. They have offered the buyer, *for his money*, a slice of motoring pleasure that was at least equal to that provided by any other sports car manufacturer, and often much more generous. From time to time there have been flashes of technical brilliance out of all proportion to the size and resources of such a small organization. At one period, M.G.s successfully upheld British prestige in racing when other more illustrious names had gone to the wall. Subsequently (and this is no less praiseworthy, though often overlooked by the sporting enthusiast) they opened up a whole new sports car market overseas to earn sorely needed foreign currency for this country—and having done so, maintained that export drive over the years. I think it shameful that so few people know, since it has never been publicized, that almost half-a-million M.G.s have been exported since the last war.

It is, I believe, a story of achievement that should not be ignored. I only hope my telling of it has preserved the balance that has been my aim, so that the reader may judge for himself whether M.G. is a marque that deserves our respect.

Abingdon-on-Thames, 1971   *F. W. McC.*

Chapter 1

Cecil Kimber (1888–1945)

A study of the M.G. sports car must inevitably begin with that of its creator, Cecil Kimber. 'It is impossible in the minds of those who had known him . . . to dissociate the man and the car. . . . He had been closely identified with the car . . . to a degree shared by few others in a comparable position.' Thus wrote H. S. Linfield in his *Autocar* obituary notice.

Moreover, Kimber's personality was so forceful that its influence persists to this day: on his family (it came as no surprise that his younger daughter had named her first child 'Kim'); on those who worked with him (more than a quarter of a century later they still speak of him with mingled respect and affection); and even on young M.G. enthusiasts who were born long after his death.

Yet the very clarity with which he is remembered makes it the more difficult to understand the complicated picture that emerges. Harold Hastings, former Midlands Editor of *Motor*, who knew him for many years, says:

'You are quite right in thinking that he had a very complex personality. In some ways he was quite ruthless and uncompromising, but in others there was a very kindly streak. Above all, he had an enormous enthusiasm, and this, I think, produced the uncompromising ruthlessness which could make him a distinctly prickly personality at times.

'There is no doubt that he was an idealist. . . . What part he could have played in the post-war motoring world . . . is difficult to foresee, as his idealism would have become steadily more out of keeping with the hard commercialism of recent years. Of one thing I am quite sure, however, and that is that he would have battled on to keep the M.G. an exclusive enthusiast's car.'

Cecil Kimber's ancestors left him a family crest, a motto ill-suited to the prevarications of a modern world (*Frangas non flectes—* Break but not bend), and no money at all. In the light of subsequent events it is an intriguing coincidence that the Kimber family lived for many years in North Berkshire; it has been traced back to the early seventeenth century, when one Richard Kimber lived only a few miles from Abingdon-on-Thames.

Cecil Kimber (1888–1945)

Richard Kimber left the ancestral home during the Civil War to serve under Cromwell as an officer of horse. His grandson, Isaac, preferred the pen to the sword; he wrote a biography of Cromwell, and edited the *London Magazine* from 1732 to 1755. Isaac's second son, Edward, followed a similar career and anticipated *Debrett* by half-a-century with his Baronetage and Peerage. But Edward's son, Richard, turned to the mechanics of the trade by working as a journeyman compositor, and one of the next generation became foreman printer of the *New York Herald* after emigrating to America.

So an association with the printed word had become a tradition in the family. Moving forward a further two generations into the early nineteenth century, we find another Edward Kimber working for W. H. Smith, the London bookseller—as, oddly enough, Henry Royce was to do some forty years later. But whereas Royce was a mere newspaper boy, Cecil Kimber's grandfather started as a clerk and built up a substantial business after his marriage to Sarah Ann Hughes. The firm of Hughes and Kimber became one of the largest suppliers of material and equipment to printers, lithographers and engravers. Edward Kimber is said to have introduced steam-operated lithographic printing machinery into Britain and the U.S.A.; certainly he enjoyed sole selling rights in China, which helped him to amass a considerable fortune.

Kimber's grandfather was also an erudite man, who became a Fellow of the Royal Geographical Society and was awarded an honorary doctorate by Rostock University in Mecklenburg-Schwerin (now a part of the German Democratic Republic). From his two marriages he fathered ten children, the seventh of whom, Henry Francis Kimber, was educated at Dulwich College, London, and Heidelberg University.

Next on the scene comes the romantic figure of Frances Newhouse Matthewman from Brook Hall, Derbyshire. Fanny Matthewman studied art in London—a bold venture, one feels, for a well-bred young lady in Victorian England—and fell for a novelist named Morley Roberts. The family thought this a highly unsuitable match; much better that she should marry a rich manufacturer of printing equipment in the shape of H. F. Kimber. Fanny did as she was told, and in due course there were three children: Cecil, born on 12th April 1888 at Dulwich; Phyllis, born in 1890 at Merton; and Vernon, born in 1894 at Streatham.

The financial decline of 'H.F.' seems to date from his move to

Lancashire about 1896 to open up a printing-ink business with one of his brothers. He had to leave £10,000 behind in the family business, which eventually failed, and although the Lancashire offshoot lingered on for many years, it never really prospered. Consequently there appears to have been no suggestion of university for his two sons. It was printing-ink for young Cecil when he left Stockport Grammar School; and, a few years later, for Vernon also.

A distinct mechanical aptitude was evinced by the teen-age Cecil when he bought (for £18) his first motor-cycle, a secondhand 1906 3⅜ h.p. Rex, which he had completely dismantled within three weeks of its purchase. This was followed by a 5–7 h.p. Rex twin, and many experiments to make this faster machine even more rapid. There is no evidence that Cecil raced his motorcycles, or even competed in hillclimbs until years later, but his brother recalls an illicit dawn duel on a public road. Cecil's opponent owned a new 1910 Triumph, but the older Rex machine won easily.

Kimber was not racing, or even riding particularly fast, when he was hit by a car shortly afterwards at a crossroads between Grappenhall and Lymm. The machine, yet another Rex borrowed from his brother-in-law, was wrecked completely. Kimber's injuries included a broken knee-cap and a badly smashed right thigh. For the next couple of years he was on crutches, a regular visitor at the Manchester Royal Infirmary, where the thigh-bone was at first 'plated' but did not mend. In a second operation the bone was cut back and bound with wire, again unsuccessfully, after which came a third operation to remove the wire binding. At this stage the surgeons despaired of making good the damage, and decided to amputate the entire right leg. This was to be done three weeks later.

But a final X-ray revealed that the bone had at last begun to set. If the leg was now some two inches shorter, leaving Kimber with a limp for the rest of his life, at least he still had two legs— and could drive a car.

The other party involved in the accident, a local stockbroker, was held responsible, so Kimber was awarded reasonably substantial damages: some say £700, some £1000. With a small part of this, £185, he bought a Singer 10. The 1912 Singer was one of the first successful 'baby cars', almost as significant in its day as the Mini of fifty years later. Kimber's, delivered in February 1913, was the first to be seen in the streets of Manchester and greatly amused the Mancunians. But by August 1914 he had covered over 17,000 miles, using the little Singer two-thirds for pleasure and one-third for business (he was now being paid £1 a week to sell printing-ink for his father's firm). A remarkable enthusiasm for detailed cost analysis is revealed in an article he wrote that year for *The Light Car and Cyclecar*, in which running expenses are calculated to three decimal places of a penny. This may well have been Kimber's first attempt at motoring journalism; it was certainly not his last.

Nor had he lost his taste for speed, despite the prevalence of police traps in Edwardian England. Somehow he acquired for the Singer an Irish registration number, NI.91. This must have caused grave embarrassment to the Manchester motorist who held N.191. History does not record how many summonses were successfully diverted in this way.

In 1914 Kimber was in his mid-twenties, but clearly unfit for military service because of his injured thigh. His mother had died of cancer three years earlier, his sister had married, his younger brother went off to the war, and Cecil's relations with his father began to deteriorate. The business was going downhill, and 'H.F.' asked his son to contribute the remainder of the compensation money. So far from agreeing, Cecil wanted an increase in salary in order to get married. Furious, his father refused to have anything more to do with him. He never spoke to his eldest son again, not even on his death-bed, although Cecil made many attempts to heal the breach.

By this time Kimber had somehow attracted the attention of A. W. Reeves, the well-known designer of the Crossley car, which was built in Manchester. Crossleys found great favour with the Royal Family and became famous as R.F.C. staff cars during the war, but since another of the company's directors was Charles Jarrott, the pioneer racing driver, it is not surprising that they were frequently seen in races and hillclimbs, too. There is no evidence that Kimber actually worked for Crossley, but his association with Reeves fostered a growing conviction that the motor industry might offer him a promising career.

In this he was fortunately supported by his fiancée, Irene (known as Rene) Hunt, of Ladybarn, on the southern outskirts of Manchester. So at the comparatively late age of twenty-seven Cecil Kimber took up his new occupation, moving to Yorkshire to join Sheffield-Simplex. This was one of the older and more respected companies in the industry, and the Sheffield-Simplex of that period was a well-appointed 30 h.p. luxury car of considerable refinement.

Rene and Cecil were married on 4th September 1915. If she did not already know, the unfortunate bride had a foretaste of life with a motoring enthusiast when she beheld his choice of honeymoon transport. It was a fierce-looking T-head sporting Singer 14, formerly raced at Brooklands and now fitted with a stark Hispano-Suiza body. With no doors, no headlamps, little tread on the rock-hard tyres, scarcely any weather protection and bristling with levers, it must have been the acme of discomfort for a touring holiday. Kimber's honeymoon car naturally bore that useful registration number, NI.91. Afterwards the young couple set up house at Norton Woodseats, near Sheffield.

About this time Kimber was joint author of a paper on works organization. One wonders where he had acquired such experience at this stage of his career, but perhaps his innate self-assurance overcame any shortcomings on that score. As a child he had never hesitated to lord it over his younger brother and sister, and Vernon Kimber remembers an occasion when, exasperated beyond endurance, they took their revenge by giving him chocolate creams filled with soot, pepper and other non-standard ingredients.

It seems that throughout his life Kimber found it difficult to accept a subservient role. In later years he told his daughters that he had once resigned on the spot because his employers showed little enthusiasm for an innovation he had put forward. This may have happened at Sheffield-Simplex, for by 1916 he had moved to Thames Ditton, in Surrey, to work for A.C. Cars. He was their buyer, and Rene acted as his secretary. A.C. had by that time designed their first four-wheeler, with 1100 c.c. engine and gear-box in the back axle—not unlike Kimber's Singer 10 of a few years before. But he missed the great days of the company's racing and record-breaking activities under S. F. Edge, for in 1918 he made another move—this time to E. G. Wrigley Ltd of Birmingham.

Wrigley's were suppliers of steering gear, transmission assemblies and axles to many manufacturers in their day, and had produced several components for the original pre-war Morris. There are conflicting accounts of the work that Kimber did for them; one has it that he was a draughtsman, another that he was a works organizer. While there he became involved in the not very successful project to build a mass-produced car known as the Angus Sanderson, Wrigley's having gambled fairly heavily on it by accepting the contract for gearbox manufacture (the engines, perhaps regrettably, were made by a company better known for its lavatory cisterns). Cecil Kimber designed the quite shapely radiator. Later he made brief mention to his family of an enterprise in which he had lost all his savings. This suggests that he may have been unlucky enough to invest some of his own money in the Angus Sanderson. It has also been stated that Kimber contributed to the design of the original Aston Martin, for which Wrigley's were again making the gearbox.

Reeves, the Crossley designer, was in Birmingham by this time, working for Enfield-Allday, and Kimber arranged for his young brother to be given a trial there when he left the army. Two other employees were Renwick and Bertelli, who subsequently left to build a car of their own, the 'R and B', which was essentially an Enfield-Allday. When Aston Martin went bankrupt in 1925 the 'R and B' was adopted as the basis of the next Aston Martin; Bertelli remained with the company, but Renwick eventually joined the M.G. design team. This inter-relation of personalities and companies is typical of the post-war motor industry; so many of them took in each other's washing.

But it was an uncertain period for the industry, and things began to look black for several promising concerns as the post-war boom started to collapse towards the end of 1920. Wrigley's were among those who suffered. Unfortunately they were no longer suppliers of major components to Morris Motors Ltd, who turned the ill wind into a good one by a series of dramatic price cuts which brought a dramatic increase in sales.

William Richard Morris owned two businesses at this time, each quite separate from the other. He had started by making bicycles in the late eighteen-nineties, then turned to motorcycles. In 1908 he had sold his motorcycle rights to a friend, Edward Armstead, but retained some old stables in Longwall Street, Oxford, which he had rebuilt and opened as The Morris Garage in 1911. With the acquisition of additional premises this concern became known as The Morris Garages in 1913.

Simultaneously, however, he had embarked on building cars of his own design in the Oxford suburb of Cowley with a company called W. R. M. Motors Ltd (renamed Morris Motors Ltd in 1919). His attention mainly engrossed by this, he left the Morris Garages in the hands of a general manager, a position taken up by Edward Armstead in March 1919.

So on the one hand Morris controlled a motor manufacturing company of rapidly growing reputation, and on the other he had a group of retail garages which was no less successful in its own way. And Cecil Kimber had the good fortune to be appointed sales manager of the Morris Garages in 1921, when his current employers, Wrigley's, were within a year or two of bankruptcy. Then came a curious twist of fate. In March 1922 Armstead suddenly resigned as general manager, and gassed himself a few weeks later; almost unheard-of in a suicide case, he left no letter, no explanation at all. Kimber, just turned thirty-four, was given the job of general manager, and it goes without saying that he seized the opportunity with both hands.

Not content with the considerable task of administering the day-to-day business of the Morris Garages, Kimber started to design special bodywork which could be fitted to the standard chassis produced by Morris Motors. He moved from a rented cottage at Clifton Hampden to a small Georgian house in Banbury Road, Oxford. Here his sister-in-law, Kathie Stevenson, paid the Kimbers a visit in 1923, and she remembers how absorbed Cecil and Rene were in sketching car bodies and discussing every aspect of their shape. When the cars were built, Rene would often model for the photographs used in Morris Garages advertisements.

Before long the Kimbers moved again to a new semi-detached house at 339 Woodstock Road. And here they were often visited by H. N. Charles, a very gifted engineer who worked for Morris Motors. Hubert Charles, then unmarried, had little hope of escaping the Kimber charm, and soon found his evenings and weekends taken up with design work on the new cars. He, too, recalls the important part played by Mrs Kimber: 'Kimber and Irene together amounted to far more than any one person ever could. She was a most cultured, charming, wonderful person.'

The special cars marketed by Morris Garages under Cecil Kimber's direction met with such acclaim that he now found himself approaching a major turning-point in his career. He was managing 'the Garages' extremely well, but he had turned the prosaic Morris Oxford into a car so different in personality that it could be sold at a price one-third higher than its Morris counterpart, and in such quantity that in 1927 a separate factory was built to produce it.

Early the following year the M.G. Car Company officially came into existence. Much of Kimber's time was now spent trying to be in two places at once. Clearly he had to choose between the two, sooner or later. M.G. activities continued to expand until three different chassis were being produced, with a wide range of bodywork.

This was a remarkable achievement by a fledgling organization that had scarcely existed only five years before. Without the backing of W. R. Morris, Kimber obviously could not have done it, but it would be a grave error to see Morris as a fairy godmother who handed out funds without hesitation. His public benefactions might be the talk of all England, but his business managers got nothing unless they presented a sound case for every new project.

Morris Garages, or M.G.? For a man of Kimber's temperament the choice was obvious. One offered security in an old-established business; the other, total commitment in a new and exciting venture that would be practically under his sole direction. When the M.G. Car Company was transferred to Abingdon-on-Thames in September 1929, Cecil Kimber resigned as general manager of the Morris Garages Ltd. He had decided to back his faith in the future of M.G. Not until 21st July 1930, however, was the new organization registered as the M.G. Car Company Ltd. The governing director was Sir William Morris, Bart. (as he had then become), and Kimber was named as managing director.

The move to Abingdon coincided with the beginning of another depression which could well have brought the new company to a premature end, as it did so many others. That M.G. weathered the storm was primarily due to the success of the original Midget sports car, which offered better value in terms of sheer enjoyment than any other on the market. Nevertheless, even the best of products needs publicity if it is to be sold in quantity, and the Midget would scarcely have made quite such an impact without the tremendous boost furnished by M.G.'s racing and record-breaking achievements.

From the close of the 'twenties Kimber displayed more and more interest in competitions, though one can only guess at the influences that fostered this interest. He may have been impressed by Crossley's pre-war successes under Charles Jarrott's direction, or noted how A.C. made a name for themselves in the early 'twenties by similar activities when S. F. Edge was at the helm. But it is just as possible that he was simply an enthusiast, unable to resist the glamour of racing, and making use of commercial arguments (as so many have done) to justify his involvement in an activity he enjoyed.

Whatever the motivation, it is ironic to consider that while Kimber's stubborn championship of racing was the very basis of

M.G.'s eventually world-wide fame, it also sowed the seeds of serious dissension with his chief, Sir William Morris.

In earlier days Morris himself had gone racing to publicize his bicycles, winning many a championship title by exerting his own stout leg-muscles. When he first turned to car manufacture, he himself drove in several speed hillclimbs and long-distance trials. Later, however, he became progressively more opposed to motor sport as a publicity medium. It was doubtless at his instigation that Miles Thomas wrote in a *Morris Owner* editorial of May 1924: 'For anyone to suggest that a concern that builds a successful racing car must *ipso facto* produce a good touring model is sheer rubbish.' This, the concluding sentence of a lengthy diatribe on the useless-ness of motor racing, was a practical exercise in making a virtue of necessity. One or two enthusiastic masochists did try their luck with modified Morrises at Brooklands and elsewhere, but they were merely the exception that proved the rule; the Morris was strictly in the 'shopping' category.

Between Morris and Kimber, then, the subject of racing was a distinctly thorny one, and it is a measure of Kimber's persuasive personality that M.G. maintained a full programme of motor sport for over five years despite the basic disapproval of the man who owned the company. It is almost as if an English prime minister had persuaded his Sovereign to support a bill for the abolition of horse racing.

But Kimber used many other methods to publicize his cars, with particularly intelligent use of the visual media. For example, Gordon Crosby was commissioned to paint a series of pictures for M.G. advertisements on the front covers of *The Autocar*. Another artist of the period, Harold Connolly, illustrated all the M.G. catalogues and leaflets from 1929 to 1939. Cecil Kimber worked very closely with both of them, and this raises the interesting question of his own artistic ability. His mother was no mere Victorian dabbler; many of her water-colours survive, and show real talent. Yet Vernon Kimber denies that Cecil inherited any of their mother's skill: 'To me he wasn't artistic. He never sketched, he couldn't play the piano or anything like that—he played the flute, badly. . . . Of course his life was motor-cars, so naturally he would study every angle of the subject: appearance, design. He was creative, yes. But not artistic.'

This judgment seems a little hard on the man responsible for the beautifully bodied Bullnose M.G.s; who drove his employees to distraction by insisting that every curve should be *exactly* right to the last eighth of an inch; who was an ardent photographer, one of the first Leica owners in England, and spent hours wading about in the sea in an attempt to capture the appearance of wave motion; who delivered to the Design and Industries Association a paper on *The Trend of Aesthetic Design* illustrated by his own charcoal sketches, making a detailed study of the relationship between shape and movement.

Harold Connolly remembers their many discussions very clearly: 'He generally sent for me about February or March and said we'd better start getting out some ideas for next year's Show. He couldn't stand a shoddy catalogue: "If the car's good, let's make the literature good." I don't think he ever counted the cost. I once said to him, "These cost a packet, don't they?" He said, "Price of a couple of door-handles, that's all. If they sell the car it's worth it. Remember, the catalogue is the salesman that goes home with you."

'He always asked me what I thought, but I don't say I influenced him in any way—if he liked it that way it stayed that way, and you could talk till you were blue in the face; he'd just dig his heels in. He liked to have a pretty girl in his cars, and a touch of the country house or a college background. I couldn't draw girls as pretty as I'd have liked, but I did my best. Kimber said he liked my drawing because the cars looked as if they were made of metal—the air-brush drawings of those days made cars look like silk stockings. He didn't think much of my figure work, but it was getting better, he said; he was frank like that. . . .

'Kimber always said a sports car should look fast even when it's standing still. That was the basis of all his designs. Every car he made looked quick, even the bullnosed ones. He prided himself that his cars were made to be good-looking anyway, so I shouldn't need to drop the roof-line, lengthen them and so on, the way I had to do for Morris and Austin. He was damned fussy about the work I did for him, and it had to be right.

'He had a lovely flair for line, a lovely idea of what the young lad of the village wanted, and that's what he built. I always went by his choice of colours entirely in designing a catalogue. . . . Kimber was a dreamer, he was after something beautiful, attractive—efficient insofar as it performed what he wanted it to do, but what it cost didn't seem to worry him a great deal. I don't think he could grasp it. I can add up three lines of figures and get four different totals—always could. And Kimber was the same, I think.'

So Connolly, an artist himself, saw Cecil Kimber as a man of artistic perception if not talent. Yet he also considered he had no head for figures—the same Kimber who had kept such a precise record of running costs with his little Singer 10. Vernon Kimber agreed that his brother had little head for figures, but added: 'I think his organizing ability was outstanding. I've seen a chart on the wall of his office showing the translation of an order from start to finish. And he had a passion for tidiness. By the time he'd finished with Wrigley's you could eat your dinner under any of the machines.'

The evidence remains conflicting. In March 1934 Kimber presented to the Institute of Automobile Engineers a paper entitled *Making Modest Production Pay*, in which every aspect of costing was considered and budgetary control discussed at length; nothing could be more down-to-earth than the decision not to employ two night-watchmen at the factory because their combined salaries would cost more than the petty pilfering they could prevent!

When this paper was shown to R. C. Jackson (the famous 'Jacko' of M.G.'s racing days), he said, 'I don't think Kimber wrote that; not his way of thinking at all.' But Kimber's own daughters, Betty (later known as Lisa) and Jean, insisted that their father was extremely cost-conscious and expected his wife to record every item of household expenditure in 'an enormous account-book'.

'They had an awful row once about her not keeping proper accounts. . . . He was parsimonious about a lot of small things. We didn't get our pocket-money unless we worked for it—we didn't just get a handout. I had to make a mash for the chickens in the morning and feed them.' 'Every night it used to take me an hour to boil the dogs' food.' 'I had to chop logs, all sorts of things. And he started me off keeping accounts, which, for heaven's sake, I still do!'

On one point, however, all are agreed: Cecil Kimber was no egg-head intellectual. 'He was childish in a lot of ways,' said Vernon Kimber. 'Simple things amused him. I've never seen him laugh so much as the time we went to see *Charley's Aunt*—he was roaring with laughter.'

This was how his daughters remembered him, too, with a liking for practical jokes and a not very highbrow taste in literature: 'He loved that Owen Wister book, *The Long Rifle*. Oh, and Adrian Bell's farming one, *Corduroy*.' 'Yes, he loved that, and *Owd Bob*, the sheepdog thing. I had a volume of Rupert Brooke's poems, and he

Cecil Kimber (1888–1945)

was a great fisherman, as you know, so I showed him the poem about the trout—you know:

> *In a cool curving world he lies*
> *And ripples with dark ecstasies.*

'He read those two lines and said, "Rubbish!", and threw it in the fire; he advised me to read Izaak Walton instead. He had a habit of throwing books of mine in the fire if he didn't like them. Another he chucked in the fire was a biography of Bix Beiderbecke the jazz trumpeter—he hated anything to do with jazz. That was a library book, too, and I had to pay for the damned thing; I was most annoyed.

'He quite enjoyed a sort of beer-drinking jolly party, like those M.G. Car Club affairs when we once had a band of buskers in from the street.' 'They once pushed a grand piano down seven flights of stairs, and he related this as quite okay.' 'When they all got going on a jolly party like that—bachelor party, not a mixed one—anything went.' 'But he was very strait-laced about blue jokes and things in front of us, in front of women. He was very hot about bad language; I never heard him swear.' 'Yes, he even considered "damn" a bad word.'

'The Earl of March [now the Duke of Richmond and Gordon] met my father when he was up at Oxford, and they were really friends all his life; he used to come and stay with us. One night Mother and I went to the theatre. We got back about eleven, and couldn't make anyone hear. Eventually we found the nursery windows all lit up, so we went and threw stones at them. Daddy and Uncle Freddie, as we called him, were playing with my trains, and completely absorbed in them.'

When the M.G. Car Company was transferred to Abingdon late in 1929, the Kimber family did not at first go with them; instead, they took a larger house in Hernes Road, Oxford. Three years later, however, they rented the Boundary House in Abingdon, from which their 1933 Christmas cards emanated with good wishes from 'CK, IK, BK, JK, two dogs, one yellow cat, one canary, and eight (at the moment) piebald mice'.

It was a full house and a full life. Despite continually recurring pain in his right thigh, Kimber would rise early every morning to do 'keep-fit' exercises, and danced or played tennis with equal enthusiasm. At every possible opportunity he would go fly-fishing or sailing, and later he cruised his own six-tonner on the Solent.

Every day, friends or favoured M.G. customers would be brought home to lunch, and Rene Kimber's considerable linguistic skill would be put to good use if it were someone like the Luranis or Tazio Nuvolari ('I liked Nuvolari, he was sweet. He was terribly jolly and played with us children in the garden. We liked him.'). While enjoying an ample social life, Kimber still found time to entertain his daughters with stories or adventurous outings: 'I don't think I brought out sufficiently what a good father C.K. was in the sense of doing things with us. . . . He was always taking us sailing, fishing, swimming, skating and just exploring generally.'

At the factory, of course, Kimber presented a somewhat different figure. He could be and often was a martinet. His terse memoranda, always signed in green ink, were something to be dreaded. When a shop-floor employee was summoned to Kimber's mock-Tudor office, it was understood that first one removed greasy overalls and made oneself presentable. He might make unreasonable demands of his men, as he often did when they were working against the clock for some race or record attempt, but his scrupulous fairness made every one of them—it sounds so archaic, nowadays—a loyal servant who would have done anything for him.

By the mid-'thirties the name M.G. had become as much a synonym for 'sports car' as Kodak was for camera or Hoover for domestic vacuum-cleaner; literally a household word. On one of Morris's many trips abroad, shortly after he became Baron Nuffield in 1934, he was introduced to an assembly as the man who made Morris cars. This was greeted blankly; Morris cars had never made much impact overseas. But broad smiles broke out when someone chanced to mention that he also owned M.G. Ah, yes, M.G.—who had not heard of the little English racing-car called M.G.?

This incident left Nuffield with mixed feelings. He was now spending much of his time away from Morris Motors Ltd, and if Abingdon was a 'happy ship' things were rather different at Cowley. There was a great deal of intrigue in his absence, important decisions were often motivated by personal gain, and some of the new Morris models proved disastrously unsuccessful, so that the company's fantastic growth of earlier days was not maintained. Nuffield had therefore appointed a tough, sandy-haired Yorkshireman named Leonard Lord to put things right. In the palace revolution that followed, several of Nuffield's best men

—good friends, some of them, to Cecil Kimber—were dismissed along with those who really deserved such treatment, while Lord's position grew steadily more powerful.

It was also unfortunate that in May 1934 a very prominent racing driver was brought to court following a crash with an M.G. —not in a race, or even during practice, but the night before a race—in which his mechanic was killed. Until that time M.G.s had hardly ever been involved in fatal racing accidents, with all the unfavourable publicity they bring. To quote H. N. Charles: 'From then on, Billy Morris didn't want to be connected with racing. Besides, the M.G. Car Company was an advertisement for Cecil Kimber, not Billy Morris—and of course you couldn't do that.'

There were other considerations affecting the whole financial structure of the Nuffield Organization. The upshot was that on 1st July 1935 Lord Nuffield sold the M.G. Car Company Ltd to Morris Motors Ltd. The new managing director was L. P. Lord; Cecil Kimber became merely director and general manager.

Things could never be quite the same again. Kimber's personality flourished only when he had freedom of action, when he was in a position to make quick decisions. He was anything but a committee man; still less a company man. M.G. owed their success to his personal control and direction, under which the Abingdon factory had become a close-knit unit owing loyalty to him, the personification of M.G.

The new managing director of M.G., however, was not a dedicated enthusiast but a hard-mouthed and ambitious business-man who gave not a damn about sports cars, save only as items on a balance sheet. The company might achieve a greater measure of commercial success in the future—and, to be fair, it did exactly that—but a vital part of the sporting image would be lost for ever. Any doubts on this score were quickly resolved when Lord paid a visit to Abingdon, surveyed the racing shop, and said, 'Well, *that* bloody lot can go, for a start.'

On a personal level Kimber and Lord managed to remain quite friendly, but they both knew who was boss. 'Remember, Kim,' said Lord briefly, 'the higher you are, the nearer you are to your hat.' Oddly enough it was Lord who picked his hat up first, less than twelve months later. He had demanded a substantial increase in salary and a share of Nuffield Organization profits. Nuffield refused, Lord departed in 1936, and his various directorships passed to his arch-rival, Oliver Boden. By the end of the year

Cecil Kimber had regained a little ground, for Boden was appointed vice-chairman and Kimber once again became managing director of M.G. Yet all these changes merely served to emphasize the extent to which he had lost control of his company.

On top of his business worries, things were no longer going smoothly at home. For some years the attractive Rene Kimber had suffered from a miserably debilitating illness which had made a travesty of her former good looks and left her incapable of playing a normal part in family life. Relations between Cecil and Rene worsened steadily until eventually they agreed to separate. Jean went to boarding school, and Kimber now found himself at loggerheads with his elder daughter. If he hated make-up, could not bear jazz music and was ever a staunch Conservative, Lisa insisted on wearing lipstick, expressing an undying love for jazz and voicing her emphatic adherence to Left-Wing politics. Basically, of course, they were very similar in temperament, and therefore clung to their differing views so tenaciously that they couldn't possibly agree.

Rene Kimber's sufferings came to an end in the spring of 1938, and Kimber married again in the summer. His new wife, Gillie, had all the *joie de vivre* that poor Rene had lost. 'He used to be so grim, so stern,' says Jean McGavin (*née* Kimber). 'I can remember him sitting there for ages, not saying a word. He changed so much after he married my stepmother, I sometimes felt I couldn't recognize the same man. She was very good for him. Liberated him. He was more relaxed, happier. . . . I loved Gillie on sight, she had that sort of charm and spirit.'

Kimber must have needed the consolation of his second marriage, for his influence on M.G. design was now very limited. New models were born at Cowley, not Abingdon, incorporating many components common to other cars in the Nuffield range and some features that Kimber himself actively disliked. However, he did what he could to ensure that the bodywork, at least, would reflect some credit on the name of M.G. Now fifty, he had perhaps become to some extent resigned to the position in which he had found himself. Shortly after the change in M.G. management he had been approached by a group of London financiers to form the C. K. Car Company, in which he would again enjoy control of design and marketing. He decided not to pursue the idea.

When the war came in September 1939, sports car production ceased, and for a long time the Abingdon factory had virtually nothing to do; the most menial tasks were gladly accepted, such as making fish-frying pans for a local military depot. In 1940, Miles Thomas was appointed vice-chairman and managing director of the Nuffield Organization after the sudden death of Oliver Boden. He considered that the whole group should be regarded as one unit for the purposes of armament production, with completely centralized control.

Kimber, however, had already secured an aircraft contract for Abingdon, which caused no little annoyance at Cowley, and Kimber's behaviour was interpreted as 'a policy of non-conformity'.

The result is related by Thomas himself in his book, *Out on a Wing*: 'I therefore went to see him at Abingdon in November, 1941, and told him that he had better look out for another outlet for his energies because he did not fit into the wartime pattern of the Nuffield Organization.' Thomas seems to have entertained no doubt about the justice of his action. Indeed, his account of the interview is made the opportunity for a homily on how to fire a high-level executive, doubtless of great assistance to others who found themselves in Thomas's unhappy position.

Cecil Kimber called his staff together and with quiet dignity told them he was leaving. There were no explanations, no recriminations. One member of the staff, Reg Jackson, was out on a service job, so a message was left asking him to call at the Kimber home that evening. On that occasion Kimber revealed something of what had occurred, but Jackson always respected his chief's confidence. Not until more than twenty years later, when *Out on a Wing* was published, was the story made public.

In normal times the reaction to Kimber's dismissal might have been different, but the war made it otherwise. Some of the motoring magazines expressed regret, others did not even record his departure. There was so much else to think about. The enemy was in control of all Europe, Hitler's troops within 30 miles of Moscow, Rommel victorious in North Africa, and many of Britain's major cities ravaged by continual bombing. The Kimber family contemplated legal action, but decided that it would be both untimely and undesirable.

Early in 1942 Kimber joined Charlesworth, the former coach-builders, to reorganize their factory for aircraft production. This occupied him until the end of the year, after which he went to the Specialloid Piston Company as works director, again to reorganize the plant, but this time with a contract for the duration of the war.

For almost the first time in his life Kimber gave way to illness.

'While he was at Charlesworth,' said Jean Kimber, 'he had his hernia done, and also had a little finger removed [because it would not straighten]. Strangely enough, it hurt him almost more afterwards than before. Then when he was with Specialloid he was at home for several months with some kind of nervous trouble, which was most unlike him. . . . I think he was broken-hearted. He used to play patience by the hour together; he always had a habit of doing that when he wanted to think.'

Kimber also got in touch with Harold Connolly again.

'He said, look, I'm with Specialloid Pistons now, would you like to do some drawings for me? So I picked up with him again. He hadn't changed a bit—still just as nice. Kind, thoughtful, and never, never went up-stage. But he was very unhappy. He wouldn't discuss it with me, I'll say that for him—he was loyal enough. But I knew they had hurt him badly. After all, he did found the firm, he'd put it where it was, and they could afford to put up with his peccadilloes.'

By early 1944 Kimber's health had improved. In April he presented a paper (*The Sports Car, its Past and its Future*) to the Institute of Automobile Engineers, and also attended one of the wartime meetings of motoring enthusiasts held at the Rembrandt Hotel in London. He was approached by Harry Ferguson, the tractor manufacturer, and had some negotiations with John Black of Triumph. He seems to have been in a very uncertain frame of mind about his own future:

(Jean Kimber) 'My stepmother says he used a characteristic phrase, "You know, Gillie, cabbage isn't good boiled twice. I'd like to retire to a cottage and write, and come up to London now and then." Gillie was quite happy to fall in with this, but she thinks he would not have been allowed to.'

(Harold Connolly) 'He told me, oh, he'd love to be back doing cars again. I know he was longing to get out of the piston business. "Y'see", he said, "there's nothing to it, you just make a piston and there it is, it's either a good one or a bad one."

'He was going to take me up to see Black for the weekend, to talk about cars and shapes and designs. I felt Black thought Kimber would make a lovely head for Triumph, with the reputation he had, because he was concentrating on his sports cars then —in spite of the bloody awful thing he was trying to sell, with its coal-scuttle mudguards; it was a dreadful-looking crate. And that's what Kimber said to me, he said you come up with me, we'll talk to Black, we'll get some shape into that Triumph.'

Cecil Kimber (1888–1945)

Kimber had for some time kept up a correspondence with Harold Hastings, an old friend and founder member of the M.G. Car Club. This had arisen from a chance meeting with Mrs Hastings: 'Although he had not seen her for three or four years, he immediately recognized her and stopped for a chat. When Brenda told him I was in India he said, "I must write to him", and asked for my address. Brenda gave it, thinking that this was the usual polite gambit and that he would forget all about it—instead of which, he wrote me several long and interesting letters.'

In his last letter to Hastings, dated 30th January 1945, Kimber wrote: 'I don't think you will find me making cars again as I want to retire, or semi-retire, in a very few years, and if I once got caught up in the whirl, heaven knows when I should be free again. Instead we have bought a cottage at Itchenor, that delightful little yachting centre on Chichester harbour, and we are looking forward to getting down there after the war . . . and, until I can give up working altogether, having a small flat in Town. I'm determined to retire whilst I am still young enough to enjoy going off sailing or fishing when I feel inclined.

'I feel somewhat pessimistic about the future of the real enthusiast's car. Sunbeam-Talbot, Riley and now M.G. have been or will be wrecked by the soul-deadening hand of the big business interests, and recently I have been staying with John Black who has just bought Triumphs, and what he proposes to do with that old name makes me want to weep. Lea-Francis appear to be the only concern left to cater for the real enthusiast, but of course Singers may come into the picture, but I think this is doubtful.'

By the time this letter reached India, Cecil Kimber was dead. The end had come on a Sunday, 4th February 1945, nine weeks short of his fifty-seventh birthday.

There was little petrol available even for business journeys then, so when he had to visit Perkins of Peterborough on behalf of Specialloid, he caught the 6 p.m. train from King's Cross, London. Less than 100 yards from its starting-point the train had to pass through three tunnels on an uphill gradient. Wheelspin was not uncommon, and trains were often assisted through by a second engine, but not on this occasion. The main line had been returned to service only a few hours earlier after renewal of the rails, which wore heavily on this section; the first train to use it had slipped to a standstill in the tunnels, but four others got through without trouble.

The 6 p.m. to Peterborough also came to rest, and in the dark-

Cecil Kimber (1888–1945)

ness of the tunnels the driver failed to realize that it had actually begun to run backwards, though at little more than walking pace. Seeing this, a signalman pulled the points to divert it to another line. He was a fraction of a second too late; the end coach had already started to pass over them. Consequently the coach overturned against the main signal bridge, the steel stanchions of which sliced diagonally through the compartment. Two passengers were killed, one of them Cecil Kimber, and twenty-five suffered from shock or minor injuries. At the subsequent inquiry the accident was attributed primarily to mishandling by the driver and guard, neither of whom had applied their brakes while the train was running back.

For a final comment we may turn again to Jean Kimber: 'Charles Russell of Specialloid opened a memorial fund after my father was killed, and my stepmother was somewhat upset to hear that Morris Motors headed the list with £100. . . . Due to misunderstanding, if you can call it that, the money, about £1500 [it was actually £1899], was put into Lord Nuffield's general Benevolent Fund.'

Not long afterwards the Nuffield Organization could note with satisfaction a steady rise in profits derived from export sales of the post-war M.G. sports car, the established reputation of which contributed so much to its ready acceptance overseas.

19

Chapter 2

Bullnose Days (1922–1926)

For almost fifty years the story of M.G.'s earliest days has been obscured by repeated attempts to oversimplify it, sometimes with scant regard for the facts. However dear it may be to a publicity man's heart, there is no more than a grain of truth in the romantic tale of Kimber building himself a Bullnose Morris special in an Oxford back-street, 'winning' the Land's End Trial with it and, flushed with success, announcing a whole range of M.G. models based on this one car. It is scarcely more logical to select one particular Morris Garages product as 'the first M.G.' than it would be to pick out one particular animal in the evolutionary series as, say, the first elephant. The M.G. did not appear overnight; it was developed gradually.

Moreover, before being dogmatic about the first M.G. sports cars one must define both M.G. and sports car—either of which tasks this writer will gladly leave to braver men than he. M.G. enthusiasts cannot agree among themselves to accept any one model as a 'real M.G.', and attempts to define a sports car have broken up many a happy discussion at the bar.

One other red herring to dispose of is the notion that the earliest M.G.s found a ready market among eager Oxford undergraduates. They did not, being somewhat too expensive for the average college man, who in any case displayed surprisingly little interest in cars at that time. The novelist Evelyn Waugh went up to Oxford in 1922, the year Cecil Kimber became manager of Morris Garages, and he has written:

'Oxford then was very much closer to my father's (and, indeed, my great-grandfather's) university than to my children's. . . . The town was still isolated among streams and meadows. . . . Its only suburb comprised the Ruskinian villas and well-kept gardens round the Woodstock and Banbury Roads. The motor works at Cowley existed, but were far from sight and sound of the university. During term tourists were few. The surrounding woods and hills were those the Scholar Gypsy haunted and could be reached on foot in the middle of the road. We walked up the tow-path and practised sortilege at Binsey, as we believed our predecessors had done. In the quiet streets predatory shopkeepers waited on the university and tempted the young into debts that were seldom repudiated. At Canterbury Gate and in the Broad hansom-cabs and open victorias were for hire. Bicycles and clergymen abounded and clergymen on bicycles were, with the cattle coming to market, the only hazards of traffic. I doubt if there were thirty cars in the university owned by dons or undergraduates.'

In this curiously Edwardian atmosphere the Morris Garages plied their trade from half-a-dozen showrooms, depots and workshops scattered about the town; the largest organization of its kind in Oxford. They sold and repaired cars and motor-cycles, their customers drawn from a wide area all around Oxfordshire and beyond.

If repair work brought an occasional exotic make to their attention, the new cars in their showrooms were for the most part solid, reliable and uninteresting: Arrol-Johnston, Belsize, Humber, Hupmobile, Singer, Standard and Wolseley. Plus, needless to say, the 11.9 h.p. Bullnose Morris in both its cheap 'Cowley' and more fully equipped 'Oxford' versions, the Ford Model T of England. Built in quantity to a no-frills specification, it was the sort of car that served you well but never impressed the neighbours.

Saloons—especially small saloons—were still something of a rarity in England. In the early 'twenties the Morris could be bought as an open car, two-seater or four, on either chassis, or as an Oxford coupé. A sports version was catalogued but it was quite astonishingly ugly, having neither the functional grace of a true sports car nor the homely charm of the standard bodies. The latter were beginning to look a little old-fashioned with their essentially pre-war lines, the stubby radiator and short bonnet swelling out to a high and wide body with an aggressively vertical windscreen.

Kimber can hardly have felt inspired by the cars that he had to sell. Soon after taking over Morris Garages he arranged to buy the Cowley in chassis form, and have it fitted with a body not included in the standard Morris Motors range. This was a simple two-seater with a space in the back for occasional passengers, but the hood was so arranged that when erected it covered all the occupants. Hence, perhaps, the generic term of 'Chummy', which distinguished this body style from the more common two-seater with dickey seat *outside* the hood (a touch of *apartheid* which may have led to the ordinary dickey becoming known as the 'mother-in-law seat').

To lower the high tail a simple modification was made. The Morris rear spring was in two parts, a semi-elliptic carrying the axle and a quarter-elliptic attached below the frame. Kimber had it fixed above the frame, effectively dropping the back end. The bodies were painted in pastel colours, unusual for the period, and finished with leather upholstery instead of the Cowley's standard Rexine.

Nobody can remember the price of the Morris Garages Chummy, save to suggest that it cost about the same as a standard Cowley four-seater (which does not help much, as the price of this model was reduced three times in little over a year). But it sold extremely well. At first, it was produced at Longwall Street by a handful of men—Bert Molden, Charlie Swinnard, Cec Cousins, Jack Lowndes and Frank Stevens—who combined this work with many other duties, Longwall being the main service depot of Morris Garages.

In the summer of 1922 'production' was transferred to a tiny workshop in Alfred Lane, where Cousins found himself in charge of a labour force answering to the name of Stan Saunders. They were shortly joined by Lowndes, and the three of them—while still doing other work for the firm—contrived to collect chassis from Cowley, modify them as necessary (doing all the drilling with a hand-brace), deliver them to Carbodies of Coventry for bodying, collect them again, and finish off. At one time they reached the remarkable output of twenty cars a week—but then, a working week of eighty hours was not uncommon.

Early the following year Kimber sent his own grey Chummy to Longwall for a number of modifications, including minor engine tuning, and at the end of March 1923 he drove it in that classic long-distance event, the London to Land's End Trial. Passengered by a restaurateur friend, Russell Chiesman, he qualified for one of the fifty-three gold medals awarded, but elected to take the optional award of a pair of cuff-links.

This small success may have prompted thoughts of a more sporting version of the Cowley. Kimber ordered six two-seater bodies from Charles Raworth of Oxford (who had built the original pre-war Morris bodies). These, again, were fitted to slightly modified Cowley chassis. They carried a raked windscreen supported at the sides by triangular glazed frames, and the scuttle was provided with two marine-type ventilator cowls. Knowledgeable M.G. enthusiasts will recognize this combination as distinguishing features of the marque (sometimes imitated by other builders) which persisted until late 1929. In the terminology of the period the Raworth two-seater was a sports body, and Cousins, who was responsible for building these cars, regards the Raworths as the first Morris Garages product that may be considered M.G.s. A small booklet issued by the Company in 1928 states that M.G. sports cars were first introduced in 1923.

The exact date when the first Raworth was built is unknown, but at least one existed in the summer of that year. On 11th August 1923 a young man named Oliver Arkell came to Oxford to buy himself a Chummy, but found something more interesting in the Queen Street showrooms. 'I saw this yellow sports car in the window—an unusual yellow, the colour of good butter, and it had black wings. Mr Kimber was there. He said it was £300. It wasn't much more than the Chummy, so I said very well, I'll have that.'

Arkell paid a deposit three days later, his Raworth was registered (FC.5855) on 16th August, and on 5th September it was delivered to the family home in Wiltshire, where his father christened it 'Oliver's Beetle'. There were neither front-wheel brakes nor starter; Arkell had wanted to have these fitted, but Kimber had explained that their weight would spoil the performance. One delirious day the Beetle did achieve 60 m.p.h., and the magdyno collapsed under the strain.

Shortly after the purchase Arkell was told that the price should have been £350, and this is the figure quoted in advertisements some six months later. This uncertainty does suggest that his Raworth was the first one sold to a private customer.

At £350 the sports two-seater was rather too expensive for a car based on the very simple Cowley chassis, then sold at only £175. It took about a year to find buyers for all six cars, so Morris Garages' first essay into sports car production was hardly a success. A further blow came later in 1923 when Morris *Motors* announced a model called the Occasional Four at £215. This was practically indistinguishable from the Morris Garages Chummy but appreciably cheaper, so the once-popular Chummy became almost unsaleable overnight, after several hundred had been built.

Kimber tried several expedients. The Occasional Four being on the Cowley chassis, Kimber had his Chummy body fitted to the Oxford chassis, but this aroused little interest. Then he tried to take advantage of the more powerful 13.9 h.p. engine which was at first offered as an option in the Oxford chassis, and later adopted as its standard power unit. He had a sedate and well-finished saloon body mounted on the 14/28 Oxford chassis, as it was called, and placed it on the market at £460 as the 'M.G. vee-front saloon'.

But this, too, was somewhat overpriced, Morris Motors having announced their own Oxford saloon at £395. The main claim to fame of this model lies in the fact that it was the first M.G. to be advertised in a motoring magazine. The first issue of *The Morris Owner*, which appeared in March 1924, carries a Morris Garages advertisement for this car with a photograph showing Rene Kimber stepping gracefully from its interior.

There were also experiments with a single landaulette, a vee-front coupé and a cabriolet, but by early 1924 there was something else in the wind. Kimber had been visited by Reg Brown, a member of the racing staff of John Marston Ltd, makers of Sunbeam motor-cycles, who had dealings with Morris Garages because they were Sunbeam agents. This time, however, he called to show Kimber a car. It was a 14/28 Morris Oxford chassis that Brown had modified with flattened springs, raked steering, Dunlop wire wheels, and an open four-seater body in polished aluminium with red leather upholstery, tonneau cover and hood. This body had been built on the lines of Brown's own 30/98 Vauxhall by Clarey Hughes, a Birmingham sidecar maker.

Brown has stated that Kimber, impressed by this car, built a similar one for Mrs W. R. Morris. But this seems unlikely. A Morris Garages car was built for her late in 1925, but it was a Weymann-bodied coupé.

There was, however, a young salesman at Morris Garages named G. S. ('Jack') Gardiner who planned to celebrate his 21st birthday by having a car of his own. He, too, bought a 14/28 Oxford chassis and asked Kimber to do the rest. Opinions differ about where this body was built: Gardiner thinks it was somewhere in Coventry; Cousins, who delivered the chassis for bodying, thinks he took it to Birmingham. Wherever it was bodied, Gardiner's car was registered (FC.6333) on 13th March 1924, the day before his twenty-first birthday, and featured in the *Morris Owner* advertisement the following month, at £395.

The photograph of this 'M.G. Special 4-seater Sports', as it was called, shows an open tourer corresponding to the general description of Brown's car, except that it has the Morris artillery-type wheels. There are no scuttle ventilators, but the windscreen is the 'triangulated' type used on the Raworth two-seaters. Just how much Kimber was influenced by Brown's car when designing this one can only be a matter of conjecture, but the connection assumes more significance if the body was built by Hughes of Birmingham.

The standard Morris Cowley sports model had been discontinued during 1923, and Billy Cooper, a well-known trials driver who had owned three of them, expressed interest when Kimber told him that Morris Garages were bringing out a new sports model of their own. The car that Kimber built for Cooper was a 14/28 open four-seater somewhat similar to the Gardiner car, but with a number of subtle alterations which greatly improved the appearance. The work of Carbodies, this tourer was appreciably lower overall, and Ace discs hid the ugly artillery wheels. The now familiar M.G. windscreen was used together with scuttle ventilators, and the body was finished in polished aluminium, with blue wings, valances and upholstery. The springs were flattened, the steering raked, and it was perhaps on this car that Morris Garages first adopted their practice of mounting the steering-box higher up on a specially made bracket, with a longer drop-arm which provided more direct steering.

Cooper's car was registered (MF.8068) on 31st May 1924 and given an illustrated half-page description in *The Motor* of 24th June. For the next two years it was a familiar sight in British sporting events, gaining several awards not only in reliability trials but in the first M.C.C. High-Speed Trial, held at Brooklands. Here, Cooper was assistant to 'Ebby', the famous starter and timekeeper, so his M.G. was frequently parked near the starting-line on race days.

It could hardly have been publicized in a better place. 'It was a novelty, y'know, in those days,' says Cooper. 'It looked—well, everyone, when I had it down at Brooklands, they all thought, "How did he get it—who made it?" They all wanted to know then. . . . It wasn't really a sports car as we know 'em today. It was just a little sports body, and it looked nice.'

The April 1924 *Morris Owner* advertisement included, for the first time, the stylized M.G. motif enclosed in an octagon, exactly as it is used today. The car illustrated was a Raworth two-seater priced at £350 and referred to as 'the M.G. Super Sports Morris'. This suggests that although one or two more Oxford-based tourers were being built by this time, M.G. had not yet got around to putting a two-seater body on the more powerful 14/28 Oxford chassis; they were still trying to dispose of the remaining Raworths.

Yet another Morris Garages effort at this time was a striking landaulette body on the short-lived six-cylinder 'F-type' version of the Morris Oxford chassis, with wire wheels. This first M.G. six-cylinder car was never advertised; nor was an exceptionally attractive open four-seater on the same chassis. It seems that Kimber, after a few experiments with the six, realized that the engine was unsatisfactory and decided not to proceed with it. By September 1924 he had started advertising the 'M.G. Chummy De Luxe Morris', an odd-looking body suggestive of the later Sporting Salonette. But the advertisements were illustrated by mere line drawings and no price was quoted, so it may have existed only in his fertile imagination.

It is time, now, to take stock of the situation on the eve of the 1924 London Motor Show—but with due caution, bearing in mind that no accurate production records survive, no leaflets or catalogues seem to have been produced, and too few cars had been built to establish a 'standard' specification.

The preceding twelve months or so, which might be called the immediate post-Chummy period, had seen Morris Garages experiment with several body styles to replace their popular Cowley-based car, killed by the announcement of the Morris Motors Occasional Four. Most of these new bodies were on 13.9 h.p. Oxford chassis. The closed types had met with only limited success, and the same was true of their first two-seater sports cars, the 11.9 h.p. Cowley-based Raworths. On the other hand the first open tourers on Oxford chassis had been well received, and not less than four had been built. Sticking rigidly to cars that are *known* to have existed (because photographs or other reliable evidence survives), Morris Garages had built at least thirteen after the death of the Chummy and before the 1924 Show.

Firm prices were quoted for four different models: open two-seater (£350); open four-seater (£395); vee-front saloon (£460); and single landaulette (£395). Advertisements had been placed in *The Morris Owner* each month, starting in March 1924. The octagon motif had been devised and featured regularly from May onwards. All these advertisements referred to the cars—open or closed—as M.G.s, but on the rare occasions when they were mentioned in other publications they were usually called specially bodied Morrises; a practice that continued on and off for years, to the intense irritation of Cecil Kimber. Can M.G. be regarded as a separate marque at this stage? That is a very moot point; but there can be little doubt that Cecil Kimber's ambitions already lay in that direction.

Several important changes were announced in the standard Morris range on 1st September 1924, apart from a substantial price cut and the inclusion of a year's free insurance with every car sold. All models were fitted with wired-edge 'balloon' tyres, much more comfortable than the high-pressure beaded-edge type that preceded them. All Oxford chassis had larger brakes front and rear, and a larger radiator. Closed and four-seater open Oxford bodies were now mounted on a longer chassis, of 9′ 0″ wheelbase instead of 8′ 6″.

Nothing makes a coachbuilder happier than a long wheelbase to work on. If the open four-seater M.G. had been a handsome car before, it was now transformed into one of the most beautiful ever built.

It could still be bought with the entire body and wings in polished aluminium, but Kimber now offered an optional two-tone effect most unusual in the mid-'twenties and derived, some said, from marine practice. The wings, side valances, bonnet top and upper portion of the body could be painted, with leather upholstery and hood bag to match (claret or smoke blue were suggested, but alternative colours could be provided without extra charge). Beneath a bold horizontal waistline running straight from radiator to tail, the sides of the body retained their natural finish of polished aluminium, with wheel discs to match. The result was breathtaking in its effect and bore not the slightest resemblance to the plebeian Morris from which it sprang. Small wonder that Kimber, in his first printed leaflet, quietly dropped the name of Morris and called it simply the M.G. Super Sports Model.

M.G. modifications to the chassis were small but significant. The springs were almost completely flattened and the steering steeply raked, using the modified steering-box mounting mentioned earlier. At the rear, Hartford shock-absorbers replaced the standard single-acting Gabriel snubbers. A higher final-drive ratio was employed. The Rubury-type braking system was slightly altered and the handbrake came on the right instead of being fitted centrally. The accelerator pedal was also transferred to the right and modified to operate fore-and-aft instead of vertically, as the Morris pedal did. At this stage the 13.9 h.p. Oxford engine retained its standard Lucas magneto and Smith carburetter, except for some experiments with the S.U. 'sloper' and other types. The 1924/5 leaflet mentioned that 'certain modifications are made to the engine to obtain the maximum r.p.m.', but did not go into details.

On this chassis M.G. offered three body styles. There was the open four-seater, now reduced to £375 with free insurance. There was a new 13.9 two-seater at £350, the price of the old 11.9 Raworth. And there was a remarkable new model called the M.G. Super Sports Salonette, the GT car of the mid-'twenties. It had an all-aluminium two-door closed body with vee-shaped windscreen, and an odd little duck-tail for luggage. Behind the front seats was a space with a folding seat which could be used to accommodate more luggage, two children, or two adults in a fair degree of discomfort. Priced at £475, the Salonette appeared early in 1925 and looks a strange device in photographs, but the one surviving example reveals it as a surprisingly attractive little car.

The open four-seater body was on the long-wheelbase chassis, the others on the 8′ 6″ chassis, but all three retained the smaller Cowley radiator. Sporting motorists being suspicious of the new-fangled balloon tyres, the open cars still carried beaded-edge Dunlops on their disc-covered artillery wheels, while the Salonette used balloon tyres on steel disc wheels. Various authorities have often stated that no M.G. carried an octagon until the late 'twenties, so it is worth mentioning that these 1925 models had a Morris Garages tread-plate, complete with two M.G. octagons, fitted at the bottom of each door opening.

In addition to these cars in the M.G. Super Sports range, Morris Garages still marketed a variety of closed bodies on unmodified Oxford chassis, together with a new model, a fabric-bodied Weymann Sedan at £435. The name was not being used as a synonym for saloon, as in transatlantic practice. This car was intended to simulate the lines of the 17th-century sedan chair first used in the French town of that name. Such experiments in body styling, not infrequently a complete failure commercially, were entirely characteristic of Cecil Kimber, who seemed to find in them a necessary *obbligato* to the many successful bodies that he designed.

The meanest-minded efficiency expert could hardly complain of the results achieved with the new M.G. sports car range. By comparison with most earlier Morris Garages models they went straight to the top of the hit parade, achieving success almost overnight. In the twelve months following their announcement no less than 160 cars were turned out of that little workshop in Alfred Lane: 93 open four-seaters, 36 open two-seaters, 6 Salonettes, and 25 assorted closed bodies on unmodified chassis.

Press publicity must have helped considerably. A picture of the new two-seater had appeared in *The Motor* in January 1925. In May came the first-ever M.G. road test in *The Autocar*, featuring M.G.'s demonstrator car, a tourer registered FC.8004. They found it 'a sports model with unusually attractive lines and well-balanced appearance . . . [with] as high a turn of speed as most drivers would care to use . . . a very lively performance with little ostentation.' *The Motor* followed up by describing the Salonette in July ('a very happy combination of harmonious yet racy lines'), and in October the new magazine, *Motor Sport*, also published a report on FC.8004. Like *The Autocar* they managed a top speed of around 65 m.p.h. and reached 50 from a standstill in about 24 secs., which was rated as 'remarkable acceleration, the engine leaping into life immediately the accelerator was touched'.

In June *The Motor* reported on the 14/40 Vauxhall 'Princeton' tourer, which had a 2300 c.c. side-valve engine and a four-speed gearbox. No figures were given for acceleration from rest, presumably better because of the four-speed box, but the top-gear acceleration was poorer and the maximum speed 5 m.p.h. less than the M.G. had achieved with its similar engine of only 1802 c.c. The M.G. cost £375; the Vauxhall £595.

Harry Charnock, later famous for his motoring verses, owned a Bullnose M.G. tourer and expressed its appeal in a slightly different way. Perhaps he provided the best explanation of M.G.'s success when in 1960 he wrote: 'Mine was a pretty early one (August 1925), and it was bought blind on the strength of the modest leaflet put out by Morris Garages. The two illustrations showed the prettiest motor-car I had ever seen, a scaled-down 3-litre Bentley at one-third the price; what young man could ask for more?'

The reader might well wonder where 'Old Number One', pride of the M.G. stand at so many motor shows, fits into this picture. Back in the spring of 1924, about the time the first octagon-embellished M.G. advertisement made its appearance, the men at Longwall (not Alfred Lane) started modifying a Morris Cowley chassis frame to Kimber's instructions. The rear portion was sawn off and replaced by two new side-members, hand-forged by Frank Stevens to sweep up over the rear axle and provide mountings for two outrigged semi-elliptic springs. Meanwhile Charlie Martin, who had recently joined Morris Garages, was given the job of preparing a special Hotchkiss engine of overhead-valve design. This was not a conversion (although such conversions were in fact marketed), but an engine of the type used in the 11.9 h.p. Gilchrist, a Glasgow-built car of which about twenty examples were produced between 1920 and 1923. Martin was much impressed by its appearance: 'Such a nice, clean, tidy thing—all new to me.'

This special chassis must then have been put aside for several months, for when completed it carried, front and rear, the larger Oxford brakes which did not appear until September 1924. Moreover, Carbodies of Coventry did not start building the narrow two-seater body until 13th March 1925; it was the forty-eighth body they had produced for Morris Garages. Work on the car now speeded up, for reasons that will shortly become obvious. The body fitted, it was painted the dark 'shop grey' which M.G. customarily used for prototypes and experimental models. On 27th March the completed car was registered FC.7900. This, oddly enough, was six days *after* the registration date of FC. 8004, M.G.'s first four-seater demonstrator. When several registration numbers are reserved in advance, the actual dates of registration do not necessarily follow the same sequence as the registration numbers.

The finished 'special' was an ingenious combination of standard and non-standard Morris components, though the chassis frame broke during test runs and had to be hurriedly repaired. Over the Easter weekend Cecil Kimber and Wilfrid Mathews, an Oxford insurance broker, took FC.7900 on the 1925 Land's End Trial. The car proved both fast and roadworthy, so that Kimber had no difficulty in qualifying for a gold medal. He sold FC.7900 to a Lancashire friend soon afterwards, and not until 1932 did it return to the M.G. Car Company to be hailed as 'Old Number One'. From that time on, more unlikely tales were woven around its ancestry almost every year, reaching Munchausen proportions when the Nuffield Group eventually assumed responsibility for M.G. publicity material.

It is a pity the professional publicists have so clouded the identity of FC.7900, which deserves an honoured place as what it really was: Kimber's first attempt to build a car from Morris components which was designed specifically to use in a sporting event, and for no other purpose. To quote Cousins, 'It wasn't Number One, it was a one-off bastard. I argued until I got so unpopular that I gave up; I was flogging a dead horse.' The word is used in its engineering sense, of course. The Kimber Special performs like a car of unblemished parentage.

There were three other M.G.s in the 1925 Land's End Trial, driven by Billy Cooper, Russell Chiesman and R. V. Saltmarsh. Cooper, as a travelling marshal, was not eligible for an award. Chiesman and Saltmarsh, like Kimber, both gained gold medals. It is interesting to note that in Morris Garages advertisements which appeared after the Trial, the 'golds' of Chiesman and Saltmarsh only—not Kimber's—were recorded as M.G. successes.

The tremendous increase in demand for M.G.s during 1925 made conditions at Alfred Lane almost impossible. The men worked from 6 a.m. (bringing bitter complaints from the neighbours) until 10 p.m. or even midnight. The entire space at their disposal was 20 ft wide and 100 ft long; mathematically inclined readers may care to work out how they packed into this about twenty-five cars, each of them 5 ft wide and nearly 13 ft long, leaving room for workbenches, tools and a few simple machines—not to mention stores. To make working-space the cars were pushed out into the lane every morning, and every evening they all had to be pushed back in again. On one occasion, understandably, a few were left outside. In the morning it was found that an unexpected snowfall had filled all the open cars to the brim.

Cecil Kimber drove to Queen Street from the upper end of Woodstock Road each morning, often dropping in to see how things were going at Alfred Lane. This journey also took him past the factory at Bainton Road where Morris Motors made their radiators. He could see for himself that Alfred Lane was bursting at the seams, and Radiators Branch not entirely filled by their bull-nosed products. He asked W. R. Morris if one bay of the factory, at least, could be rented by Morris Garages for M.G. production. Presumably W. R. M. was pleased with the sales figures, for he gave his consent.

A partition was erected at Bainton Road, and in September 1925 M.G. made their second move. This time there were about fifty employees instead of only two, so a works manager was appointed in the person of George Propert. With bowler hat, sober suit and rolled umbrella, Propert sufficiently resembled a well-known cartoon character to be christened 'Pop'.

'Pop' inhabited a glass-sided office just 8 ft by 5 ft and had no secretary, which was just as well, since with any measure of decency there was not room for one. When he wanted to have a letter typed he got on his bicycle and rode to Queen Street. A great man for charts and diagrams, Propert covered the partition wall with myriads of coloured labels, whose significance nobody else understood, and every morning he would spend happy hours playing draughts with them. But one evil day Radiators Branch mounted several electric motors on their side of the wall, switched on, and all the little labels were shaken from their hooks. Broken-hearted, Propert never hung them up again, so the men concluded that even he did not understand what they meant.

In addition to the move, September 1925 brought a few changes in Morris specifications and the now customary price cuts, which allowed M.G. to reduce theirs also. A clear distinction was now drawn between M.G. Sporting Models (on modified chassis) and M.G. Special Models (on unmodified chassis). In the former category came the open two-seater (now £345), the open tourer (£360), and the Salonette (£450), followed later by a four-seater Salonette without the stumpy tail and priced at £495. Of the unmodified cars, the landaulette was dropped from the catalogue, though a cheaper version of it was built for a time, while the Weymann sedan was reduced to £399 and the vee-front saloon reappeared, listed first at £440, later at £450. All prices again included one year's free comprehensive insurance.

The longer-wheelbase Oxford chassis was now used exclusively, for two-seaters as well as four-seaters, and the open M.G.s were fitted with three stud, open-hub wire wheels— still, however, with the old beaded-edge high-pressure tyre. Wire artillery wheels were of course more 'sporting', but the discs on the artillery wheels perhaps suited the lines of the Bullnose M.G. better. A Clayton Dewandre vacuum servo was now fitted to M.G. brakes, which were still of Rubury type. A 17″ steering-wheel was standardized, slightly larger than the Morris wheel, and a Lucas automatic wiper replaced the earlier Bowden-controlled device which was worked by hand. Like Morris, M.G. adopted the simple but effective Barker arrangement which allowed the headlamps to be dipped by a long lever similar to a gear-lever. This was on the right-hand side, the equally long gear-lever on the left, and there was no door for the driver. The M.G. enthusiast, leaping aboard, stood a very good chance of collecting one lever up each trouser leg. If he wore mid-'twenties Oxford bags he was quite likely to get the handbrake as well. Some M.G. owners took to wearing trouser-clips.

Bullnose M.G. exhaust systems were unashamedly rorty, an early 1926 catalogue making special reference to the 'deep mellow note increasing to a dull boom when the throttle is opened'. After the move to Bainton Road this sonic bang was more likely to signify effective forward motion. Every engine received from Morris Motors was now dismantled, carefully checked over, the valve ports polished, the engine re-installed in the chassis and run-in before the body was fitted. A special magneto replaced the standard one used by Morris, and after various experiments with carburetters the Solex was standardized.

Increased production called for standardization of several other features. It was no longer possible to specify one's own free choice of paint colours except at extra cost (bodies could also be finished in 'cellulose unscratchable paintwork' for £12 extra on open cars, £18 on Salonettes). Steel wings were standardized instead of allowing the option of polished aluminium, so they had to be painted. The same applied to the upper portion of the body, which was now steel, only the sides remaining aluminium. However, a 2" increase in width made the bodies more roomy.

The 1926 Morris Garages catalogue consisted of a standard Morris Motors single-colour catalogue with a special M.G. cover in cream paper, printed in black and orange. Inside, a sixteen-page insert in the same colours provided lavishly illustrated details of the M.G. range. This replaced the previous year's simple brown loose-leaf folder with pasted-in photographs and type-written captions. The new catalogue stated: 'Such is the popularity of M.G. models that a special factory has been erected to cope with the demand.' This was stretching the truth somewhat, or at least anticipating it by nearly two years.

When the General Strike came in May, it seems to have made little difference at Bainton Road. Propert, something of a disciplinarian, had been shocked by free-and-easy M.G. ways when he first came there, but when he left to join Harper-Bean in the summer of 1926 he remarked to Cousins: 'I don't know, I've never seen men *enjoy* working like this. They seem to work just for the fun of it.' Most mornings, Kimber would call on his way to Queen Street. Once a fortnight everyone would be on their best behaviour for the regular visit from Morris, who came to check the accounts.

Billy Cooper covered an enormous mileage during the Strike delivering mail in his second Bullnose M.G., which he had bought earlier in the year. He also took it to Brooklands and succeeded in putting fifty-five miles into the hour at an M.C.C. High-Speed Trial with a Miss M. G. Chiesman, cousin of Russell Chiesman, as his passenger.

A more distinguished 1926 M.G. buyer was the Prince of the Asturias, the Spanish equivalent of Britain's Prince of Wales—in other words, the heir to the throne. His mother had been Princess Ena of Battenberg, a grand-daughter of Queen Victoria and great-aunt of the Philip Mountbatten who, twenty years later, bought an M.G. of his own. The Spanish prince's 1926 tourer was finished in royal purple with a gold band along the waistline. One hopes that his choice of car was a free one, uninfluenced by his royal father. It was also in 1926 that W. R. Morris made his first gift to Oxford University: £10,000 to found the King Alfonso XIII Chair of Spanish Studies.

As mentioned in Chapter I, the Kimbers had by this time become acquainted with H. N. Charles, who had joined Morris early in 1924 after a varied early career in engineering. He had followed his honours degree by doing some remarkable aircraft development work with the famous No. 56 Fighter Squadron, subsequently joined the Zenith carburetter firm, and then helped to found Automotive Products Ltd. Although fully occupied at Cowley during the day, he devoted much of his spare time to experimental work for Kimber. One of his inventions was the 'Comparator', a device similar to the 'rolling road' testers widely used in the motor industry many years later. The back wheels of a car could be placed on two pairs of rollers which were connected to a fan, with blades of suitable dimensions to represent frontal resistance and air drag at speed.

This allowed stationary testing in all gears up to maximum speed, while an accurate speedometer connected to the rollers gave an immediate check on the car's speedometer. First installed at Bainton Road, the Comparator proved extremely useful for tuning carburetters under load, setting ignition timing and making other adjustments. For more than ten years M.G. used a similar device not only for production cars, but even when tuning racing models and record-breakers.

The assistance of H. N. Charles was much needed later in the year, when Kimber had to face a major problem. If the Bullnose Morris had looked a little dated in 1922, by 1926 it was distinctly old-hat and sales began to fall. W. R. Morris had already appreciated the need for modernization, having visited the U.S.A. in 1925 to study American methods in pressed-steel body construction, and in September 1926 the latest Morris models appeared with a flat-fronted radiator. Paradoxically, many regretted the passing of the Bullnose, and Morris published an explanation:

1. Cecil Kimber, originator of the M.G. marque, in his Abingdon office.

2. The mews garage in Alfred Lane, Oxford, where most of the early M.G.s were built.

3. The 11.9 h.p. 'Chummy' of 1922/3 was one of the earliest examples of special Morris Garages coachwork produced under Kimber's direction.

4. The first Morris Garages sports car was the 1923/4 Raworth-bodied two-seater on the 11.9 h.p. Cowley chassis. This one is parked in Alfred Lane.

5. Billy Cooper's 14/28 tourer of 1924—almost certainly the second four-seater M.G. to be built—photographed outside W. R. Morris's office at Cowley.

6. Rene Kimber with the all-aluminium M.G. vee-front saloon of 1924. This photograph illustrated the M.G. advertisement in the first issue of *The Morris Owner*, dated March 1924.

7. A 14/28 M.G. tourer of 1924/5 type with the two-tone finish that was then optional, but subsequently adopted as standard.

8. Mid-'twenties G.T. car: Kimber's unusual Sporting Salonette, which appeared early in 1925, provided closed accommodation for two adults and ample space for luggage or children.

9. Kimber climbs Bluehills Mine during the 1925 Land's End Trial with his specially built o.h.v. car, often erroneously referred to as 'M.G. Number One'. He gained a first-class award.

10. Complete with trilby hat and lady passenger, Billy Cooper puts 55 miles into the hour with his second M.G. in the 1926 M.C.C. High Speed Trial at Brooklands. He, too, won a first-class award.

11. An M.G. owner collects his 14/40 model from the Edmund Road service department, and signs on the dotted line while Albert Eustace (*left*) fills the under-bonnet tank with petrol.

12. The first-recorded M.G. racing victory came on 30th October 1927, when Alberto Sanchiz Cires won an event on the San Martin track outside Buenos Aires.

13. The running-in bay at Edmund Road, early in 1928. Every chassis was run-in on coal gas for the equivalent of 750 miles, at varying speeds in each gear.

14. This 14/40 salonette, photographed at the Olympia Motor Show in 1927, carries the new M.G. radiator badge but still has the earlier cut-out M.G. motif fixed to the honeycomb.

15. The first M.G. Midget, the M-type, in chassis form.

16. Two early 18/80 Mark I models, tourer and saloon, at the finish of the 1929 Land's End to John o' Groats Trial.

17. D. K. Hall's 18/80 Mark II tourer basks in Mediterranean sunshine on the Côte d'Azur.

18. A group of M.G. staff at the Company's inaugural luncheon on 20th January 1930. Second from the left is H. N. Charles, fourth is Cecil Cousins, fifth Cecil Kimber, sixth George Propert, and seventh is Sir William Morris, Bart.

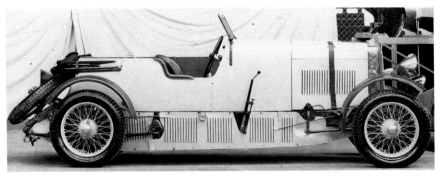

19, 20. The two M.G. models prepared for the 1930 Double Twelve at Brooklands were the massive 18/100 Road Racing Model (*top*) in cream with brown mudguards, and the diminutive modified M-type (*centre*) in brown with cream mudguards.

21. The Hon. Mountjoy Fane seated in one of the two special M-types built for the 1930 Le Mans race. His car was driven by Murton-Neale (in beret) and Jack Hicks.

22. A line-up of standard M-type Midgets at the M.G. factory, early 1930.

23. EX.120, the first 750 c.c. car in the world to achieve 100 m.p.h., at the Montlhéry track in February 1931. Eyston is in the cockpit; behind are Jackson, Kindell, Eldridge, Cousins and Phillips.

24, 25. Two C-types: (*above*) the Earl of March (now the Duke of Richmond and Gordon) at the 1931 Brooklands 500 Miles Race with his supercharged car; the mechanic in very dirty overalls is Syd Enever. (*Below*) the unsupercharged car with which Norman Black won the 1931 Irish Grand Prix.

26. First non-racing model to use the C-type chassis design (but not its engine) was the D-type, available only in four-seater form.

27. Sir Francis Samuelson at the finish of the 1931 Monte Carlo Rally with an M-type Sportsman's Coupé, the third M.G. in which he had completed the event.

28. One of several body styles on the F-type Magna chassis was this close-coupled Salonette.

29. M.G.'s first small six-cylinder engine, the F-type, was virtually a Midget unit with two additional cylinders, and closely related to the Wolseley Hornet.

30. With the J.2 two-seater of mid-1932, M.G. achieved a classic shape that set the fashion in sports cars for many years to come.

31. Ronnie Horton's strange-looking single-seater C-type averaged 96.29 m.p.h. to win the 1932 Brooklands 500 Miles Race. This super-charged 750 c.c. car lapped the Outer Circuit at 115.29 m.p.h.—faster than the best 1100 c.c. cars of that time.

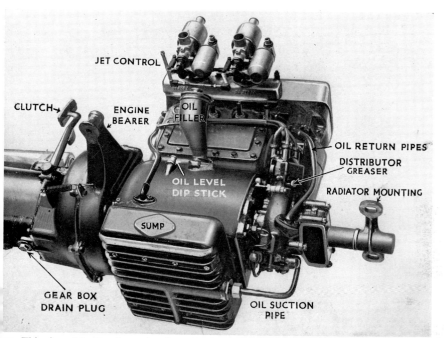

JET CONTROL

CLUTCH

ENGINE
BEARER

OIL
FILLER

OIL LEVEL
DIP STICK

SUMP

OIL RETURN PIPES

DISTRIBUTOR
GREASER

RADIATOR MOUNTING

GEAR BOX
DRAIN PLUG

OIL SUCTION
PIPE

32. This view of the J-series engine shows the tubular front mounting which also carried the radiator, a simple but effective feature of M.G. design.

33. W. T. Platt and A. W. Archer at Folkestone during the 1933 Monte Carlo Rally. Their car is a J.3, the supercharged version of the J.2 Midget.

34. First of the Magnettes was the K.1 pillarless saloon, shapely but underpowered until later fitted with an improved engine.

35. A brisk demand for J.2 Midgets kept the Abingdon production lines busy in 1932/3.

'We have adopted this new radiator so that we can obtain a more fashionable body line. I decided that it was not practical to fit the new longer and roomier bodies we are standardizing for next year behind the old familiar radiator. Since a change had to be made, I have made it as definite and sweeping as possible.'

It was actually much more than a change of radiator. Morris had brought out a completely new chassis frame which was wider, shorter in the wheelbase, and a good deal heavier than its predecessor. For M.G. this was a near-disaster. Their bodies would have to be completely redesigned from end to end. Many of their special chassis components were now quite useless; they, too, would have to be redesigned. And after all this work the new M.G. would have less performance than before because of the increase in weight.

Harry Charnock's comments are again significant, though the flat-radiator M.G. that he bought after the Bullnose one was a 1928 model: 'My first reaction was one of violent disappointment; it seemed impossible that the prettiest car of 1925 could have grown into the ugliest one of 1928, but such seemed to be the case. It looked like the drawing mistress who used to teach perspective at my prep. school: angular, flat-chested, all straight lines and vanishing points. . . . Closer examination, however, made me forget all about looks. Here, although the specification read the same, was every improvement I had ever wanted on my earlier M.G., and at a price a few pounds lower than the 1925 figure.'

But the improvements that Charnock found in 1928 were, many of them, not available in late 1926. They came only gradually after continual effort to make the flat-radiator a worthy successor to the earlier M.G.s. In the words of Cousins, 'We had an awful job to make those cars go as fast as a Bullnose.'

Nor were matters helped by considerable difficulty in obtaining any of the new chassis from Morris Motors so that a start could be made on the mammoth (for the tiny M.G. organization) task of redesigning the whole car.

Meanwhile it was necessary to produce sales literature of some sort for the 1926 Motor Show (M.G. could not yet afford a stand at the Show, but their salesmen had to attend to gather in what orders they could). This, in the circumstances, called for a good deal of inspired guesswork. The only charitable assumption is that Kimber must have been elsewhere at the time, for the late 1926 leaflets are undoubtedly the worst that ever carried the name of M.G. An excruciating sales slogan made its appearance: 'The car that takes the ills out of hills'. As there was no car to photograph, the leaflets were illustrated by the most appalling drawings, done by an artist completely unfamiliar with M.G. technique. Even that deceptively simple trademark, the M.G. octagon, was incorrectly drawn. After the dignified Bullnose M.G. catalogues the whole thing was atrocious.

Despite this inauspicious start the new M.G.s were eventually improved in many respects until they, in their turn, gave way to newer models. How that was done, and how Kimber continued his uphill struggle to establish the separate identity of M.G., belongs to the next chapter. The Bullnose days were over.

Chapter 3

Adolescence (1927–1929)

The large-quantity production of any manufactured article, be it armchair or aspirin tablet, neither guarantees excellence nor precludes it. Some of the finest examples of automobile engineering ever built have failed to reach a two-figure output; some cars produced in their thousands have been extremely bad ones that nevertheless satisfied a public demand.

It has become fashionable to sneer at the Bullnose M.G. as 'just a rebodied Morris'—but what has that to do with its quality? Joe Soap and Joshua Reynolds will produce very different results from the same paints and canvas. In terms of sheer performance the Bullnose M.G. was not and could not be an outstanding sports car, but as a complete transformation of an ugly and uninteresting utilitarian vehicle, it was a stroke of sheer genius. The excellent reputation that it enjoyed during its production period, though now forgotten, was well deserved.

Nevertheless, the total production in more than three years was just over 400. Its immediate successor, inferior in both looks and performance, equalled that figure in 1927 alone, its first full calendar year of production. During that time many small but significant improvements were made to the flat-radiator M.G. The following year, production dropped by 25 per cent. Any attempt to draw a logical conclusion seems pointless, but in the writer's opinion there is usually a considerable time-lag in public reaction—so much, indeed, that an appreciable overlap occurs, and every new model leans on the reputation of its immediate predecessor.

This leads us in a roundabout way to the complicated question of nomenclature. The vague notion has long persisted that the Bullnose M.G. Super Sports, with 14/28 side-valve Morris engine, was succeeded by a similarly-powered flat-radiator model known specifically as the 14/40, which in turn was developed into the octagon-bedizened M.G. Mark IV. About ten years ago somebody was bright enough to observe that the first 'flats' had an odd-looking radiator, different from those of later cars, and dubbed them 'Flat-rad 14/28' on the assumption that no significant modifications to increase engine power output were being made at that stage. This, however, raised another question: what, then, was the difference between a 14/40 and a Mark IV? A few more octagons hardly called for a brand-new model designation.

The present writer, after making many inquiries, abandoned as hopeless the attempt to distinguish between the two. A different approach explained the difficulty—they were indivisible! The 1926/7 flat-radiator cars were actually called M.G. Super Sports, just like their Bullnose predecessors. The earliest mention of '14/40' that could be traced came late in 1927 *accompanied* by the designation 'Mark IV'. In fact the full and correct title of a 1927/8 car is '14/40 M.G. Mark IV', and no earlier model was called 14/40 in M.G.'s own sales literature. This car continued in production for most of 1929, with several alterations in specification, but no further change was made in its type number or name. All things considered, it seems a good idea to abandon the Mark designation altogether for side-valve cars, whatever the shape of their radiators, and reserve it for the later 18/80 range, where the distinction is clearly defined. The models of 1924/5 and 1926/7 may obviously be called Bullnose, and contemporary practice condones our adding a '14/28' tag to this. As M.G. seem to have made appreciable alterations to the 14/28 engine from some time in 1927, perhaps we may stretch a point and refer to all post-September 1926 side-valve M.G.s as, quite simply, 14/40 models. This avoids the unmelodious 'flat-rad', and takes advantage of the fact that a considerable hiatus in production occurred around this time.

In the last chapter we left Cecil Kimber and Hubert Charles scratching their heads over the new Morris chassis of September 1926: wider, shorter, appreciably heavier, and with a very angular radiator that clashed violently with the subtle curves of the Bullnose M.G. body. They certainly had a problem on their hands, and perhaps Kimber for once appreciated the seasonal nature of the British motor trade. During the nineteen-twenties and 'thirties (even, to some extent, today) the arrival of each spring turned the British motorist's thoughts lightly, not to Tennysonian love, but to the purchase of a new car. He would remain in this receptive state, easily transfixed by the arrow of some Cupid-like salesman, until about mid-July, when he could still be persuaded to buy a car for his annual holiday. Then, however, he would recall the manufacturers' incomprehensible practice of announcing *all* new models in September, and, conscious of heavy depreciation, remain deaf to all entreaties until the following spring. Only a few ardent automobilists sought the distinction of buying a new car at the Motor Show in early October (which was just as well, for the manufacturers were seldom ready to build them). Consequently the average British car factory lay almost idle for the greater part of each winter. During this particular winter the normally hard-working lads at Bainton Road were reduced to playing cricket with shock-absorber rubbers while the chosen few deliberated over a new M.G. design.

Eventually it emerged. To be fair, the flat-radiator Oxford chassis was more stable than its predecessor, with its sturdier frame and semi-elliptic rear springs. M.G. made it even more so. They used flatter springs fore and aft, removed the woolly, rubber-mounted Morris steering and replaced it by a new Marles assembly with $17\frac{1}{2}$-inch René Thomas spring-spoked wheel. The new Smith shock-absorbers were retained at the front, but the rears replaced by Hartfords, as in Bullnose days. Once again the M.G. used a higher final-drive ratio than its Morris equivalent. The new Morris braking system was not at all clever, and in any case there was no room for M.G.'s massive B-type Clayton Dewandre servo. The whole system was redesigned, incorporating the smaller C-type servo. Unfortunately M.G. ended up with a veritable forest of brake-shafts and levers, little better than the Morris arrangement.

The new five-stud hubs were fitted with open-hub wire wheels and, at last, balloon tyres instead of beaded-edge. The improved Morris petrol tank and mounting were also used, but in a modified version of the Cowley sheet-steel bulkhead. The radiator, too, was of modified Cowley type for the open cars, but the larger Oxford version was fitted to the closed models. A much quieter exhaust system was employed. The battery having been moved from the running-board to beneath the nearside front seat, the toolbox was displaced to a new position between the rear dumb-irons, outside the body; people must have been more honest in those days.

The wings and running-boards were attached to the chassis, quite separate from the body, and the front ones fitted with C.A.V. 'streamlined' sidelamps instead of the fat little replicas of the headlamps. The doors, instead of being small and shallow, were cut right through to frame level. The traditional M.G. two-tone finish was retained, but an engine-turned effect (the catalogue called it 'curled') was applied to the aluminium body and bonnet sides, which were then lacquered.

In an attempt to reduce the apparent height of the lofty flat radiator, Kimber had a false piece soldered to the lower portion so that it overlapped and obscured the front chassis cross-member, seeming to sit lower in the frame. The radiator still carried the Morris badge, but a cut-out M.G. badge in German silver was fixed to the honeycomb. Some cars were fitted with an earlier Morris type with an outer ring bearing the words, 'The M.G. Super Sports', as on most Bullnose M.G.s, and there were also a few with a Morris badge to which a small M.G. octagon was fixed in the centre. The subject of badges is a tricky one. Several survivors of the period carry enamelled octagonal M.G. badges, but contemporary photographs and catalogues suggest that these may have been substituted later in the life of the car. On the other hand, the situation is confused by M.G.'s occasional habit of using old photographs in their catalogues, sometimes unretouched, in a sudden access of economy. All one can say with reasonable confidence is that no M.G. built before late 1927 is likely to have had an enamelled M.G. radiator badge as an original fitting.

The new specification was accompanied by some price cuts, the open two-seater to £340 and the four-seater to £350. For the two- and four-seater versions of the Salonette, a new price was fixed midway between the two at £475. One Salonette buyer was the actress, Madeleine Carroll, who was to make a name for herself in Hollywood ten years later. Kimber always had the knack of meeting 'show-biz' personalities, who would be shown around the factory and, if possible, sold a car with which they would be photographed.

By now, M.G. made a practice of polishing the combustion chambers as well as the ports, and fitted stronger valve springs. To emphasize that the engine differed from its Morris counterpart, the cylinder head was stove-enamelled black and secured by nickel-plated dome nuts. But the 14/40 two-seater tested by *Motor Sport* and *The Autocar* early in 1928 proved no faster than a 1925 14/28 four-seater, and acceleration to 50 m.p.h. was actually a little poorer because of the heavier chassis. However, both magazines remarked that the roadholding was quite exceptional, and the new body also met with approval, *The Autocar* commenting: '. . . splendidly balanced. . . . The car looks a thoroughbred.' *Motor Sport* referred to 'lines reminiscent of Cowes'. They were certainly different from Bullnoses.

To encourage production once the design was settled, early in March the men at Bainton Road were offered a bonus on all cars built over fifteen a week, though it was emphasized that this would be immediately withdrawn if inspection revealed any decline in standards of assembly. But the supply of chassis from Morris Motors was still inadequate, and less than a fortnight later the bonus was made payable on anything over ten cars; this in a working week of fifty hours.

In the middle of this pressure to build more cars, Radiators Branch suddenly decided that they needed the space occupied by M.G. A hurried move to another bay of the factory was made one weekend, so that work could start normally on Monday morning. A depot in Merton Street was taken over for servicing cars, and another in Leopold Street for coachpainting and repairs. As production continued to rise, the need for more room became obvious.

Kimber now went to see W. R. Morris and, with understandable hesitation, put forward a startling request—for £10,000 to build a special factory at Cowley exclusively for M.G. production. He was surprised as well as relieved when Morris smilingly agreed. It promised a big step forward in the history of M.G.

The factory at Edmund Road took about six months to build and cost a great deal more than the estimate; £16,000, in fact. It was ready for occupation in September 1927, so the removal came at a highly inconvenient time, only a few weeks before the Motor Show. Probably for this reason, no new Show literature was printed. Instead, the previous year's leaflets were overprinted '1928' and some but not all of the latest modifications marked in; several, indeed, may have had to be postponed until production settled down at the new factory. A preliminary announcement in the motoring press quoted new and slightly reduced prices for the open two-seater (£335) and tourer (£340); the Salonette was at first quoted at £475, as before, but the duck-tailed two-seater version was shortly discontinued and the four-seater Salonette catalogued at £445. These were the last price cuts to be made during the production life of the 14/40 range.

An additional model was also announced at this time, providing further evidence that Kimber, although nowadays famous for his sports cars, always liked to experiment with closed coachwork. Satisfactory saloon bodies were difficult to produce during the vintage period, when the relatively flexible chassis frames caused them to rattle, twist, and often break up. Hence the popularity of fabric-covered wooden bodies, which were quieter and more supple. For some time Kimber had been approaching various coachbuilders to produce sample bodies on M.G.'s version of the

Morris Oxford chassis, and his choice finally fell on Gordon England, already noted for his specialized versions of the Austin Seven. England produced for M.G. an ingenious saloon body in which the floor and seats were fixed directly to the chassis, and the body mounted flexibly at only three points. The price of the 'M.G. Featherweight Fabric Saloon' was £445—the same as the Salonette.

Kimber's choice of colour schemes for this model was a little peculiar, one of the strangest being 'grained black fabric sprinkled with gold dust'—which, at Edmund Road, earned that particular demonstrator the name of 'Old Speckly Hen'. He had perhaps laid an egg with the Featherweight Fabric Saloon, only thirty-two of which were built in two years. Another oddity to appear during the 1928 season was a high and unwieldy-looking Sports Coupé, £445 with folding head or £455 as a four-light fixed head. Only two of each were made, although both were catalogued.

In July 1927 The Morris Garages had been registered as a limited company, which in November accepted responsibility for M.G. guarantees instead of passing them on to Morris Motors Ltd. A brass guarantee plate was fixed to the nearside bulkhead bracket of each new car, which was then identified by an M.G. car number instead of the original Morris chassis number—although this was still stamped on the frame.

A further step towards independence came in the spring of 1928 with the establishment of a new company which was called The M.G. Car Company (Proprietors: The Morris Garages Ltd.). A start was made on the task of producing owners' handbooks, preparing service manuals and drawing up parts lists. In fairness to existing owners the handbooks had to cover earlier models, and an attempt was made to go back as far as 1925, but it was impossible to deal with all the cars—well over 700—that had been built before the move to Edmund Road. Service work at first continued in Merton Street, and was later transferred to a separate department in the new factory. Under Kimber's control the M.G. Car Company was noted for its good servicing arrangements, which contributed much to the enviable reputation of the marque.

November 1927 brought news of M.G.'s first victory in a genuine motor race—and this, of all unlikely places, in South America. At the San Martin track outside Buenos Aires, a meeting had been organized the previous month to celebrate the crossing of the South Pacific by two French airmen. The first race, a one-hour event, had been won at an average speed of almost 62 m.p.h.

by a 14/40 M.G. tourer driven by Alberto Sanchiz Cires, comfortably ahead of seven other finishers. This must have come as something of a surprise, for M.G. certainly did not see the 14/40 as a racing car. The side-valve Morris engine still had splash-fed big-end bearings, and the late 1927 catalogue stated: 'For continuous high speed track work—for which the M.G. Mark IV Sports is *not* designed—we naturally would recommend a high pressure oiling system to all bearings. This can be provided at extra cost.'

Nor were any extravagant claims made for performance in the first M.G. Salesmen's Booklet, which appeared early in 1928: '. . . We give no definite speed guarantee. We do say, however, that every M.G. when properly and thoroughly run-in should be easily capable of over 60 m.p.h. . . . We do sincerely claim for the M.G. acceleration, steering, road holding and braking as good as, if not better than, anything else in its class, and in consequence the ability to put up as high an average on any give-and-take run as is safely possible under modern road conditions, which so seldom allow a really high maximum speed to be used. . . . The M.G. . . . offers as fine a "value for money" proposition as is obtainable among fast touring cars today.'

The main purpose of the 1928 Salesmen's Booklet was to emphasize the separate identity of M.G. and counter the 'rebodied Morris' criticism that cropped up so often. It was pointed out that the cost of a finished M.G. chassis, with all the special components and assembly work that went into it, was almost twice that of the standard Morris Oxford chassis.

And indeed, this was no idle boast. A great deal of special attention was lavished on the M.G. chassis now that there was space to carry out the work in a separate factory. The engine, in particular, was the subject of more meticulous assembly, perhaps, than any subsequent M.G. power unit with the exception of those intended for racing or record cars.

The Morris engine was removed when the rolling chassis arrived, and completely dismantled, as had been M.G. practice for more than two years. The valve guides were removed, the ports taken out to maximum diameter with a high-speed grinder, and polished. The combustion chambers were also polished but the head was not skimmed, the compression ratio wisely being left at the standard 5:1 figure. Every bearing was checked for clearance, alignment and end-float. Piston and connecting-rod clearances and alignment received the same attention, all faults being corrected. The whole engine was then carefully cleaned, reassembled with its stronger valve springs and specially-wound Lucas GA.4 magneto, and reinstalled in the chassis. Also fitted were the radiator and a special carburetter designed for use with coal-gas— for there was more to come.

The chassis was now pushed to a most unusual running-in bay, where supplies of coal gas and cooling water were laid on and arrangements made for disposal of exhaust gas. Beneath the rear wheels were sets of rollers connected to the under-floor paddle fans to provide a suitable load—a simplified multiple version of H. N. Charles's Comparator. There were five 'pits' in all, each with two sets of rollers. In the first the engine was run at 1000 r.p.m. in first gear. In the second the speed was increased to 1100 r.p.m. and second gear engaged after a time. In the third the speed went up to 1200 r.p.m. in second gear. In the fourth the engine ran at 1400 r.p.m. in second gear, then in top. Finally the engine was run at 1600 r.p.m. in top gear in the fifth pit. With a total of thirty hours in this running-in bay, every engine *and* transmission system had the equivalent of 750 miles' road work. Then the head was removed, the engine decarbonized, the valves ground in, and a Solex carburetter fitted.

Work on the remainder of the chassis included removing the Morris brake gear and fitting the M.G. type, now much simpler in design but more effective than the 1926/7 version, so that the servo motor was not required. The brake drums were fitted with aluminium cooling fins and the shoe assembly thoroughly checked. The standard Morris road springs were replaced by M.G.'s flatter ones, the Hartford shock-absorbers fitted at the rear, and M.G.'s wire wheels all round. The back axle, as supplied, already contained M.G.'s higher final-drive ratio. The Morris steering assembly was also removed and replaced by M.G.'s Marles steering, now with 18″ Bluemel steering wheel. Next came M.G.'s new exhaust manifold, more efficient than the Morris type, and the remainder of the exhaust system.

On the chassis was mounted a sturdy, cast-aluminium bulkhead which had replaced the earlier sheet-steel device, together with the fuel tank, wings, running-boards and valances. With a standard loaded test body it was taken out on the road so that brakes and shock absorbers could be adjusted. This was followed by a session on the Comparator to ensure that performance came up to M.G. standards, with further adjustment to carburetter and ignition settings if necessary. Then—and only then—was the chassis considered ready to be driven up to Coventry so that Carbodies could mount the coachwork. When the car returned the wiring was completed and various accessories fitted, including a Smith wiper driven off the camshaft instead of from the gearbox, as before— which, of course, meant that the wiper no longer stopped when the car stopped.

The practice of soldering a false piece to the radiator had now ceased; instead, there was a neat metal apron between the front dumb-irons through which the starting-handle passed. With a proper enamelled M.G. badge on the radiator, there was no need for a cut-out metal one on the honeycomb, although some cars did carry both.

Indeed, the 14/40 now started to break out in a perfect rash of octagons. In June 1928 the oval instrument panel with Smith instruments was changed for an octagonal one carrying Watford instruments. An octagon was cast in the aluminium toe-board, and the (right-side) accelerator pedal bore an M.G. octagon. Special hub-caps with M.G. motifs replaced the standard Morris type. Scuttle ventilators were usually octagonal. The holding-down bolt for the lid of the toolbox, prominently visible at the rear of the car, carried an M.G. octagon.

One can laugh at all this, of course; Kimber's obsession with the octagon was always faintly absurd and frequently overdone. However, considering what went into the basic Oxford chassis before it was considered fit to carry an M.G. body, is it surprising that he hated his cars to be called 'rebodied Morrises' and went to such lengths to accentuate the difference?

After a time it was thought illogical to buy in complete rolling chassis from Morris Motors and tear them apart to make so many alterations, so M.G. arranged to have separate deliveries of bare frames, engine/gearbox units, and axles complete with brakes. The latter were supplied by Wolseley Motors Ltd (which concern, together with the S.U. Carburetter Company, W. R. Morris had bought in 1927). Before long, M.G. had a telephone call from a worried Wolseley engineer. They had, he said, run into trouble when shrinking the cast-aluminium fins onto the standard brake-drums: if overheated they distorted; if heated insufficiently, they would jam halfway on and then split. Clearly, he said, the oven temperature was extremely critical, probably within a range of 5 degrees Fahrenheit. Would M.G. please tell him the correct setting? 'No idea,' said Cousins cheerfully. How, then, had M.G. fitted their brake fins so successfully? 'We heated them up with a gas-pipe and spat on 'em,' said Cousins. 'If they sizzled, we knew they were right.'

As mentioned earlier, demand for the 14/40 M.G. fell gradually throughout 1928 and production dropped to just under 300 for the year, compared with just over 400 the previous year. Morris sales also fell in 1928, and there was reason to suspect that Father Time was beginning to overtake the basic design. Any sports car enthusiast might well feel disappointed when he opened the impressive bonnet of the 14/40 M.G. to find, under a great deal of fresh air, only a modest four-cylinder side-valve engine.

However, some minor alterations in specification were made: new wheels with smaller hubs, much less ungainly than the open-hub type; cellulose paintwork; an electric wiper; vacuum head-lamp dippers instead of Barker. The 1928 Motor Show literature mentioned that Malcolm Campbell owned a 14/40, and boldly announced: 'We make no apology for continuing the 14/40 M.G. Sports Mk IV at its existing specification and price. During the past season we have incorporated many improvements and this popular model still remains by far the best value in its class.'

And indeed, the old side-valve M.G. continued in production for more than a year. But the 100-odd cars built following the Show formed only a small proportion of the total number of M.G.s produced during that exciting year of 1929. By that time, several interesting things had happened.

What Kimber needed, of course, was a more sophisticated engine for his sports cars. The story of how he acquired one involves a trip backwards in time and the invocation of that statute so dear to the British motor industry, the Old Pals' Act. First, however, it must be recorded that when W. R. Morris bought Wolseley Motors in February 1927, he did so because they had gone bankrupt, and their bankruptcy had resulted mainly from heavy investment in an admirable overhead-camshaft car known as the Silent Six. When, therefore, Morris Motors surprised everybody by bringing out an o.h.c model in October 1927 after so many years of side-valve Morrises, most people assumed that the engine was a Wolseley design. But it wasn't.

Back in 1918, it was a friend named Frank Woollard who secured for Cecil Kimber his job with E. G. Wrigley Ltd. Woollard, like Kimber, pulled out of Wrigley's before they finally went bankrupt in the early 'twenties, and in 1923, when Morris bought the Hotchkiss factory at Coventry to turn it into Morris Engines

Branch, Kimber recommended Woollard as its manager. Morris accepted this recommendation and Woollard became one of his most valued men, a pioneer of advanced mass-production methods in England. It was not too difficult, therefore, for Kimber to suggest to Woollard a few years later that Morris Engines *might* like to produce something better than the old Hotchkiss-designed side-valve four-cylinder unit. And his old friend instructed Pendrell, the chief designer, to do so.

The new 2468 c.c. overhead-camshaft six-cylinder engine was presented to W. R. Morris as a *fait accompli*, which was never a good idea with him, and probably looked far too complicated to a man who preferred his engines to be almost agriculturally simple. He grudgingly allowed it to be used in three mediocre motor-cars, one after another.

It was first installed in a 'stretched' Morris Cowley chassis of 9′ 6″ wheelbase which, with a fairly light body, appeared at the 1927 Motor Show as the Morris Light Six. The advanced engine design quite overwhelmed the motoring press, and *The Autocar* devoted no less than six pages of one issue to describing the new wonder car, which, they said, '. . . is destined to compete in price, equipment, coachwork, and performance with anything produced within, or outside, the confines of the British Isles'.

This paean of praise might have been stifled had someone looked more closely at the long and willowy chassis frame, which flexed so much that it affected the steering—something of a misfortune in a relatively fast car. Sir Miles Thomas, one of the few people who have ever driven a Morris Light Six, described it later as 'an absolute bitch to hold on the road'.

So eight of the 4′ 0″-track chassis that had been built were hurriedly dismantled, leaving only three survivors. Morris Motors went back to the drawing-board and produced a much sturdier chassis with wider (4′ 8″) track and even longer (9′ 9″) wheelbase, but still retaining the Cowley brakes and steering. Since this was a great deal heavier they called it, logically enough, the Morris Six, which *The Autocar* tested in May 1928 and *The Motor* in March 1929. Neither magazine ever criticized a car much in those days —especially a British car—so when it was gently suggested in print that the brakes and steering 'might be improved', this meant they were indescribably awful.

The third attempt with the new o.h.c. engine was the Morris Isis of late 1929, with Bishop cam steering and Lockheed hydraulic brakes. These were a great improvement, but the car had now grown so heavy and cumbersome that its flat-out maximum was found to be only 62 m.p.h., a speed that it took more than 40 secs. to reach from a standstill.

One of the surviving three narrow-track Morris Light Six chassis, fitted with a fabric saloon body, was bought by Morris Garages on 29th December 1927. The first thing M.G. did was to throw away almost everything but the engine, doubtless repressing a shudder as they did so. A completely new frame was designed with particular thought for the suspension and an ingenious design of front shackle. The Cowley back axle was rebuilt by E.N.V. incorporating some Morris parts and some new ones. A new front axle was made by Alford and Alder, but the brake gear was a mixture of Morris and M.G. The track remained at 4' 0". Modified Marles steering was installed, and the five-stud hubs retained but fitted with M.G. wheels.

Many of the prototype parts were roughly traced out, at Kimber's insistence, by Cousins, who had drawn nothing since he left school fourteen years before, and despite the fact that M.G. did not own even a drawing-board (he used a sheet of plywood instead). From these very elementary drawings the first prototypes were made. As a temporary measure the chassis was fitted with a bulkhead of basically 14/40 type. The final touch was a completely new radiator, designed by Kimber with assistance from Ron Goddard of Radiators Branch. The first M.G. radiator of all, it was so exactly right in appearance that the same basic design was retained for a quarter of a century. There were, later, murmurs of complaint from Daimler, who said Kimber had pinched their vertical centre rib. Quite unabashed, Kimber answered that *they* had pinched it from the London General Omnibus Company.

Two prototypes were prepared so that they could be shown to Morris, any attempt to go ahead without his personal approval being foredoomed to failure. Fortunately he was pleased with M.G.'s very first essay into chassis design (apart from the Kimber Special of 1925), and on 17th August 1928 *The Autocar* was able to publish details and pictures of the six-cylinder M.G. This aroused so much interest that an initial order was placed with Carbodies of Coventry, even before the Motor Show opened.

Most new cars, if they have any personality at all, acquire a nickname in the prototype stage, and this model was known at Edmund Road as the 'Quick Six'. For this reason most of the components still carry the prefix 'QS' in the official parts list. Mention of factory nicknames recalls that M.G.'s first full-time draughtsman, one Keith Smith, was taken on about this time to draw the 'QS' components for quantity production. His employment lasted until one Monday morning a couple of years later, when it was found that he had 'borrowed' Old Speckly Hen, the Feather-weight Fabric Saloon, for a weekend's illicit motoring. Speckly had then degenerated into a factory hack, but even hack cars were not used without prior permission.

When the M.G. Sports Six appeared on Stand 150 at the 1928 Motor Show, it was a very different car from the single-carburetter prototype of a month or two before. For a start, a completely new cylinder block had been cast for use with two carburetters, the induction tracts passing through the block and curving upwards to mate with a new cylinder head. Several major engine components had been produced in handsome polished aluminium. Otherwise the JA-type Pendrell design was followed closely. The bottom end assembly was an exceptionally rigid one and almost every bearing was pressure-fed, with an additional oil feed to the cork-lined clutch. There were shell-bearing big-ends and mains. The over-head camshaft was driven by a long duplex roller chain, with spring-loaded eccentric tensioner. Every valve rocker had its own separate oil supply, and the back of the camshaft was drilled to provide a tachometer drive. The high-tension distributor con-tained two contact-breakers instead of one.

There was a new bulkhead supported by cast-aluminium brackets which incorporated an M.G. motif (totally invisible, alas, when the body was fitted!), and two bulkhead tanks, one for reserve petrol and the other for a reserve supply of engine oil. The handbrake—for the first time—was of the 'fly-off' racing type that engages only when the knob is pressed down. The wheels, too, suggested racing practice, being of authentic Rudge-Whitworth centre-lock design. Pedals and steering were fully adjustable. The instrumentation was nothing short of magnificent, with a splendid array of Jaeger instruments mounted in a black-crackle panel.

Prices were a long way above the tentative figures previously quoted, the chassis alone costing (at £420) almost as much as a complete tourer was expected to be. The actual price of the tourer was £485, the two-seater £5 less. A two-door Salonette cost £545, and a four-door saloon £555.

Approval of the 18/80 M.G. Six, as it was now called, was un-stinted when the first road test appeared in *The Motor* in March 1929. The new M.G. would out-accelerate a 3-litre Lagonda Six or an Alvis Silver Eagle, steering and roadholding were rated admirable, and a top speed of almost 80 m.p.h. was achieved. By the standards of the period this speed was truly exceptional, and the 18/80 M.G. made the 14/40 seem a poor relation indeed.

But the 18/80 and 14/40 models had not been the only inhabitants of Stand 150 in October 1928. There was something else, attracting so much attention to itself that the others were almost in danger of being ignored completely.

W. R. Morris had made his name with an 11.9 h.p. car, added to this a 13.9 h.p. model, and by 1925 held 41 per cent of all British car sales. In the later 'twenties he moved further up the horsepower scale, mainly in a pursuit of export business which proved unsuccessful and nearly lost him his home market, too. The design of smaller cars had greatly improved, so that more motorists were turning to vehicles of 10 h.p. or less, encouraged by the British system of taxing cars in direct proportion to their R.A.C. formula horsepower. The imposition of a petrol tax in 1928 gave a further boost to small-car sales.

Morris's own position was not helped by the rather uninspired design and appearance of the flat-radiator Oxford and Cowley, and it must have been particularly irritating that his arch-rival, Herbert Austin, had been doing extremely well with the Austin Seven from as far back as 1922. By 1927 Morris had already realized that he would have to produce a 'baby car', as they were popularly called. And when he took over Wolseley early that year, he found that they had already designed an engine in the 8 h.p. class for their own use.

This was a brilliantly clever little four-cylinder unit derived, via the post-war Wolseley Ten, from the big Type W4A Hispano-Suiza aero engines that Wolseley had built under licence during the war. It was of only 847 c.c., but it had a tiny overhead camshaft driven through bevel gears by a spindle which formed the armature of the vertically mounted dynamo. Although the crankshaft had only two main bearings, it was quite short and very rigidly supported, an ingenious arrangement having eliminated main-bearing caps completely.

When this engine was installed in a prototype chassis it provided such a startling performance that Morris Motors Ltd decided it would scare the hell out of Mr and Mrs John Citizen. So Wolseley were instructed to produce a detuned version for use in the new Morris baby car, rumours of which were rife throughout the spring of 1928. *The Autocar* published the first full description of the

Morris Minor on 31st August, exactly two weeks after their announcement of the new M.G. Six.

Only two weeks later they told their readers that the M.G. Car Company was going to produce a sports model based on the new chassis. For some strange reason they referred to this as the 'Morris Midget', which must surely have brought a scathing letter from Cecil Kimber.

Kimber had managed to borrow one of the experimental Minors, fitted with the engine that had been thought too powerful for that chassis. He removed the Minor body and replaced it by a light two-seater sports job which Carbodies built early in September—just a week before *The Autocar*'s Midget announcement was published, indeed, making it one of the slickest scoops in the history of motoring journalism.

For M.G., the operation must have brought back memories of early Bullnose days. Very few chassis alterations were needed: the standard Minor suspension was lowered, the steering rake increased, the gear-change and pedal layout slightly altered. The body was as simple as could be, panelled in fabric-covered plywood on an ash frame and incorporating a pointed boat-tail for luggage and spare wheel. There was a little vee windscreen, an elementary hood that normally lived in the tail, fixed cycle-type mudguards, and a scaled-down version of the new M.G. Six radiator. The wheels were the standard Minor wire-spoked type with three fixing studs, but adorned with M.G. hub-caps. Two louvred metal panels served to reduce the apparent height of the chassis frame.

This body was finished in blue. Another, in red, was built a fortnight later and mounted on another chassis, but an engine for this could not be obtained before the Motor Show opened the following week. So the bonnet was firmly fastened, a dummy exhaust pipe protruded from underneath, and the red Midget became of necessity a stationary exhibit on the M.G. stand, while the blue car served as demonstrator. Both Show cars had swept-up scuttles which later proved too expensive to make (the complete body costing £6 10s.!) for quantity production.

So it was that three M.G. models were seen at the 1928 Motor Show, the first in which the Company had their own stand at Olympia. There was the 18/80 M.G. Six at anything from £480 to £555, depending on coachwork; there was the faithful 14/40 at £335 to £445; and there was the Midget, carrying a price tag of £175, which was exactly £50 more than the new Minor on the

Morris stand. With its hotter-than-Minor engine and all-up weight of just over 10 cwt., the little Midget turned out to be almost as fast as the 14/40 two-seater in all gears, with better acceleration all the way. And it cost hardly more than half as much. No wonder the new M.G. baby attracted attention, but *The Autocar* were being more prophetic than they could possibly have imagined when they said, 'The M.G. Midget will make sports car history.'

Production of the Midget did not commence immediately after the Show, but it aroused so much interest that M.G. ordered 498 bodies from Coventry and laid down a new assembly line at Edmund Road. During March 1929 the first Midget chassis started coming off the line. They went to Leopold Street for body mounting, then came back to be finished at Cowley. The Midget engines were sent direct to Edmund Road from Wolseley Motors.

After the familiar side-valve unit of the 14/40, these little o.h.c. engines—and, of course, those of the bigger 18/80—were looked upon with a certain amount of awe, and the men at M.G. were instructed not to tamper with the valve gear. Indeed, they were not even allowed to remove the rocker-box cover.

This restriction was considered rather irksome by a fairly new employee called Reg Jackson. He had had some experience with o.h.c. engines when he ran a little garage of his own before joining M.G. the previous October. He was possessed of a most inquiring nature, and when one of the Midgets failed to show up its anticipated performance on the Comparator, he wanted to know why. The forbidden cover was soon removed, after which a few experiments seemed to suggest that the camshaft bearings were too tight.

Low power outputs were not uncommon, and 'Papa' Dring, chief experimental engineer of Wolseley, paid several visits to Edmund Road. He was an amiable soul with a long and curly waxed moustache and soon became friendly with Jackson, whose diagnosis he confirmed. Already it seemed that the complicated new engines were beginning to lose their aura of mystery. Within the next few years, M.G. were to achieve more with them than Wolseley Motors would ever have thought possible.

A new spirit was beginning to stir within the M.G. Car Company. In January 1929 the prototype 18/80 saloon had been prepared for entry in the Monte Carlo Rally, driven by Francis (now Sir Francis) Samuelson, a familiar figure on the racing circuits. He drove to Monte singlehanded, his co-driver having been delayed, won an award in the coachwork competition with the M.G., and made third best performance of the day in the Mont des Mules speed hillclimb which followed. At Easter, four Midgets and three 18/80s showed up well in the Land's End Trial. Three Midgets were next prepared for Callingham, Parker and the Earl of March to drive in a J.C.C. High-Speed Trial at Brooklands in June. All three gained gold medals, as did two privately owned Midgets driven by Dunham and Scott. This success was repeated in a similar M.C.C. event later in the season.

More and more emphasis was placed on performance now that Kimber had two models which, each in its class, could give competitors a run for their money. A rather mediocre 1928 sales slogan, 'It Passes—and Surpasses', was replaced in 1929 by the crisper-sounding 'Faster than Most'.

And M.G. now started to design yet another new car. Competition work had already shown that the 18/80 Six was handicapped by its Morris three-speed gearbox, the Morris-derived brakes were no more than adequate, and the Morris-based final drive would soon give trouble if more power had to be transmitted. Besides, the 4' 0" track—yet another Morris legacy—was somewhat narrow and restricted the width of the coachwork.

In retrospect, these considerations alone do not fully explain what followed. One suspects that, with the design of the 18/80 Mark II, Kimber was looking still further ahead. Certainly the Mark II had a four-speed box, redesigned brakes, a sturdier final drive and 4' 4" track. But the whole chassis had been 'beefed up' to an extraordinary extent. The frame was deeper and stiffer, although the Mark I frame had never given trouble. The rear springs, shock-absorbers, axles and steering connections all went up in size to such an extent that the Mark II chassis weighed some 3 cwt. more than a Mark I. With the normal 18/80 engine, a good deal of the performance was actually lost.

So many changes were made that the new Mark II chassis cost £105 more than the Mark I, every part—excepting certain engine components—being made specially for M.G. by suppliers from inside and outside the Morris empire. It was, indeed, the first complete production chassis to be conceived specifically as an M.G., and this was marked by the prefix 'A' to the range of chassis numbers. However, a growing M.G. tradition was observed. The first car to carry an M.G. number, a 14/40 of late 1927, had been allocated number 2251. The first production

18/80 Six had carried 6251, and the first Midget had been M.0251. Obviously the first 18/80 Mark II had to be A.0251.

On the eve of the 1929 Motor Show M.G. had almost trebled the previous year's output of cars. About 12 per cent of the season's total were 14/40 models, something over 30 per cent were 18/80 Mk I, and the new Midget accounted for the remainder. In the near future, even discontinuing the 14/40, the range of body styles on three different chassis would represent a total of no less than fourteen models.

They had not only established themselves after a long struggle as a distinct and separate marque in their own right, with an admirable reputation among the car-buying public. They had in just two years completely outgrown their new factory at Edmund Road, Cowley. So they moved for the fourth and last time to another one at Abingdon-on-Thames, where the telephone number—by accident or design—was, and still is, Abingdon 251.

Chapter 4

Road and Track (1930–1935)

A few miles from Oxford the River Thames takes a sudden sweep westwards before recollecting itself and continuing on its way to London and the sea; at the most westerly point lies Abingdon, scarcely a teeming metropolis at any period of its existence. In the 7th century a minor Saxon king named Cissa had established a Benedictine monastery there, but Henry VIII did it no good at all at the time of the Dissolution, and Cromwell's men made an even worse mess of the entire town a century later. In 1929 it still had not quite recovered, and the arrival of the M.G. Car Company was about the fourth most important thing that had happened to Abingdon in a couple of thousand years. A small sports car factory achieved what kings and conquerors had failed to do, by making the name of Abingdon known throughout the western world.

The factory that M.G. took over was an extension of the adjacent Pavlova Leather Company's premises, which had fallen into disuse after the war. Here, during the first few months, Kimber gathered his team around him. H. N. Charles was the obvious choice for design and development. George Propert, who had returned to the M.G. fold at Edmund Road, was appointed general manager, with Ted Colegrove as sales manager and George Tuck in charge of publicity. From A.C. Cars came Maynard and Vines to look after buying. Most of the 'old-timers'— Cousins, Saunders, Stevens, Tayler, Morris, Martin, Hounslow, Nash and many others—were among those transferred from Edmund Road, as was Reg Jackson. Two newcomers were Gordon Phillips, a highly skilled fitter, and Sydney Enever, a former Morris Garages shop-boy who was to reveal a rare talent for original design. Such men might lack theoretical qualifications, but H. N. Charles was often amazed by their insight into mechanical problems; they were, he says, exceptionally gifted in their own way.

The inaugural luncheon party was held on 20th January 1930. Only a few weeks later, in faraway Detroit, the son of Henry Ford bought an M.G. Midget for his own private amusement. This was an intriguing portent of things to come, but probably made not the slightest impact on Abingdon at the time, for the men of M.G. had something else on their minds; they were building their first racing car.

Its basis was the new 18/80 Mark II chassis, into which was fitted an exciting development of the 18/80 power unit incorporating a new crankshaft and pistons, a new camshaft, dry-sump lubrication, a cross-flow cylinder head with twin sparking-plugs, and a host of other improvements including a new clutch and a higher second gear.

The convenient remote control gearchange of the Mark II was retained, together with the transmission. Nor were many changes necessary in the immensely strong chassis apart from a modified mounting (reminiscent of Bullnose practice) for the steering box, an additional pair of shock-absorbers at the rear, and increased fuel tankage. The admirable Mark II braking system—a stout central cross-shaft carrying a double lever at each end, from which cased cables ran fore-and-aft to roller bearing camshafts, with large aluminium brake-shoes and finned 14-inch drums—was modified only slightly. In accordance with correct racing practice, the front axle and steering-arms were draw-filed and polished.

On this chassis was mounted an exceptionally handsome four-seater body conforming with AIACR regulations. There was a fold-flat windscreen and cycle-type mudguards, the front ones secured by massive cross-bracing made up from special steel tube of 'streamlined' section. It was all tremendously impressive and—predictably—appallingly heavy, the total weight being about 27½ cwt.

The vexed question of nomenclature now arises again. This M.G., as a development of the 18/80 Mark II or A-type, naturally became the Mark III or B-type. Contemporary catalogues called it the M.G. Six Sports Road Racing Model, and hopes of greatly increased power output provided the designation '18/100'. Over the years, however, it has come to be called the Tiger or Tigress, and it is now difficult to decide how this arose. A jungle cat of indeterminate sex admittedly appears on the cover of Mark III leaflets, but this identical drawing was used to advertise the M.G. 14/40 model in a Brooklands programme as far back as July 1928. It therefore seems safer to call M.G.'s first racing car simply the Mark III—noting, nevertheless, that the future was to bring other Mark III models of very different shapes and sizes.

One can only guess at Kimber's motives in producing this

splendid monster. It has been suggested that he nursed Bentleyish ambitions, and it is noteworthy that Bentley had just scored their third successive Le Mans victory in 1929 (and were about to win again in 1930). Moreover, the new M.G.'s first event was to be a 24-hour race, the Brooklands Double Twelve on the second weekend of May.

But while the Mark III was nearing completion, Kimber was approached by two friends, Edmondson and Randall, who contemplated entering three Midgets for the team prize in the same race. The Midget had been much improved in detail during its first year of production, the most notable advance being a complete redesign of the braking system, for which Reg Jackson had been mainly responsible. Now that the Midget would stop, Jackson was instructed to make it go, and so began intensive work on the engine of a spare car. To discourage fatigue fracture, he brought most of the engine components to a mirror finish with a metal polish called 'Shinio', and in due course this name rubbed off, so to speak, on the car. H. N. Charles, who did not share Kimber's enthusiasm for the Mark III project, began to take an interest in the progress of Shinio. For an engineer of his ability it was natural to alter the rather staid valve timing, and this brought an immediate power increase—from 20 to 27 b.h.p.

Five cars were built with similarly modified engines, larger fuel tanks, Brooklands regulation exhaust systems and bonnet straps, and stronger road wheels. The bodies were basically of Midget shape, but with deep cutaways in the doors and folding gauze windscreens. Two cars were for private owners who had become interested in the race, and the remainder formed the team known to M.G. as 'The Tomato-Growers', Edmondson and Randall having a business interest in market gardening. A sixth Midget, privately prepared, was also entered.

It has long been a tradition of motor-racing that, when a car 'blows up', some ingenious excuse for its demise must be found. Leslie Callingham and H. D. Parker, the drivers of the Mark III, produced a classic example when their big M.G. displayed sudden and fatal symptoms a couple of hours after the Double Twelve started. A throttle butterfly, they said, had come loose and jammed in the valve gear. According to *The Autocar* report it was a broken piston, but Cousins describes the trouble more succinctly: 'When we took the sump off the crankshaft was *purple*. There wasn't a bearing left anywhere.'

The little Midgets, however, ran almost faultlessly throughout the race, although the privately prepared one retired towards the end of the first day. At the end of the second day the car driven by Cecil Randall and F. M. Montgomery finished fourteenth overall, averaging 60.23 m.p.h. for the twenty-four hours against a handicap speed of 62 m.p.h., and the other four Midgets also survived the long grind over the bumpy Brooklands track. Two works Austin Sevens finished ahead of the M.G.s, but their third car lay far behind after continual engine trouble, so the Team Prize went to the Tomato Growers. There was great rejoicing at Abingdon.

Kimber had intended to build at least twenty-five of the big Mark III road-racing M.G.s, and was reluctant to abandon the idea because of the model's unsuccessful debut. Callingham, who was with the Shell company, did much experimental work after the race in association with Reid Railton, and the standard engine's 83 b.h.p. at 4300 r.p.m. was eventually raised to within 4 b.h.p. of the target 100 at the same r.p.m. But the Mark III engine continued to dislike sustained high speed. Moreover, at £895 the car appealed to a very limited market in 1930; one was bought by Victor Rothschild, but there were not enough Rothschilds among M.G. fanciers to justify production. No further orders came from the 1930 Motor Show, so production ceased after only five cars had been built. The remaining twenty engines were sold, and the unused bodies fitted to 18/80 Mark I chassis.

At the 1930 Show the Midget appeared with further improvements in addition to the Double Twelve valve timing which was now being used on all production engines. But the bigger M.G.s still occupied a prominent position on the stand; in fact there were two new 18/80 models, the stately Mark II De Luxe Saloon at £699 and a lively Mark I Speed Model at £525, making up a total, with various options in coachwork, of no less than nineteen M.G.s. The 18/80 Mark I continued in production until the summer of 1931, when 500 examples had been built in all. The Mark II lingered on right into 1933, but it was always handicapped by its greater weight and higher price, and total production reached only 236 cars.

By that time, however, hardly anybody thought of the M.G. Car Company as builders of large, well-appointed and relatively expensive motor-cars. They had won fame with a bewildering array of Midgets, Magnas and Magnettes, and achieved so many successes in races, trials, rallies and record attempts that one cannot hope to chronicle more than a fraction of them. The Company had adopted a new sales slogan—'Safety Fast!'—late in 1930, and in two words it seemed to embody the essence of the marque's appeal. About the same time, a group of enthusiastic owners had formed the M.G. Car Club. Their first honorary secretary, a young accountancy student named John Thornley, joined the Company in 1931; he was to be appointed its general manager twenty-one years later.

Even before its good showing in the Double Twelve the original M-type Midget had become widely known as a small sports car that was inexpensive to buy, cheap to run, yet suitable for the amateur to use in almost any form of motor sport. F. M. Montgomery had successfully completed the 1930 Monte Carlo Rally with a privately owned car and gone on to break the 1100 c.c. class record in the subsequent Mont des Mules hillclimb. No less than thirty were entered for the Land's End Trial, and eighteen of them won gold medals. The Midget's successes in 1930 included awards in races and hillclimbs as far apart as South Africa, Czechoslovakia and Singapore. The factory had built two cars for Le Mans, one driven by Murton-Neale and Hicks, the other by Samuelson and an M.G. employee named Freddie Kindell. Although neither of the Midgets had completed the race, Samuelson had taken his on to the Belgian G.P. a fortnight later and finished this twenty-four-hour event, despite continual clutch-slip.

The M.G. Midget was not, of course, the only small sports car sold in England. The Austin Seven, for example, had a record of racing successes that was remarkable for a side-valve car, and in supercharged form it won the 1930 Brooklands 500 Miles outright at an amazing 83.41 m.p.h. average. Had Longbridge built their sports Sevens in quantity instead of leaving that field mainly to a host of small specialist coachbuilders, M.G. might have faced sterner competition in selling as well as in racing their cars. But the Midget was far better looking than the Austin Seven, cost no more, and above all it was available.

Moreover, the Seven had changed comparatively little since its introduction in 1922. M.G. were already planning their next Midget when the Double Twelve was run, and it was to differ considerably from the Minor-based M-type.

Kimber had somehow acquired an example of a little-known French sports car, the Rally, a most purposeful 1100 c.c. machine rather similar to the Brooklands Riley Nine in appearance. The chassis side-members were of channel section and, apart from curving up over the front axle, were straight for most of their length, the low lines being achieved by passing the chassis *beneath* the rear axle. M.G. adopted this unusual arrangement to build a prototype chassis, EX.120, which, like the Rally, carried centre-lock wire wheels on Rudge-type hubs. The Rally had square-section cross-members, but square tubing was costly and required end-brackets that were difficult to make. Abingdon found that mild-steel tubing could be bought quite cheaply from the cycle trade; it was made to extremely fine limits and allowed the use of turned brackets, pinned and brazed in place, bicycle fashion. In this way a dead-true frame could be built even with the limited facilities available at the factory. The opportunity was taken to lengthen the M-type's inconveniently short wheelbase to 6' 9", and the braking system was a simplified version of that used on the 18/80 Mark II.

Thus was evolved the basic chassis frame that was to remain in use on M.G. Midgets for nearly twenty years. It incorporated some unusual but highly effective features. As on the Lanchester of the mid-'twenties, the main leaves of the springs were eyeless at the rear; instead of being shackled they passed through phosphor-bronze trunnions which provided considerable lateral rigidity. The engine, instead of having a four-point mounting, was carried by two tubular supports, one fore-and-aft at the front, the other passing laterally below the bell-housing. The radiator was not carried by the chassis, but on an extension of the front engine mounting. This arrangement was the work of H. N. Charles, whose wartime experience with the airframes and engine mountaings on fighter aircraft had taught him that, in his own words, 'the heavy things must stand still'.

It provided many advantages. Although the chassis was intended to flex there was no relative movement between radiator and engine, thus reducing the likelihood of hose leakage. It gave a stable radiator and bonnet line—very reassuring to the driver—however much the chassis weaved about. When swept front wings replaced cycle-type mudguards a few years later it was possible to brace them to the radiator, which in turn was fixed to the engine, and the whole of this considerable mass was unaffected by chassis movement. Again, supporting the engine at the rear by a transverse tubular mounting prevented chassis flex being transmitted to the rear main bearing. This cured one of the main faults of the M-type, in which clutch slip frequently resulted from an oil leak in the rear main bearing. The trouble reappeared in subsequent models that reverted to the earlier engine mounting.

But the EX.120 chassis was destined to serve as something more exciting than a mere factory prototype. Two well-known figures in the record-breaking world, Capt. George Eyston and Ernest Eldridge, had been planning an attack on the Class H (750 c.c.) Hour record, using either a Ratier or a modified Riley Nine engine in the chassis of the original Thomas Special. Then they found that an old friend of Eyston's, Jimmy Palmes, had done some work on two M.G. engines with a similar aim in mind. A visit was paid to Abingdon, where Kimber pointed out that a suitable M.G. chassis also existed. He offered to put one of his men on full-time experimental work under Eldridge's direction.

That man was Reg Jackson, who was soon installed in a top-secret workshop within the factory, its walls lined with white ceiling-board. Before the job was finished they were covered from end to end with drawings, each of which, as Jackson puts it, represented a visit from Eldridge. By that time, too, little remained of the basic M-type engine as modified by Palmes. Eldridge had designed a new counterbalanced crankshaft, the most painstaking work had gone into the bottom-end bearings and their lubrication, and the valve gear was a highly ingenious roller-bearing arrangement incorporating some Bugatti parts and turned-down J.A.P. motor-cycle valves. Most of the assembly work had been shared by Jackson and Gordon Phillips, whose skill as a fitter was tested to the full. Seldom has any multi-cylinder unit been so beautifully put together. With the sparking-plugs removed, the pressure of the valve springs on the camshaft would turn the engine over.

Fitted with a faired-in body of generally M-type appearance, M.G.'s first record car was taken to Montlhéry track, where on 30th December 1930 Eyston covered 100 kilometres at 87.3 m.p.h. before one of the turned-down valves broke. He had failed to capture the 'Hour' by almost twenty minutes, but his speed was high enough to wrest several other records from Austin.

A conference ensued back at Abingdon, where it was known that Malcolm Campbell was shortly to attempt 100 m.p.h. on Daytona Beach with a specially built Austin Seven. Kimber said firmly that M.G., not Austin, must be the first to achieve 100 m.p.h. with a 750 c.c. car. Eldridge said it would take anything up to a year's development work unless M.G. used a supercharger, as Austin did. And Eyston reminded them both that he had a business interest in the Powerplus supercharger.

Frantic work followed, including lengthy tests with blowers fitted to standard M-type engines. Within four weeks the Eldridge engine had been converted for use with the Powerplus, and Jackson and Kindell set off for Montlhéry to install it in EX.120. Despite all that they could do, Eyston was unable to better 97.07 m.p.h., so Cousins and Phillips were sent out to help the weary pair. Further work on the record car included fitting the radiator with a frontal cowl, beaten out from an old oil-drum over a convenient drainage channel in the concrete track. Despite a considerable cross-wind the courageous Eyston tried again, late in the evening of 16th February 1931, and secured four records at speeds up to 103.13 m.p.h.

The impact of this achievement can scarcely be imagined nowadays. At a time when the average small car had a top speed of about 50 m.p.h., it was tremendous. Two weeks later, Kimber celebrated with a luncheon party in Abingdon, the guests including many of the Double Twelve drivers, Earl Howe, the Earl of March, and Capt. Arthur Waite, son-in-law of Sir Herbert Austin and head of the Longbridge racing department. The guests had a reception beyond their wildest dreams, hundreds of people crowding the streets and displaying a boisterous enthusiasm that even the 100 m.p.h. record hardly seemed to warrant. What had happened was that one of the regular Austin drivers (not, in fact, present at all) was named Chaplin, and somehow the rumour had got about that *Charlie* Chaplin was coming to the party.

The M.G. factory had little chance to rest upon their laurels, for Kimber stood up after lunch to announce that a new 750 c.c. racing model, the Montlhéry Midget, would shortly be produced on the lines of the record-breaker. He even had a mock-up chassis ready to show to the guests. The price was to be £345 in supercharged form or £295 unsupercharged, which seemed fair enough by comparison with the Double Twelve Replica M-type already marketed at £245. Six months later the price of the new model had crept up to £575 supercharged, £490 unsupercharged, which must rate as one of the most startling increases in the history of the motor trade.

It was an odd time to put a racing car on the market. Widespread depression had brought many small companies to a standstill. Although M.G. had doubled their production the previous year, they had had to cut their labour force by one-third, and the staff had volunteered to accept a 10 per cent reduction in salary. But Kimber had managed to persuade Sir William Morris that the attainment of 100 m.p.h. must be quickly followed up by further M.G. successes on the track. In fact he instructed the men at Abingdon to have fourteen of the new cars ready in time for the 1931 Double Twelve, just two months ahead. This, on the face of it, was impossible. Most of the parts for the new chassis had yet to be made. New bodies would be required to suit the longer and lower chassis. As for the engine, it had yet to be designed, let alone built. Eldridge had turned the 57 by 83 mm (847 c.c.) engine of the M-type Midget into a highly specialized 54 by 81 mm (743 c.c.) unit for the record-breaker. Recognizing the limitations of a relatively long-stroke engine, H. N. Charles was engaged in redesigning it with the original 57 mm bore but reducing the stroke to 73 mm, giving 746 c.c. Almost every component was different in detail. Even the clutch was redesigned, and the engine mated to a new four-speed gearbox with a remote-control lever. A downdraught Solex carburetter replaced the horizontal S.U. of the M-type, and a special float-chamber fixed to the sump controlled a reserve supply of oil from a separate tank —an idea borrowed from Panhard.

Drawings were whipped from the drawing-board and sent straight to suppliers so that components could be made. There was no time for proper testing, even if M.G. had possessed a test-bed in those days. Yet the essentials of the engine design were retained for all subsequent racing Midgets with complete success. The new valve timing that Charles developed at this time was used on almost every o.h.c. M.G. engine, four-cylinder or six, in production sports cars and supercharged racing cars alike.

Somehow all the components were gathered together, and the fourteen Montlhéry or C-type Midgets were built in fourteen days, every soul in the factory being pressed into service to assist in one way or another. Jackson was inflicted with a youngster bearing the unlikely name of Baden-Powell—quickly transmuted into Bathing-Towel—who broke almost every twist-drill that M.G. possessed when trying to make split-pin holes. Jackson set him to work connecting up ignition control levers, assuming that Bathing-Towel could hardly make a mess of such a simple job as this. He did, though; he connected them upside-down.

The doorless bodies were of aluminium, with cutaway sides and pointed tails. Just as the record-breaker had carried a humped wind-deflector on the scuttle, so the C-type had a pair of similar humps riveted in place. As a further reminder of EX.120, a shaped cowl enclosed the radiator.

The fourteen C-types, delivered triumphantly to Brooklands in time for the first Double Twelve practice period, were divided into four teams of three entered by the Earl of March, Cecil Randall, a Major A. T. G. ('Goldie') Gardner who had raced small cars for several years, and the Hon. Mrs Chetwynd, a relative of Sir Henry Birkin. One of the single entries was a non-starter; the other was for a University Motors salesman named Hugh Hamilton, who had driven a Riley Nine into third place in the previous year's race. The handicap allowance for 1931 made a small-car victory so certain that only two cars of more than three litres were entered. However, the new M.G. Midgets faced ten Austin Sevens, four of them supercharged, and plans were carefully laid. Graphs had been prepared in the Abingdon drawing-office showing the precise handicap position throughout the twenty-four hours, and the average speeds that had to be maintained. Every driver was thoroughly briefed on race tactics, refuelling procedure, pitwork and signals. This sort of advance planning was to play its part in many M.G. racing successes over the next few years.

Practically the entire M.G. factory—more than 200 of them—made their way by coach, car or train to Brooklands for the race. When it ended they went wild with delight, for the first *five* places were occupied by Midgets, and the March/Staniland C-type had won the 1931 Double Twelve outright at an average speed of 65.62 m.p.h. This was faster than the highest-placed 1100 c.c. Brooklands Riley (64.14 m.p.h.) and almost as fast as the best supercharged Austin Seven (68.2 m.p.h.). Of forty-eight starters only twenty-four cars completed the distance, and seven of them were M.G.s; not surprisingly, they won the Team Prize. It was an incredible achievement by a brand-new and untried model in any race, let alone a twenty-four-hour event that was generally considered tougher than Le Mans itself. If the motoring press condemned the handicapping, they conceded that M.G. had scored 'one of the greatest one-make triumphs in the history of motor-racing'.

In that fantastic first season the C-type Midget went on to take the first three places in the Saorstat Cup Race, Norman Black's winning average of 64.76 m.p.h. also giving him outright victory in the handicap Irish Grand Prix. Nine of the eleven M.G.s entered completed the Irish race, and again they took the Team Prize. A few weeks later, their M.G.s now supercharged, Black won the Ulster T.T. at 67.90 m.p.h. and Crabtree finished third, while Hamilton established a new class record for the Newtownards circuit. Finally there came the Brooklands 500 Miles, in which the handicappers set the 750 c.c. cars an impossible target of 93.97 m.p.h. E. R. Hall achieved the near-impossible with his C-type by averaging 92.17 m.p.h. for the full distance, which gave him third place overall, and yet again the Team Prize went to M.G. The Brooklands 500 Miles was at that time the fastest long-distance race in the world, Indianapolis not excepted. As for the Double Twelve, the Irish Grand Prix and the Ulster T.T., they were regarded as the three most important races held in the British Isles. Moreover, the two Irish races were held on circuits that—unlike Brooklands—tested every aspect of a car's behaviour to the full. M.G. could scarcely have given the motor-racing world a more convincing demonstration of their virtues.

Before the 500 Miles Race was held, M.G. had announced their range of models for 1931/2. The faithful M-type two-seater was still listed, but in two versions: the old fabric-bodied car, now reduced to £165, and a new metal-panelled one at £185, which is what the fabric Midget had cost since late 1929. The ingenious little M-type Sportsman's Salonette that had appeared the previous year was now called the Sportsman's Coupé, and its price reduced by £10 to £235. Also catalogued was the 18/80 Mark II in a range of six body styles at prices from £625 to £699.

There were two new chassis derived from the C-type with its sliding-trunnion suspension and centre-lock wheels, both offered with either open four-seater bodywork or a closed body somewhat similar to the M-type Coupé. One of these chassis was the D-type, with a wheelbase of 7′ 0″, and the other the 7′ 10″ wheelbase F-type which bore a new M.G. type-name, 'Magna'. The D-type cost £210 open, £250 closed; the F-type £250 open, £289 closed.

The D-type merely had the M-type 847 c.c. engine, complete with three-speed gearbox, though the latter was provided with a neat remote control. The F-type, however, was greeted with much more excitement, for it was powered by a 1271 c.c. six-cylinder o.h.c. engine with twin carburetters and a four-speed gearbox, and carried an impressive '12/70' designation.

Alas, it was nothing more than an M-type engine with two additional cylinders, retained the early valve timing that the M-type had abandoned after the 1930 Double Twelve, and gave a mere 37.2 b.h.p. at 4100 r.p.m. It was in fact a Wolseley Hornet engine, to which pieces of sheet metal had been attached in an attempt to conceal its identity. Nevertheless, the F-type Magna was well received and sold steadily despite its disappointing performance. Dick Seaman's parents bought him a tourer during his first year at Cambridge, and he used it not only in minor events but for his first international competition, the 1932 Alpine Trial. Even the under-engined D-type sold quite well, though it was still more lacking in performance.

A fortnight after the new M.G. models had been announced, George Eyston took the EX.120 record car out for its historic last run at Montlhéry, when he covered 101.1 miles *in* the hour before the car burst into flames. Only seven months earlier, it had been a struggle to exceed 100 m.p.h. for about five minutes.

The demise of EX.120 was accepted lightly, for M.G. had already built a new 750 c.c. record-breaker, EX.127, which had an asymmetric rear axle so that the transmission line could be offset to one side. This allowed the driver to sit very much lower under a new body designed by Jackson with, as H. N. Charles put it, 'a nose like a whale and a tail like a mackerel'. As the Magic Midget, the new M.G. record car was to become even more famous than its predecessor. With Eyston in hospital, Ernest Eldridge decided to drive EX.127 on its first outing, and covered five kilometres at 110.28 m.p.h. When Eyston had recovered he donned a specially made pair of asbestos overalls and, on 22nd December 1931, covered the same distance at 114.77 m.p.h. Already, 120 m.p.h. had begun to look like a possibility—less than eleven months after the first 100 m.p.h.

Unquestionably, 1931 had been a remarkable year for M.G., and it would be satisfying to report that their sales had risen steadily throughout the twelve months. Unfortunately they had not; on the contrary, production had fallen by more than 25 per cent. This was partly due to the depression, which reduced every British car manufacturer's output that year, but it is also true to say that the design of M.G.'s production models simply had not kept pace with their more glamorous racing cars at that time. For most of the year they had been endeavouring to sell the now out-dated 18/80 models. The C-type, for all its racing success, was too expensive to sell in quantity; indeed, only three more were built after the 1931 T.T., bringing the total to a mere forty-four cars. The new models they had introduced towards the end of the year, the D-type and F-type, were both underpowered. Their only pro-duction two-seater Midget was the ageing M-type, whose design owed almost nothing to racing practice, and Olympia 1931 was its fourth Motor Show.

M.G. had produced an excellent new chassis layout and developed Wolseley's 847 c.c. engine into one that gave almost twice as much power, unsupercharged, even when reduced to 746 c.c. capacity. It was now high time to combine this chassis and engine —or something very like them—in a new production two-seater.

All the engines still had their inlet and exhaust ports on the same side, so the first step was to design a new cross-flow cylinder head for the four-cylinder unit, allowing two carburetters to be used instead of one. The new head, which used 14 mm sparking-plugs instead of 18 mm, was fitted to the C-types which ran unsupercharged in the Brooklands 1000 Miles of June 1932. It gave an immediate power increase of 18 per cent, but the cars encountered various troubles and Norman Black was lucky to finish third at 75.5 m.p.h. The new head also went on the super-charged C-type that Black and Samuelson drove at Le Mans a fortnight later, but the car retired with a leaking fuel tank: one of the troubles that had afflicted the C-types in the 1000 Miles. This was Samuelson's third Le Mans race with an M.G., his third retirement. Hamilton brightened the racing outlook a month later when his blown C-type won the 800 c.c. class of the German G.P. by thirteen minutes, but then he crashed in practice for the Ulster T.T., a disastrous event for M.G. relieved only by Eddie Hall's third place at 69.93 m.p.h. A small point, significant only in retrospect, is that most of the C-types were by now fitted with lighter bodies incorporating a squared-off tail to which a large 'slab' fuel tank was fixed, and the radiator cowl had been discarded.

Kimber did not wait for the 1932 Motor Show with his new two-seater Midget; he unveiled it at the beginning of August— and what a sensation it created! It was the most delicious-looking little sports car, every line derived straight from racing practice. Here were the deep cutaways to the doors which M.G. had first used on the Double Twelve M-types, together with a fold-flat windscreen and fixed cycle-type mudguards. Here was a refined version of the double-humped scuttle first seen on the C-type. Here was the cut-off tail with large external fuel tank, the spare wheel strapped on behind. It was a classic blend of functional com-ponents, a thoroughly practical car for a keen youngster, and a certain recipe for commercial success. There has never been a better argument for keeping the stylists right out of the car-design business. The new Midget set the fashion in sports cars for years to come, and its brilliantly simple shape was used in essence for every two-seater M.G. until 1955. As George Oliver has commented in

Road and Track (1930–1935)

A History of Coachbuilding, 'The M.G. Midget was one of those
inspired designs that show no signs even now, more than twenty-
five years after its introduction, of dating in any significant way.'

Superior individuals have since become loud in their contempt
for 'pseudo racing cars', but the new Midget owed more than its
shape to the racetrack. The chassis came, via the D-type, from the
Montlhéry Midget, using the 7' 2" wheelbase adopted midway
through the D-type's production life. The engine was a production
847 c.c. version of the 750 c.c. C-type unit, with an output of 36
b.h.p.—almost as much as the 1271 c.c. F-type six-cylinder—and
had a four-speed gearbox with a particularly neat remote control,
not to mention the cross-flow head and twin S.U. carburetters.

Several letters of the alphabet had been mislaid, for the new two-
seater was known as the J.2. Its price, £199 10s., was not £15
more than that of the old M-type. The new chassis was also offered
as the J.1 with open four-seater (£220) or Salonette (£255) bodywork. Although none had yet been built, it was announced that a
'super-sports' J.3 and racing J.4 would shortly be available.

Kimber made one grave error of judgment. He told Jackson to
ensure that the first J.2 Midget was capable of at least 80 m.p.h.
before it was handed over to *The Autocar* for road test. Jackson did
so, S. C. H. Davis duly reported that he had achieved 82 m.p.h.,
and a few days later the crankshaft broke. A lower compression
ratio had to be adopted for the production cars, and for the rest of
the J.2's life M.G. were pestered with complaints from owners
whose cars would not do what *The Autocar* had said they would.

By Showtime 1932 the pretty two-seater Midget body was also
available on the Magna chassis at £250 (the four-seaters going up
in price slightly). Moreover, the Magna brakes were wisely
increased to 12-inch diameter, a great improvement on the 8-inch
brakes of before, which were still retained for the Midget range.
The improved chassis was called the F.2, but this designation was
later confined to the two-seater Magna, the four-seaters then being
referred to as F.3 models.

By this time, too, Kimber had produced another new range of
cars with a view to carrying his racing activities into Class G
(1100 c.c.). Falling midway between the 847 c.c. Midgets and
1271 c.c. Magnas, these new six-cylinder models were dubbed
Magnette. As the Magnettes cost over £100 more than the
Magnas, M.G. were at pains to emphasize in their literature that
the engine was a completely new design intended for use with a

68

supercharger, and therefore much sturdier than a mere 'touring' unit. Oddly enough they made little mention of the fact that the Magnettes had a wider (4 foot) track, larger (13 inch) brakes, and an improved steering layout incorporating a divided track-rod and a slave-arm on the front axle.

The new K Magnette chassis was available in two wheelbases, one of no less than 9 feet, the other virtually the same as on the Magna—except that it had mysteriously grown by three-sixteenths of an inch. On the long chassis was mounted either a roomy open tourer (readily distinguishable from the Midget and Magna four-seaters by its double-humped scuttle, deeply cutaway doors and sweeping front wings), or an unusual closed body with four doors but no central pillars. The 'pillarless saloon' was a very shapely car, but not particularly cheap at £445. Showtime literature was a little vague about the price of the open four-seater, and no two-seaters had yet been built on the short Magnette chassis, but the provisional list included a sports car and two racing models, one supercharged, one unsupercharged.

Few things are more bewildering than the ramifications of the M.G. Magnette series. In the K range alone there were three chassis (K.1, K.2 and K.3), four engines (KA, KB, KD and K.3), three gearboxes and at least five different bodies, while the cars were built in such minute quantities that no two of them seemed alike. When the same type-name was later used for a range of different chassis and engines with different bodies, and components from the two series subsequently combined to make yet another Magnette, the confusion became total. An admirable test for any M.G. enthusiast is to distinguish between a K.1(KA), K.1(KB) and K.1(KD). If he passes that one he can go on for honours by explaining the difference between a KN and an ND.

M.G.'s new six-cylinder Magnette engine followed the general layout of Wolseley's Hornet design, the stroke shortened from 83 to 71 mm to give a capacity of 1087 c.c. There were several detail improvements apart from the use of a cross-flow cylinder head. The ignition was by magneto and the gearbox was preselector, a type much in favour at that time, but whereas other cars had the selector lever on the steering-column, M.G. had a neat little one incorporated in a remote control on the box itself. In terms of output, however, the 1087 c.c. M.G. engine in its original KA form was not much better than the 1271 c.c. Wolseley, giving only 38.8 b.h.p. This was partly due to a faulty design of inlet manifold for the three S.U. carburetters, partly to very uninspired valve timing adopted in the interests of smoother tickover. It was used in the K.1 pillarless saloon until July 1933, but provided such disappointing performance that a much more powerful Magnette engine, the KD, was then substituted.

Meanwhile, however, the K.1 four-seater and K.2 two-seater had gone into production in February with the KB engine, which had only two carburetters and reverted to M.G.'s standard valve timing, putting the power output up by about 2 b.h.p. Most of these were fitted with ordinary 'crash' gearboxes, though the pre-selector was listed as an option. As for the KC engine, this was similar to the KB but had coil ignition instead of magneto. To add an extra touch of confusion, it was not used in a Magnette but in the F-type Magna's successor, the L-type.

Announced in March 1933, the L series Magna used the K.2 wheelbase of 7′10$\frac{3}{16}$″ but retained the earlier 3′ 6″ track. In two-seater L.2 form the body itself was almost indistinguishable from those of the F.2 and J.2, yet the car's appearance was trans-formed by the use of nicely swept wings, as on the K series. It thus bore a strong family resemblance to the two-seater K.2 on the same wheelbase, but this actually had a longer scuttle and there-fore a shorter bonnet.

The L series cars were appreciably more expensive than the earlier Magnas, costing £285 as a two-seater, £299 as a four-seater and £345 as a Salonette. They were, however, better cars, the 1087 c.c. M.G.-designed engine not only giving nearly 4 b.h.p. more than its 1271 c.c. Wolseley predecessor but being sturdy enough to stand considerable further development. In four-seater form the L.1 also looked better than the F.1 or F.3 tourers, for it incorporated the swept wings, flared scuttle and cutaway doors that had now become characteristic of the open M.G.s.

While Abingdon thus played automotive Meccano with engines, chassis and bodies, several interesting things had happened in the world of motor sport. For the Brooklands 500 Miles of September 1932, the set handicap speed for 750 c.c. cars had risen yet again to a barely credible 95.78 m.p.h., and most of the C-types appeared with the radiator cowls and pointed tails that they usually wore for high-speed events. R. T. Horton went one better by fitting his with an extraordinary offset single-seater body. After a battle with no less an adversary than George Eyston in the Magic Midget, Horton won the race outright at a truly remarkable 96.29 m.p.h., while M.G. won the Team Prize. During the race

Horton's oddly-shaped Midget lapped the Outer Circuit at 115.29 m.p.h. to establish a Class H record that was higher than the Class G figure.

This made it almost an anticlimax when, at Montlhéry in December, Eyston at last recorded the long-sought 120 m.p.h. on 750 c.c. However, Eyston and his fellow-drivers then brought out a J.3 Midget, and with this and the Magic Midget proceeded to mop up every remaining Class H record for M.G. If the 1932 season had brought comparatively few notable racing victories for M.G. it thus ended on a high note, and it was even better news that M.G. production had risen over the year by almost 75 per cent.

By the first week of the New Year, two prototypes existed of perhaps the most famous racing M.G. of all, the K.3 Magnette. The original prototype was a curious mixture on a 7′ 6″ wheelbase chassis, with supercharged 1100 c.c. engine and basically C-type body, and it was entered for the 1933 Monte Carlo Rally. Not only did it complete this highly unsuitable event; it then made fastest climb of the day in the Mont des Mules hillclimb, establishing a new class record. Meanwhile the second prototype spent some five weeks undergoing extensive testing in Italy under the watchful eye of Jackson, in preparation for the K.3's first major event.

That event was, of course, the Mille Miglia, for which a team of three Magnettes was built at the suggestion of Earl Howe. One car was driven by Howe and Hamilton, the second by Eyston and Count Johnny Lurani, and the third by none other than Sir Henry Birkin—the famous Bentley driver who, only a few months before, had written so scathingly of the 'scuttling kindergarten of M.G.s' that won races only because they were 'given such huge handicaps'. Now he found himself on the other side of the fence, and perhaps felt a little uncomfortable when, like the other team drivers, he moved into the Hotel Moderno Gallo at Brescia and found even the table-napkins emblazoned 'M.G.'.

Never the man to spare a car, Birkin assumed his natural role as pacemaker and most effectively disposed of the Maseratis during the early stages of the race before his K.3 dropped a valve. Then it was the turn of Eyston and Lurani to smash the 1100 c.c. class records, ably backed up by Howe and Hamilton, so that the conclusion of the 1000-mile road race saw the remaining two Magnettes finish 1st and 2nd in their class. If the M.G. team had not finished intact, nor had any other, and the Magnettes put up the best performance. For the first time in the long history of the

Mille Miglia, a non-Italian marque had won the team prize, the Gran Premio Brescia.

This daring raid on the very Mecca of motor racing, with three completely new cars, caused immense excitement back home. Before the race the drivers had been received by the King of Italy and Mussolini himself, a rather more important person at that time. Afterwards they returned to a celebration dinner in London attended by the Prince of Wales and Prince George, two future Kings of England. The triumphant debut of the K.3 Magnettes set the pattern for the next two years, in which M.G.s large and small achieved so many racing successes—well over a thousand in all parts of the world—that it becomes impossible to record more than a fraction of them. To quote Cyril Posthumus, the motoring historian: 'Were it not for M.G.s of Abingdon we would have had barely a shred of self-respect in Europe between the years 1931 and 1935.'

It was Horton's venerable C-type that scored M.G.'s next Continental victory, before a large crowd that included Adolf Hitler, when he won the 800 c.c. class of the Avusrennen at 90.9 m.p.h. It was also a C-type that finished sixth overall at Le Mans a month later, when Ford and Baumer won the 1100 c.c. class of that event at record speed. The meat in this sandwich was provided by the first appearance of the new 'full-race' J.4 Midget, which Hamilton drove at the Nürburgring, winning the 800 c.c. class of the Eifelrennen by an almost embarrassing 25 *minutes*. Then came another shock for the Italians at the end of July. In the Coppa Acerbo Junior, Whitney Straight and his single-camshaft two-seater K.3 took on a horde of twin-camshaft single-seater Maseratis—and beat the lot.

In such circumstances it is not surprising that the great Tazio Nuvolari, then at the height of his fame, agreed to drive a K.3 in the 1933 Ulster T.T. three weeks later. Every M.G. enthusiast knows how he broke the class lap record seven times during that race to win by a bare forty seconds from 'Hammy' Hamilton's J.4, the Magnette averaging 78.65 m.p.h. and the Midget 73.46 m.p.h. Nuvolari's average remained the fastest T.T.-winning speed until 1951, when Stirling Moss bettered it with a C-type Jaguar.

A fortnight after the T.T., Eddie Hall scored M.G.'s second successive victory in the Brooklands 500 Miles, his single-seater K.3 averaging 106.53 m.p.h. over that distance. As the year drew to a close the Magic Midget paid its usual end-of-season visit to Montlhéry. Fitted with the engine from Hammy's T.T. car, and rebodied too small for Eyston to fit in the cockpit, it was driven by the indomitable little Bert Denly, Eyston's mechanic, who covered 110.87 miles in the hour and returned a speed of 128.63 m.p.h. over the flying mile.

M.G. simplified their range considerably for the 1933 Show, cutting down from sixteen to ten models. The 18/80 models were finally dropped, as were the rather pointless little open and closed four-seaters on the Midget chassis. However, there was one new model, the Continental Coupé mounted on the L-type Magna chassis at £350. This was one of Kimber's beloved experiments in closed-car design; a two-tone variation on the Salonette theme, it featured an extraordinary reverse curve running down the scuttle side at the colour-change point, reminiscent of the Renault Reinastella or some of the Lancia Lambda bodies. Kimber confidently ordered 100 of these from his coachbuilders, but it took a long, long time to sell them.

The popular J.2 Midget now had an outrigger bearing at the front of its crankshaft and, like its larger sisters, swept front wings, but the price was unchanged. Those who wanted a more powerful two-seater could choose between the L.2 Magna, still at £285, or the K.2 Magnette, now listed at £390. For racing, the choice lay between the 750 c.c. J.4 Midget and the 1100 c.c. K.3 Magnette, the simpler J.3 having been dropped. Prices were well above the tentative ones quoted earlier; £495 for the J.4, £795 for the K.3. However, changes on the racing side were just around the corner; indeed, the last of the nine J.4s had already been built before the Show opened.

Higher prices for the K Magnette range were justified by the use, since July 1933, of the new KD engine mentioned earlier. This was a considerable improvement over the unblown 1100 c.c. units, achieved mainly by lengthening the stroke to 83 mm so that the capacity rose to 1271 c.c. (which made a slight nonsense of the type names, the Magnette engines being now larger than the Magna). With standard M.G. valve timing the new engine gave 54.5 b.h.p. at 5500 r.p.m., and even with the dismal camshaft used in the pillarless saloon the output was still 48.5 b.h.p.—an improvement of nearly 10 b.h.p. on the engine originally fitted to that model. Other alterations included the abandonment of magneto ignition and a return to the preselector gearbox for all K models, but this time with an automatic clutch to relieve strain on the first-gear band and give a smoother take-up. Confusion being inseparable from the Magnettes, it should be added that although the K.1 open four-seater was still listed (now at £399), none were actually built with the larger engine, and only five K.2(KD) two-seaters were produced.

All the M.G. literature quoted the wrong capacity for the new KD engine. The reason for this is rather intriguing.

Sports car enthusiasts are a well-informed breed, not easy to deceive, and many had been perfectly aware that the engine of the 1271 c.c. F-type Magna was a Wolseley Hornet unit, despite the tinware wrapped around it. But since then Abingdon had virtually redesigned the o.h.c. six, fitting a cross-flow head and, as we have seen, getting slightly more power at 1087 c.c. than the Wolseley engine had provided at 1271. Over that same period the Wolseley engine had become worse instead of better; besides retaining its old-type cylinder head, it abandoned the vertical camshaft drive in favour of a long and floppity chain which did nothing to improve its high-r.p.m. characteristics. Wolseley Motors were selling this engine, in a most undistinguished chassis, to a host of specialized coachbuilders who fitted thereto some of the most offensive 'boy racer' bodywork that has ever been produced. The result was the very worst kind of fake sports car.

There was some danger that M.G.'s new 1271 c.c. o.h.c. engine (which was, in fact, made by Wolseley to M.G.'s designs) might be mistaken for Wolseley's own 1271 c.c. o.h.c. engine, since the dimensions were identical. Kimber therefore 'added' one millimetre to the stroke of the M.G. engine, calling it 84 mm and making the capacity 1286 c.c. He could hardly have foreseen that this subterfuge would have to be adhered to through four M.G. models, and would cause confusion for forty years or more.

It might well be imagined that by the end of 1933 the M.G. Car Company was in a very enviable position. Abingdon was the only factory in the world devoted exclusively to the manufacture of sports cars. No marque had earned a finer reputation for consistent success in racing with engines of quite small capacity. The production cars were closely related to the racing models, and when a new M.G. was announced it was invariably greeted with great enthusiasm by the motoring press. The average motoring journalist is an enthusiast at heart, more readily stirred by a racing victory than by commercial success, and contemporary press references to M.G. suggest that Abingdon could scarcely cope with the overwhelming demand for its products.

Behind the scenes the picture was unfortunately rather different.

Despite their racing successes, M.G. sales actually dropped slightly during 1933. Their prices, after all, had been creeping up for some time. The open Magnettes were so over-priced that they were extremely hard to sell. The pillarless saloon was also expensive, and, although now provided with a better engine, had already become known to the trade as an underpowered car which was cramped and noisy inside. Sales of the L-type Magna—always excepting the disastrous Continental Coupé—were steady but not impressive. The one good seller in the M.G. range was the J.2 Midget, and even this had its faults; notably an easily broken crankshaft and rather inadequate brakes.

Kimber was also learning that the law of diminishing returns applies sharply and painfully to motor racing. Once a marque has begun to win races it is expected to continue doing so; failure will arouse considerable comment and adverse publicity, but continued success—paradoxically enough—will bring less approbation than before when one has reached the stage of being *expected* to win. Moreover, nothing becomes out-of-date so quickly as a racing car. A continuous programme of intensive development work is necessary to maintain any marque in a commanding position.

The only way a tiny concern like M.G. could produce race-winning cars, even at something more than twice the price of their standard models, was to build them mainly of components that were in fairly large-quantity production—and, contrariwise, to make use of racing to develop new standard cars. The J.4, for example, had had to wait for the 12-inch brakes of the F.2 Magna before it could go into production in March 1933, and by that time the 750 c.c. engine had become almost too powerful for such a small chassis. Very few men were brave enough to drive such a projectile as this, and only nine J.4s were built. It was obvious that the racing Midget needed a larger chassis—but nothing other than the Magnette chassis, which was too large, was available at that time. It was equally obvious that further engine development would be restricted by the two-bearing crankshaft. M.G. could afford to have counterbalanced crankshafts made specially for the J.4; they could not afford to have a completely new engine made, just for a small-production racing car.

While conscious of the need to develop a new racing Midget, M.G. were also under continual pressure from Sir William Morris to restrict their expenditure on racing, to show a profit on their sports cars, and to buy as many components as possible from within the Morris group of companies. Before the 1933 Motor Show closed, Kimber had agreed to sever his long association with Carbodies of Coventry and buy his production coachwork from Morris Bodies Branch. It had even been suggested that he should buy the complete Hornet chassis from Wolseley and merely fit a body to it, but this idea was rejected with horror. M.G. had already started designing a new Midget and a new Magnette. As for the racing models, these would in future be fitted with light, aluminium-panelled bodywork that could be quickly produced by any good panel-beater. By January 1934 the last J.2 Midget had been built, the L-type Magna discontinued (apart from the ever-lasting Continental Coupé), and K Magnette production reduced to a trickle of pillarless saloons.

At the beginning of March 1934 the new P-type Midget was announced, followed a few weeks later (in defiance of the alphabet) by the new N-type Magnette. It was immediately obvious that a great deal of thought had gone into their design with a view to improving on the earlier models while retaining their best features. Both chassis frames were sturdier than before, both longer in the wheelbase: the Midget now 7' $3\frac{5}{16}$", the Magnette 8' 0""; but while the Midget was still of 3' 6" track, the Magnette now used 3' 9" axles, midway between Midget and old Magnette size. Magnette and Midget both had 12-inch diameter brake-drums. Both used Bishop cam steering instead of M.G.'s familiar Marles-Weller, and on the N-type there was a clever modification of the twin-trackrod linkage invented by Cousins.

The P-type had a new 847 c.c. engine with three main bearings, altogether more robust than the J-type and noticeably smoother-running. In production form it actually gave a slightly lower power output than the J, a penalty often paid for increased smoothness, but it was better able to stand up to further tuning. The transmission line had also been strengthened by the use of a better clutch and gearbox, and a four-star differential instead of two-star. Although the Midget body followed the same lines as its predecessor, it was a little roomier and more comfortable.

The engine of the N-type was essentially the KD unit (1271 c.c., but still called 1286) with a manual gearbox and a number of small modifications, including standard M.G. valve timing, which brought the output up to a very satisfactory 56.6 b.h.p. The chassis frame differed considerably from those of earlier cars, being tapered, and the body was mounted on a rubber-insulated subframe. In seeking to provide greater comfort the Magnette body had 'grown up' somewhat; the fuel tank was now concealed and the scuttle was rather high. A two-tone colour scheme, with a sweeping curve running along the sides, helped to reduce the apparent height.

In pricing the new models, M.G. had arrived at a compromise. The P-type was just a little more expensive than the previous Midget at £220 (later increased to £222) for the two-seater, £240 for the four-seater. The N-type cost a little more than the superseded L-type Magna but much less than the K-type Magnette: £305 as a two-seater, £335 in four-seater form. To these four basic models was added quite a range of specialist coachwork. There was a neat closed body known as the Airline Coupé available on either chassis. The N-type could also be bought as an ingenious open 2/4-seater of very trim appearance, usually referred to nowadays as the Allingham—though in fact both the Airline and this body were marketed by H. W. Allingham of London. Cresta Motors of Worthing also brought out a special open body for the N-type chassis. In the same way, University Motors sponsored a drop-head coupé version of either chassis, known as the University Foursome. As a further variant by the manufacturers themselves, some of the left-over K.2 slab-tank two-seater bodies were fitted to N-type chassis, this combination being known within the factory as the ND.

Specialist coachwork apart, M.G. had thus simplified their range even more, but practical considerations called for one or two additions before the 1934 Motor Show, and it was noticeable that the N-type Magnettes had been announced as additions to, not replacements for, the K-type Magnettes. There was a good reason for this. When the K series had first appeared late in 1932, M.G. had rather over-confidently ordered 250 pillarless saloon bodies and 100 open four-seater bodies. It took two years to dispose of the four-seaters, but only about seventy-five saloons had been sold during the same period, leaving a considerable surplus of saloon bodies on the long-wheelbase K.1 chassis. During 1934 these bodies were given a 'face-lift' to alter their appearance; a sunshine roof, a different instrument panel, a badge bar and several other touches. The chassis were fitted with the 1271 c.c. engine in its latest N-type guise, complete with manual gearbox and better valve timing.

This meant that a model which had originally appeared with a mere 38.8 b.h.p. under the bonnet, later improved to 48.5, now had 56.6 b.h.p.—and the effect on its performance may be imagined. The price was cut by almost £50 to £399. Dubbed the KN, the revamped saloon was announced in September 1934 and sold well. It cleared the surplus K.1 components out nicely, while a few University Foursome coupés were also sold on the same chassis. But another spectre from the past lingered on in the shape of the L-type Magna Continental Coupé. It took more than three years to lay that particular ghost.

M.G. were not alone in marketing too diverse a range of models during the mid-'thirties; other, much larger, manufacturers made the same mistake and suffered thereby. The lesson had been learned, and in the new P-type Midget and N-type Magnette M.G. offered two excellent cars which achieved the commercial success they deserved. Both were extremely well received by the motoring press, though the performance figures quoted must be treated with some caution; the two press cars had been 'breathed upon' fairly extensively before being tested. The little P-type even had its share of racing victories, starting off by winning the 1934 Australian Grand Prix in the hands of Les Murphy. Another finished the 1934 Le Mans race driven by Mme Itier, establishing a precedent that was followed by a six-girl team, with three P-types, in the 1935 race, and M. H. Fleming used a P-type to win the County Down Trophy in 1935.

And if the K-type Magnette range had been a flop commercially, it had at least fathered one of the most successful British racing cars ever built. The K.3 Magnette won so many races that its few failures came as a distinct surprise. One of these was the 1934 Mille Miglia, for which M.G. prepared three cars similar in appearance to the previous year's team but with Marshall superchargers, which gave slightly less power than the original Powerplus but had a less voracious appetite for sparking-plugs (it is recorded that in winning their class in the 1933 Mille Miglia, Eyston and Lurani had used no less than 157!). The K.3s were certainly out of luck this time; Howe's car crashed, Hall's had a succession of troubles, and the Lurani/Penn-Hughes car finished almost one-and-a-half hours behind Taruffi's class-winning Maserati.

Subsequent 1934 K.3s were fitted with a most ingenious twin-lever braking system invented by Cec Cousins, largely as the result of H. N. Charles having a front brake lock on while testing at around 100 m.p.h. They also had N-type cylinder heads and, most of them, a slim two-seater body on which the fuel tank formed part of the tail. Jackson had spotted this idea on Alfa Romeos while in Italy the previous year and passed it on to Charles, who readily adopted it because increasing use of alcohol fuel called for larger tanks.

The racing M.G.s, large and small, had been designed as two-seaters with full road equipment so that they could be driven in sports-car races; many owners also used them in rallies, and a few arch-enthusiasts even drove them regularly on the road. But their performance was such that others, again, drove them—often very successfully—in what were really pure racing-car events, and there was therefore quite a demand for single-seater bodywork, not easy to arrange on a two-seater chassis. Ronnie Horton, having achieved this with an offset Jensen body on his C-type, evolved a similar arrangement for a K.3. George Eyston, for his part, had a K.3 built on the lines of *his* Midget, the EX.127 record-breaker. Abingdon produced for him a Magnette chassis with offset transmission, EX.135, on which he could mount either of two bodies— one for road racing, the other for track racing or record attempts. Many years later these two special Magnettes were to be amalgamated and turned into perhaps the most famous M.G. of all time.

Horton brought both of his offset single-seaters to Brooklands on Easter Monday 1934. With the Magnette he set a new 1100 c.c. Outer Circuit lap record at 117.74 m.p.h., which was impressive enough, but with the now quite ancient Midget he then proceeded to put the 750 c.c. record up to an amazing 116.64 m.p.h. At the Whit Monday meeting he took the Magnette around the Outer Circuit at no less than 123.58 m.p.h.

This Whit Monday meeting was also noteworthy for the first appearance of two new cars, M.G.'s Q-type racing Midget and Austin's latest single-seater Seven with modifications by Murray Jamieson. The Austin came third in one of the races and broke Hamilton's J.4 class record for the Mountain Circuit, but the M.G. won the next race outright and regained the 750 c.c. lap record.

M.G.'s new racing Midget made good use of the components that had become available with the advent of the P-type and the N-type. Its chassis combined K.3 wheelbase (7' $10\frac{3}{16}$") with N-type track (3' 9"), together with N-type steering and brakes, although special drums were used. The bodywork was so similar to that of the 1934 K.3 that it was difficult to tell the two cars apart. The engine was a toughened-up P-type with a preselector gearbox, as on the K.3, but unlike its bigger racing sister, the Q-type had a special clutch designed to slip automatically above a certain torque figure, thus protecting the N-type rear axle. For a genuine racing car the Q-type was very reasonably priced at £550.

Furthermore, the Q-type incorporated something quite new— a Zoller supercharger designed by McEvoy and Pomeroy in collaboration with H. N. Charles. Apart from being better matched to its engine than any previous supercharger used by M.G., the Zoller offered a measure of precompression before delivery. Boost pressures began to soar, and with them the power output produced by the new Midget engine. Even in a fairly modest state of tune the 750 c.c. Q-type gave well over 100 b.h.p., and in its finally developed 'sprint' form of 1936 it produced 146.2 b.h.p. at 7500 r.p.m. This represents almost 200 b.h.p./litre, a higher specific power output than any other car engine in the world at that time. As Laurence Pomeroy has pointed out, the 'fabulous' sixteen-cylinder Auto Union engine of 1935 gave less than 85 b.h.p./litre, and even in its ultimate 1939 form it still achieved only 161 b.h.p./litre, while the contemporary Mercedes-Benz engines gave slightly less power.

By any standards this was an extraordinary achievement. The German engines, chosen for comparison because they represent the absolute peak of pre-war Grand Prix development with virtually unlimited resources behind them, were designed specifically as racing units. The M.G. engine had been developed, by a handful of men working on a shoe-string budget, out of a five-year-old economy car design that had originally given 20 b.h.p. from 847 c.c.—in other words, 23.6 b.h.p./litre.

M.G.'s racing successes in 1934 rivalled those of the previous year, and they were gained in many different parts of the world. One of the most unusual race finishes occurred in the Isle of Man, where only eight cars out of nineteen starters completed the Mannin Beg—and seven of them were M.G.s; the only 'foreigner' was Cyril Paul's 1½-litre Riley, in sixth place. Two weeks later, M.G. made their closest approach to winning at Le Mans when the Ford/Baumer K.3 worked its way up to second place behind an ailing Alfa Romeo—only to be hit by another car and forced to retire. However, Martin and Eccles finished fourth overall and won the 2-litre class with another K.3.

Eyston's EX.135, which had come third in the Mannin Beg and established a new class record, scored an outright win in the

1934 British Empire Trophy, while M.G.s took the Team Prize. In mid-August, three K.3s thrashed the Maseratis again in the Coppa Acerbo Junior to finish 1-2-3, driven by Hamilton, Cecchini and Seaman. Seaman went on to gain further successes with his M.G., while Cecchini won so many events that he was awarded the 1100 c.c. Championship of Italy, an unheard-of achievement with a non-Italian car. Poor Hamilton, however, was killed before the month was out when driving a Maserati in the Swiss Grand Prix.

The final Donington event of the 1934 season, the Nuffield Trophy Race, brought a significant result when Seaman's K.3 and Kenneth Evans's Q-type were beaten by Raymond Mays's E.R.A. This was a new marque which had appeared earlier in the season, and it enjoyed two big advantages over M.G.: it had been designed from the outset as a single-seater racing car, and it was available with a 1500 c.c. engine. The E.R.A. was soon to replace M.G. as the leading champion of British prestige in motor racing.

During 1934 M.G. also faced a problem of a different kind, for supercharged cars were excluded from the most important British sports car event of the year, the Ulster T.T., and it was essential that Abingdon should be represented in such a race. An intensive development programme was instituted on the N-type Magnette engine, raising the power output to 74 b.h.p. at 6500 r.p.m. The N-type chassis was also used, but the bodywork of the NE, as it was called, was rather unhandsome by the time various race regulations were complied with.

The experiment was successful, but only just, for M.G.'s third T.T. victory was gained by the narrowest of margins. Of the six Magnettes entered for the race, four retired, one finished fourteenth, and the remaining NE won by a bare seventeen seconds in an event of more than six hours' duration. Abingdon's reputation had been effectively upheld. The year ended with M.G. still firmly in possession of all significant Class H records and a substantial holding in Class G, the latter including Eyston's 128.69 m.p.h. over the flying mile and 120.88 miles *in* the hour with EX.135.

Kimber, however, was looking to the future. By this time some of the better car manufacturers had started thinking seriously about independent suspension; even Singer had brought out a saloon with a curious i.f.s. in 1934, and outside England many cars had independent suspension, at least at the front end. Some typically suck-it-and-see experiments had been carried out at Abingdon by Jackson and Enever; they had sawn the rear end off a J.2 chassis and fitted it up with a home-brewed suspension using fabricated wishbones and old axle-shafts as torsion bars. Tests on M.G.'s private circuit within the factory grounds met with Kimber's approval, and a similar arrangement was evolved for the front end. Again the tests were successful, for they had somehow hit on an ideal combination of suspension geometry and spring rates, though the latter amounted to nothing more than turning down the axle-shafts in a lathe until they 'looked about right'. It was decided to take things further with a new racing Midget, the Q-type having already, like the J.4, become too fast for its chassis. As Hounslow comments, 'You never see a picture of a Q-type with all four wheels on the deck. For Brooklands we had to fit grab-handles on the *floor* so that the mechanic could keep himself inside the car.'

H. N. Charles needed no prompting to go ahead with an all-independent design; he had learned to drive on an i.f.s. car in Edwardian days and had never done more than tolerate cart-springs. He also knew the desirability of a rigid chassis for an all-independent car, so a Y-shaped frame was made by the same Frank Stevens who had made the chassis for the Kimber Special ten years before. Completely boxed in and welded, it was immensely strong but weighed a mere 57 lbs.

Within the arms of the 'Y' was mounted a basically Q-type engine with some modifications, including stronger connecting-rods and improved cooling, while magneto ignition was adopted so that a battery need not be carried. On a small but sturdy bulk-head was mounted a twin steering-box with two drop-arms and two drag-links, so that kick-back from one front wheel could not affect the other. The brakes were still cable-operated with 12-inch drums, but Girling backplate assemblies were used. As on the Q-type and later K.3s, the fuel tank formed most of the tail. The remainder of the body consisted of a scuttle section, a bonnet, and a number of fairings. It was a pity, really, to clothe such an advanced chassis design in such 'bitty'-looking bodywork, with a rather ponderous front cowling that did little to enhance its appearance. In one respect, however, it differed from every other M.G. offered for sale to the public, before or since. It was a genuine single-seater.

The new R-type Midget created a sensation when it was announced on 25th April 1935 at a price of £750. *Motor Sport*

36. Three of the pretty L-type Magna two-seaters, entered by the M.G. Car Club, won the 1933 Brooklands Relay Race at 88.62 m.p.h. G. W. J. H. Wright's car, seen here, was partnered by those of Alan Hess and Charles Martin. The same three cars won the Team Prize in the 1933 Alpine Rally.

37. Unsuccessful experiment: the oddly-styled Continental Coupé on the L-type Magna chassis proved almost unsaleable.

38. Successful debut: Capt. Eyston and Count Lurani won the 1100 c.c. class of the 1933 Mille Miglia with the new K.3 Magnette. Earl Howe and 'Hammy' Hamilton, also seen in this picture, finished second in the same class.

39. The great Tazio Nuvolari broke the class record seven times to win the 1933 Ulster Tourist Trophy Race with a K.3 Magnette, and his winning speed was not bettered until 1951.

40. With the 1934 K.3 Magnette, the racing M.G.s began to depart from their traditional sports car shape.

41. The J.4 Midget was too fast for most drivers. J. C. Elwes's car, seen here on the starting-line for the 1933 International Trophy Race beside Howe's K.3 Magnette, crashed on the first lap.

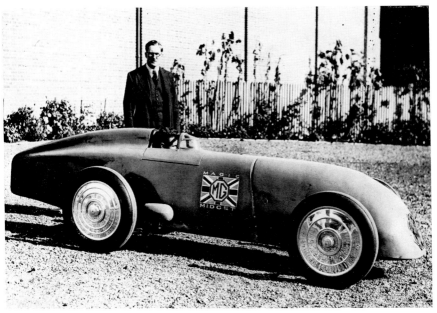

42. Eyston and Denly with the revamped 'Magic Midget' which exceeded 128 m.p.h. at Montlhéry late in 1933.

43. M.G.'s first three-bearing four-cylinder engine was the P-type, basis of the racing Q and R units which gave prodigious power outputs.

44. Eyston's all-girl team at Le Mans, 1935, with one of their three P-type Midgets, which completed the 24-hour race and were later used as trials cars. The girls are Mesdames Skinner, Evans, Simpson, Richmond, Eaton and Allan.

45. A departure from the slab-tank style of two-seater body came with the NA Magnette of 1934, noticeably roomier than its immediate predecessors.

46. The N-type and P-type chassis were both available with a body known as the Airline Coupé—a mid-'thirties 'fastback' that attracted much attention.

47. Kimber's personal 100 m.p.h. road car was a supercharged Magnette chassis with drophead coupé bodywork by Corsica.

48. Dick Seaman practises for the 1934 Coppa Acerbo Junior in the K.3 that Whitney Straight had used to win the previous year's race. In 1934 Hamilton, Cecchini and Seaman scored a 1-2-3 victory with K.3 Magnettes.

49, 50. (*Above*) The twin-lever brake of the 1934 K.3. (*Below*) Controls of the 1934 K.3 include fuel tank air-pump, gear selector, ignition advance lever and brake adjuster; some instruments and switches have still to be fitted to the dash.

51, 52. Record-breakers: (*Above*) Eyston's EX.135 in chassis form, showing the offset transmission line; (*below*) Horton's offset-bodied Magnette, later used by Goldie Gardner. Parts of these two cars were amalgamated to build the famous Gardner-M.G. which exceeded 200 m.p.h. with an 1100 c.c. engine.

53. Bill Everitt (*facing camera*) with his Q-type Midget at Brooklands, where he covered the *standing* start mile at 79.88 m.p.h. on 1st August 1934.

54. Raffaele Cecchini breaks his own class record at the Stelvio Hillclimb of 1935 with his single-seater K.3, the first non-Italian car to win the Italian 1100 c.c. Championship.

55, 56. Versatility: (*Above*) A quartet of NE Magnettes rounds Dundonald hairpin during the 1934 Ulster T.T. Race, driven by Eyston, Dodson, Handley and Black. Three of the six team cars were then converted into trials cars (*below*) and gained the Team Prize in the 1935 Welsh Rally. Dodson's NE, winner of the T.T., also won the rally in the hands of Sam Nash.

57, 58. Last of the pre-war racing M.G.s—the all-independent R-type of 1935. Above is seen the 'backbone' chassis with wishbone suspension. (*Below*) Doreen Evans rejoins the Brooklands International Trophy Race after a pit-stop at the model's racing debut.

59. For the 1935 Motor Show the N-type Magnette was rebodied and, within the factory, was known as the NB.

60. M.G. purists were shocked by the SA, the first completely new model after the Morris Motors takeover. This Tickford drophead coupé was driven by Kay Petre in the 1938 R.A.C. Rally and won its class in the coachwork competition.

61. At Frankfurt in October 1936, Bobbie Kohlrausch prepares to raise the 750 c.c. flying mile record to 140.6 m.p.h. with the ageing Magic Midget. This figure remained unbeaten for 10 years.

62. George Tuck poses with a Tickford version of the TA, M.G.'s first pushrod o.h.v. Midget.

63, 64. (*Above*) Maurice Toulmin, passengered by John Thornley, passes team-mate Ken Crawford in the 1936 Scottish Team Trial; both are driving supercharged PBs of the Cream Cracker team. (*Below*) R. A. Macdermid makes the mud fly with his 1936 Three Musketeers team car, a potent mixture of Midget, Magna and Magnette components.

65, 66. (*Above*) The 1937 Cream Crackers were unsupercharged TA Midgets, much closer to standard, but they still won the Team Championship. (*Below*) J. A. Bastock tackles a Colmore Trophy section in his 1938/9 Three Musketeers team car, basically a TA with much-modified and supercharged engine.

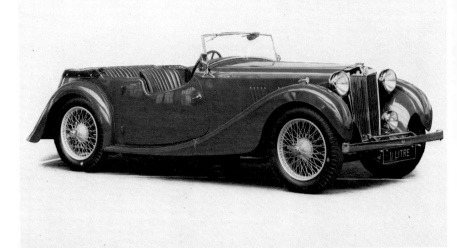

67. At the 1936 Motor Show the Magnette was succeeded by the VA, seen here as an open four-seater.

68. Biggest-ever M.G. model was the WA, announced in mid-1938. This is the standard 2.6-Litre saloon, one of three types of coachwork available on the WA chassis.

called it 'a car which will be the admiration of the rest of the world . . . a genuine Grand Prix racing car in miniature. Nothing like it has ever been within the reach of motor-racing enthusiasts at the price, either in England or on the Continent'.

That spring of 1935 had seen the M.G. factory engaged in a frantic scramble reminiscent of early C-type days. It was early April before enough parts had been gathered together to start assembling the R-types, and once again most of the men were called upon to assist. Some of them had actually worked right through from a Friday to a Tuesday, day and night with only a few hours' rest on camp-beds in the workshop, to build the engines. Six cars were completed in time for the International Trophy at Brooklands on 6th May, but it was probably a mistake to rush the assembly of such a revolutionary new design; only two R-types finished the race. However, Hall's K.3 came third overall, Campbell's R-type won the 750 c.c. class, and M.G. took the Team Prize.

Several more worthy successes were achieved with the R-type during 1935, especially by the Menier stable in France, but the car undoubtedly needed further development. It rolled a great deal on corners—indeed, the suspension geometry was such that it could not do otherwise—and the sensation was as unpleasant as it was unfamiliar to racing drivers of some forty years ago. There was a particular reason for H. N. Charles's decision to place the roll axis at ground level and anchor all four torsion-bars just forward of the driver's seat. The Mark II version of the R-type, which never saw the light of day, was to incorporate 'controlled lean' suspension, the torsion bars trimmed by Lockheed cylinders actuated by a gyro, with an engine-driven hydraulic pump included in the system.

A more serious fault—though one that could easily have been corrected—was that the frequency of the rear suspension was lower than that of the front, making the R-type unstable in pitch. Charles spotted this quite soon, but it was already too late to arrange for new torsion bars to be fitted. Within two months of the new car's announcement a sudden wind of change had swept through Abingdon and carried off M.G.'s design office, experimental shop and racing department.

The motoring enthusiasts of Britain, and of many another country, too, could scarcely believe their eyes when they read that the M.G. Car Company was to withdraw completely from racing in the middle of the 1935 season. A statement issued to the press was mainly devoted to emphasizing that the Company had not, like so many others, made itself bankrupt by participation in motor sport. Apart from that it merely said that M.G.s had been handicapped out of racing in Britain, presented the usual clichés about resting on one's laurels, and announced that M.G. would allow their production models to 'catch up with extremely advanced ideas incorporated in the present racing car, which is highly specialized and years ahead of its time'.

If Kimber wrote that statement, he may well have believed that M.G. would be able to proceed with their plans to produce an all-independent production sports car. If he did so, he was soon to find that his new masters had very different ideas.

Chapter 5

Business is Business (1935–1945)

The manner in which M.G. had gone motor racing was rather unusual. They had never maintained a full team of works cars, with paid drivers to handle them. Most racing M.G.s were bought by private individuals who either made their own arrangements for servicing or had their cars maintained at Abingdon, where a separate racing department existed for that purpose. Such work was charged, just like the servicing of any ordinary road car, and even to the most famous of 'names'. Owners whose successes were sufficiently frequent and significant were sometimes allowed special discounts because of the publicity enjoyed by M.G.—but they still had to pay. Astonishingly enough, much of M.G.'s record-breaking had been carried out on a similar basis.

Again, M.G.'s racing models were so closely related to their production sports cars that even with a fair profit margin they could be sold to the amateur driver at far from unreasonable prices; the Q-type Midget, for example, was marketed at £550, and even the highly specialized R-type could be bought for £750. By contrast, Austin's twin-o.h.c. single-seaters are said to have cost that company £10,000 apiece, and they were certainly not for sale at any price. When M.G. sold their immensely successful K.3 Magnettes at £795 they were making a profit of £75 on every car.

So M.G.'s outlay on motor racing, though it must have been substantial, was by no means ruinous, and financial considerations alone can scarcely have justified the abrupt withdrawal in mid-1935. It has been ascribed to a private truce with the Austin Motor Company, their main rivals in Class H, but if this be true it is odd that Austin went on racing for more than four years after M.G.'s retirement. The Longbridge 750 c.c. twin-o.h.c. cars, which gave 116 b.h.p. at 8500 r.p.m., appeared in the spring of 1936 and were raced regularly until the outbreak of war in 1939.

It seems more probable that the ban on M.G.'s racing activities was but one of several moves in a major reorganization of the Abingdon factory, though doubtless much influenced by Lord Nuffield's personal dislike of the sport. As soon as the Morris take-over occurred, most of the Abingdon design staff were either dismissed or transferred elsewhere. H. N. Charles went to Cowley; only Bill Renwick (who had joined M.G. the previous year to help with the R-type project) and Syd Enever were allowed to remain at Abingdon as design liaison men. The policy was to ensure that new M.G. models would be far less specialized than before; that they would incorporate as many standard Nuffield components as possible, with a high degree of interchangeability; that service problems would be minimized by simplification of design; and that each model would be given a longer production run so that development costs could be more easily recovered.

Such a policy is much favoured by accountants, and there was some justification for applying it to Abingdon. M.G. production costs were relatively high because the cars were very different from Nuffield Group cars, and built in small quantities. Total annual sales had undoubtedly fallen steadily since 1932 despite M.G.'s racing successes. This was partly due to the motor insurance companies' disapproval of M.G.'s 'helmet and goggles' image, which was expressed in unreasonably high premiums. And it was also true that many M.G. owners found their cars disappointing in use, mainly because proper maintenance of the o.h.c. engine demanded a level of mechanical skill far above that of the average *garagiste*. Correctly assembled, it was a beautiful little unit, but there has seldom been an engine that the incompetent could more readily transform into a clattering, oil-slinging abortion, barely capable of pulling the car along. Jackson deliberately overstates the case in saying, 'No o.h.c. M.G. ran properly after its first decoke', but there is more than a grain of truth in this. The technique of driving a high-revving sports car with ultra-responsive steering, non-synchromesh gearbox and cable brakes was also something of a mystery to the average motorist, and the general 'fussiness' of the o.h.c. models made them tiring on long journeys.

The new policy, then, had much to recommend it, and before long it brought more sales and higher profits to the M.G. Car Company. In some ways, though, M.G. lost more than they gained. Never again would they be regarded as leaders in sports car design, far ahead of others in the technical development of their engines and progressing rapidly towards advanced forms of chassis construction. Even from a strictly commercial point of view Abingdon's reputation suffered. Customers and dealers alike found it was one thing to do business with a small, self-contained concern whose activities were controlled by one man; quite another when it was swallowed up by a large, unwieldy and sometimes disgracefully inefficient organization that seemed incapable of adhering either to an agreed delivery date or a catalogued specification. In this respect, too, M.G. never fully regained the ground that was lost.

After the takeover the first essential was to tidy up the existing range of models for the 1935 Motor Show. The 847 c.c. P-type Midget had for some time been meeting growing opposition from Singer's 972 c.c. sports car, and this was painfully emphasized at Le Mans when M.G.'s all-girl team attracted much publicity but finished a long way behind three Singers which took 1st, 3rd and 4th places in the 1000 c.c. class, averaging an easy 10 m.p.h. more than the M.G.s for the twenty-four-hour race.

So the P-type engine was bored out to 60 mm, making the capacity 939 c.c. and giving a useful increase in power, and mated to a closer-ratio gearbox. The PB Midget, as it was called, was announced at the end of August at the same price as its predecessor. The PA (as the P-type now became) was discontinued but still catalogued for a few months at a substantially reduced price. When this move failed to dispose of existing stocks, the remaining twenty-seven PA Midgets were converted into PB models at the end of the year.

For the N-type Magnette a new body was produced with stronger, forward-hinged doors and a lower scuttle line. This new Magnette, sometimes but not always called the NB, was offered at a much lower price than the NA: £280 for the two-seater, £285 for the four-seater, £330 for the Allingham 2/4-seater and £355 for the Airline coupé. The racing M.G.s were of course withdrawn, as was the KN saloon. The type designation 'SA', which had been intended for an all-independent Magnette single-seater on R-type lines, was applied to something very, very different.

M.G. enthusiasts were astonished, not to say horrified, when the new model was announced at the beginning of October 1935. By Abingdon standards it was enormous—a saloon with a wheelbase of 10' 3" and a track of 4' 5⅜". Gone was the familiar M.G. chassis; this one was completely conventional in every way. Gone was the o.h.c. engine; the new one had its overhead valves operated by pushrods. Gone were the cable brakes; the new M.G. had the Lockheed hydraulic type, a system Kimber had always distrusted so much that he would not use it even on his racing cars.

The prototype had bolt-on wheels and, as yet another shock for the purists, a synchromesh gearbox, with a long and willowy gearlever protruding from the top, while the clutch was a cork-lined one running in oil. Actually the engine was that of the Wolseley Super Six, its capacity 2062 c.c., and the new car was simply called the M.G. Two-Litre. However, the saloon body—designed by Kimber—was exceptionally attractive, and at a mere £375 the SA looked a great deal of motor-car for the money, especially by comparison with its immediate predecessor, the 1271 c.c. KN Magnette at £399. The motoring press rallied round to emphasize its good points: 'A handsome well-found car which should be ideal for fast cruising in silence and comfort.' (*Motor Sport.*) 'The design is not that of a super-sporting saloon. The engine is not tuned to a fine edge of performance which will call for constant attention . . . just the type of design to appeal to the modern sports car enthusiast who has come to realise that speed with silence has a fascination all its own.' (*The Motor.*)

It so happened that just ten days before the M.G. Two-Litre was announced, another new sporting saloon was unveiled, by S.S. Cars Ltd of Coventry. M.G. had always looked with justifiable contempt on the so-called sports cars of S.S., but this new saloon of theirs—the first to bear the name of Jaguar—was a worthier competitor. Though it lacked the racing background and good reputation of M.G., it had a powerful 2½-litre engine, was more compact without sacrificing much in appearance, and cost only £10 more.

Most unfortunately, production of the new M.G. was badly delayed by a classic piece of ineptitude. The M.G. Car Company, when they did their own designing and dealt direct with suppliers, had reached the stage where they could get a new model rolling off the lines within weeks of its announcement. Thanks to the general inflexibility of the Nuffield Group it was well over six months before the M.G. Two-Litre got into full production. By that time most of the initial publicity had been wasted, and there were more than 500 highly dissatisfied customers waiting for their cars. As Cousins says, 'We ought to have outsold S.S., because we were making the better car.' But the Jaguar was available early in 1936, the M.G. was not, and many of Abingdon's customers must have changed their allegiance.

The existence of the 2664 c.c. Jaguar probably played its part in deciding M.G. to enlarge the SA's engine to 2288 c.c. before the now rather unsuitably named Two-Litre went into production, just as the bolt-on wheels were changed to centre-lock as used on the Jaguar. But throughout the car's production life its specification was changed continually in a way that made nonsense of the promised Nuffield efficiency. The first production gearbox, unlike that of the prototype, was a non-synchromesh unit with a remote control of sorts. Then came a new gearchange, followed a few months later by a completely new gearbox with synchromesh on top and third. These alterations were accompanied by a plethora of other modifications which could only be explained by faulty initial design; even the complete chassis frame was eventually changed. Before the 1936 Motor Show it was necessary to raise the prices. The saloon went up to £389, the Charlesworth open tourer (which had come on the market at the same price as the saloon) to £385. Only the Tickford drophead coupé was unchanged in price for a further year or so. Early in 1937 the engine capacity was changed again, to 2322 c.c. Such a small change could have no significant effect on performance, and seems to have been due to mere standardization of various Nuffield models.

Weighing almost a ton and a half and having only 75.3 b.h.p. at its disposal, the M.G. Two-Litre was not exactly noted for its sparkling acceleration; the o–60 m.p.h. figure was in fact identical to that of the old 18/80 Mark I saloon. But it had a genuine maximum of well over 80 m.p.h. and could be cruised in comfort at close to this speed. In April 1937, Tommy and Elsie Wisdom drove an SA saloon in the Mille Miglia and maintained a high average until Florence, where they crashed on a wet road. The SA was not, as some suggest, inherently unstable—it handled a good deal better than the Jaguar—but with an overall length that exceeded sixteen feet it had to be treated with respect on a slippery surface. Laurence Pomeroy, technical editor of *The Motor* and co-manufacturer of the Zoller supercharger in Britain, had a Tickford coupé for more than two years and called it '. . . certainly the best car I have owned out of a considerable number, built both in England and on the Continent. . . . For sheer pleasure in driving I have come across nothing which pleases me more.' The drophead coupé probably suffered less than the saloon from the main fault of the SA, a tendency to cook its occupants because of excess heat transmitted from the engine and gearbox. It is intriguing, by the way, to note that M.G. advertised the Two-Litre with the slogan, 'for space . . . for grace . . . for pace . . .' This was in 1937, and ten years before Jaguar started to stress the same qualities in their advertisements.

About the time the Two-Litre eventually got into production, in the spring of 1936, M.G. discontinued the o.h.c. PB Midget and announced its successor. The new Midget had a chassis frame of the traditional M.G. design, except that it was boxed-in around the engine and gearbox, but its dimensions were virtually those of the Q-type: 7′ 10″ wheelbase and 3′ 9″ track, which made it appreciably larger than any previous production Midget. This allowed a much roomier two-seater body to be fitted, with more luggage space and a larger fuel tank. But the suspension was softer than before, the brakes were hydraulic, and the weight had gone up by more than a hundredweight.

What upset the purists once again was the use of a pushrod o.h.v. engine (closely akin to the contemporary Wolseley Ten) with 'wet' cork clutch and, except on the very earliest cars built, a synchromesh gearbox. However, the Midget now had 1292 c.c. under its longer bonnet, giving 52.4 b.h.p. at 5000 r.p.m., and its price—£222—was exactly that of the much smaller-engined Midgets that it succeeded.

While retaining its Abingdon appearance and offering quite as much performance as before, the Midget had undoubtedly 'grown up', as *The Autocar* put it, and this new TA model was not altogether welcome to those who liked the compact dimensions and crisp behaviour of the o.h.c. Midgets; indeed, the original exhaust system soon had to be altered so that it made a little more noise! Really, M.G.'s new smallest sports car was in effect a Magnette, not a Midget. It was of very similar size, and though the o.h.v. four-cylinder engine gave slightly less power than the o.h.c. six at the top end, it actually gave rather more lower down the r.p.m. range; it was not only smoother, but more flexible. And if the comparison be continued, the TA two-seater weighed 1¾ cwt. *less* than the N-type two-seater, so it is not surprising that *The Light Car* took almost 2 seconds off the Magnette's standing quarter-mile, though a slightly lower maximum speed was returned (there is no record of the TA press car having been tuned before road test, like its predecessors, but of course it may have been). One tends to forget that for several months the N-type Magnette and T-type Midget were on the market together, the former costing £280 as a two-seater, the latter £222, and offering much the same performance from a very different specification. It must have been a nice test for M.G. enthusiasts to choose between the two.

Reg Jackson, who had been transferred to service work when the racing department closed down, drove the first TA to a dealer in Manchester. 'For the first half of the journey I thought I'd never get used to it, but when I arrived I said to myself, "Jackson, you've never felt less tired." There wasn't much wrong with the T-type, and it was a bloody lovely ride after getting your guts thumped out in the earlier cars.' The new Midget went quickly into production, and others soon began to come round to Jackson's opinion. Before long *The Light Car* were able to refer to it as 'one of the most popular and successful small sports cars ever placed on the market'. At first, an Airline Coupé version was listed at £295, but very few were made before it gave way to a handsome little Tickford coupé which sold well at £269 10s.

One reason for keeping the N-type Magnette chassis in production for a time was that it provided M.G.'s only small four-seater; the big Charlesworth SA tourer (known at Abingdon as 'The Haywagon') cost £100 more. Since there was no intention of marketing the TA with such a body, Abingdon having at last realized the futility of minuscule four-seaters on Midget chassis, a new M.G. chassis of intermediate size was obviously needed.

This was announced at the 1936 Show, and if it was intended as a replacement for the Magnette it was certainly a Magnette that had put on weight; in chassis form alone the new middle-sized M.G. scaled more than a complete N-type four-seater. This would have mattered less if the power output had gone up proportionately, as it did with the TA Midget, but the engine of the new M.G. actually gave slightly less power than its o.h.c. predecessor. It was based on the contemporary Wolseley Twelve, had a capacity of 1548 c.c., and once again was a pushrod o.h.v. unit with a wet clutch and synchromesh gearbox. The power output was 54 b.h.p. at 4500 r.p.m. The chassis was a conventional design similar to that of the SA, with a wheelbase of 9' 0" and track of 4' 2".

The new VA model, or 1½-Litre, as it was called, was offered as an open four-seater (£280), saloon (£325) or Tickford drophead coupé (£335). Just as its chassis and engine recalled the Two-Litre, the 1½-Litre bore a strong resemblance to its bigger sister in saloon or coupé form; only the tourer looked different, because it was made by Morris Bodies Branch instead of Charlesworth.

The unfortunate 1½-Litre M.G. resembled the Two-Litre in other respects, too, for it took just as long to get into production and suffered frequent changes in specification throughout its life. The wet clutch was changed for a dry one, the crankshaft changed twice, direct-metalled big ends gave way to shell bearings, the camshaft, the carburetters, the steering box, the rear axle casing, the road springs, the shock absorbers, the door handles—almost every component, it seems, was changed at least once. These incessant alterations must have made planned production almost impossible, and it is remarkable that M.G. managed to build as many VA models as they did. There is a legend at Abingdon of an assembly-line operator called—strangely enough—'Maggie' Buckle, who evolved a complex arrangement of ropes and planks with which to force the VA front wing into position before drilling it for the fixing bolts. One day Maggie fell ill, and almost everyone in the factory vainly tried to operate his Heath Robinson contraption. There was a long queue of VAs waiting to have their front wings fitted when Maggie at last returned to work.

It was the middle of 1937 before *The Motor* were able to road-test a VA tourer. The acceleration was predictably unimpressive (it returned the same 0–60 m.p.h. figure as an 18/80 Mark I Speed Model), and *The Motor* commented: 'If one wanted to term it a sports model, then it would have to be classed with the new régime of silent sports motoring which is becoming so popular.' However, they liked its roadholding, its brakes and its general smoothness, and managed a speed of 81.82 m.p.h. with the windscreen folded flat.

One might assume that M.G. had now left sports cars far enough behind (except with the TA Midget) and ventured as deeply into the big touring-car class, with the SA and VA, as anybody could want. But in the summer of 1938 they took things a stage further with the WA or 2.6-Litre, surely the most luxurious M.G. ever made. Its chassis was again similar to that of the SA—it even had the same wheelbase and the same front track—but the rear track was increased by more than three inches and the brake-drum diameter went up from twelve inches to fourteen inches, while Kimber wisely insisted that the Lockheed system should incorporate a dual master cylinder. The basically SA engine had the same stroke but the bore went up to 73 mm, giving a capacity of 2561 c.c., and the compression ratio was considerably increased. The power output went up by almost 20 b.h.p.—but then, it needed to. The chassis weight had increased by almost 3 cwt.

By the end of the year the 2.6-Litre was in production: a saloon at £442, a Tickford drophead coupé at £468, and a Charlesworth tourer at £450. Only about nine tourers were made, however, for the Charlesworth concern seem to have ceased building car bodies early in 1939, so that the Two-Litre tourer also had to be dropped at that time. No accurate performance figures are available for the WA, biggest of all production M.G.s, Abingdon having coyly decided not to submit any more cars for comparative road tests: 'These journals . . . only take into consideration what a car will do, and not how it does it.' From the few 'road impres-

sions' that were published it is clear that the WA offered the same
sort of performance as the smaller SA and VA: disappointing
acceleration by sports car standards, but a surprisingly high maximum speed and the ability to maintain high cruising speeds at
fairly low engine r.p.m.; good roadholding, precise steering, and
brakes that were well able to cope with the considerable weight of
the car. The 2.6-Litre was a handsome big carriage by any standards, and most luxuriously fitted out in every detail, but it was
the wrong sort of car to market when war clouds were gathering
over Europe.

Any attempt to assess the SVW range fairly is bedevilled by the
antagonism of traditional M.G. enthusiasts, to whom they are
anathema—lumbering, overbodied brutes by comparison with
their nimble predecessors, and unworthy of the name of sports
car. Yet they were never intended to be sports cars; they were a
deliberate attempt to revive M.G.'s earlier image as manufacturers of comfortable and well-equipped touring cars. Within
that context they represented excellent value for money; one has
only to compare the noisy and cramped K.1 saloon of 1932, which
cost £445, with the sleek and luxurious WA offered for £442 in
1938, or recall that the earlier 18/80 Mark II De Luxe saloon cost
no less than £699.

The atmosphere at Abingdon during the late 'thirties was
naturally very different from the intensely enthusiastic spirit of
earlier days. As Cec Cousins puts it, 'The glamour was gone, and
we set about cost-cutting. Charlie Martin and I checked the production costs every week; if any item went up by so much as a
halfpenny we wanted to know why.' Any notions of original
design were stifled almost at birth. Syd Enever followed up the
R-type with an all-independent production car—known, because
of its size, as the *Queen Mary*—and quotations were obtained from
several engine manufacturers for a V.8 power unit consisting of
two P-type blocks on a common crankcase. But Cowley put a stop
to the whole project.

As for Kimber, he paid frequent visits to Cowley in an attempt
to influence the design of new M.G. models as much as possible.
So far as the bodywork was concerned, at least, he was given a
fairly free hand. If there were features that he disliked personally,
he kept such reservations to himself and never relaxed his efforts
to 'push' M.G. publicity and sales. According to Jackson, 'When
Kimber got a few octagons on the pushrod cars he really quite

liked them—and then, of course, we got some money in the bank. I don't think we'd ever have done it under his control.'

Many private owners continued to race M.G.s, although the lack of factory support inevitably put them at a disadvantage. Prominent among them were the Evans family, who ran the Bellevue Garage in London and had their cars prepared by 'Wilkie' Wilkinson, who later worked on the Ecurie Ecosse Jaguars and subsequently went to B.R.M. The many M.G.s which Bellevue used in almost every branch of motor sport included a team of R-types, with twin-o.h.c. cylinder heads designed by McEvoy and Pomeroy. Other M.G. owners converted their ageing cars to single-seaters, fitted i.f.s., and modified them in many ways to keep them competitive. In 1935 only Bugattis won more Brooklands awards than M.G. did, and even in 1936 M.G.s still won a quarter of all the races held there. Major Goldie Gardner bought Horton's old offset single-seater K.3 and, on his first Brooklands appearance with the car in August 1936, put the Outer Circuit 1100 c.c. record up to 124.40 m.p.h. When Brooklands closed for the last time three years later, that record had still not been beaten. Two other Brooklands records also passed into M.G.'s keeping for all time: the Campbell Circuit 1100 c.c. figure, which J. H. T. Smith's rebodied K.3 secured with a 70.60 m.p.h. lap in 1938; and the Outer Circuit 750 c.c. record, which Harvey Noble set at 122.40 m.p.h., no less, with a single-seater Q-type in 1937.

M.G. successes also continued overseas. The leading M.G. driver in Germany was undoubtedly Bobbie Kohlrausch, who raced several M.G.s and eventually acquired the Magic Midget, getting Abingdon to fit a Q-type engine and a new body. With this he gained countless awards in Continental hillclimbs, much longer and more testing events than their British counterpart. One of his performances was to make fourth fastest climb of the day at Grossglockner in 1935, beating many Bugattis, Maseratis and Alfa Romeos of larger capacity.

In May 1935, Kohlrausch covered the flying mile at 130.41 m.p.h., a speed that was thought to be surely the ultimate with a 750 c.c. engine. But he then had a bronze cylinder head made in Germany, sent the engine back to Abingdon for further tuning, and at Frankfurt in October 1936 put the Magic Midget's flying mile up to 140.6 m.p.h. It was an amazing speed for a 750 c.c. car, and destined to go unbeaten for ten years.

Like Kohlrausch, Gardner had a bronze head made for his

single-seater K.3, and it was arranged that preparation of the engine should be shared between Reg Jackson of M.G. and the well-known Brooklands tuning expert, Robin Jackson. Several record-breaking forays during 1937 culminated in a 148.8 m.p.h. flying kilometre at Frankfurt, using a Zoller supercharger. During that run Eberan von Eberhorst, chief engineer of Auto Union, suggested that it was high time to fit the M.G. with a proper streamlined body. This prompted Kimber to make a careful approach to Lord Nuffield. If M.G. could not participate in racing, could they at least build a record-breaker for Gardner?

Fortunately Nuffield gave his consent. On further consideration it was thought illogical to rebody the ex-Horton car when a more suitable M.G. chassis with offset transmission still existed— Eyston's 1934 Magic Magnette, EX.135, which he had sold to Donald Letts, one of the Bellevue team drivers. So the old chassis was bought by M.G., and to it they fitted a very sleek new body designed by Reid Railton, the man responsible for the body of Cobb's Land Speed Record car. The Gardner engine was further developed, partly by Robin Jackson at Weybridge and partly by Reg Jackson and Syd Enever at Abingdon, with the Zoller replaced by a Centric supercharger. In November 1938, despite some trouble with the new supercharger, Gardner covered the flying mile at 187.62 m.p.h. An increase of nearly 40 m.p.h. over the previous 1100 c.c. record seemed barely credible, and when *The Motor* office received Pomeroy's report of the run they were convinced that the figures must be incorrect. They would have been even more startled had they known that this speed was achieved with ease; such ease, indeed, that it was agreed a further attempt must be made the following year. In 1939, only three months before war broke out, the M.G. record-breaking party returned to Germany, and Gardner covered the flying kilometre at 203.5 m.p.h. The impact of this remarkable achievement with an 1100 c.c. engine recalled the furore of 1931, when M.G. had first exceeded 100 m.p.h. with a 750 c.c. car.

If Nuffield relaxed his ban in respect of record attempts, he also allowed M.G. to continue their participation in another form of motor sport after the Morris takeover. A curious activity very popular in Britain was the so-called 'reliability trial', which had developed from a straightforward test of performance and relia-bility into a highly specialized exercise, in which competing cars were required to climb rough and slippery hills of astonishing gradient. It has been suggested contemptuously that success in

Business is Business (1935-1945)

'mud-plug' trials revealed nothing more than 'the ability to follow a duck through a sewage farm', but the sport had a tremendous following and made a special appeal to the youthful amateur who wanted a relatively inexpensive form of competition in which he could use his everyday motor-car. The smaller o.h.c. M.G.s were particularly well suited to trials work; the very simple bodywork suffered little damage over rough going, while the combination of a high power/weight ratio and ultra-low bottom gears ensured good performance on the hills.

Three very successful drivers during 1934 were J. M. Toulmin, J. A. Bastock and R. A. Macdermid, who used PA Midgets and started to run as a team under the name of 'Cream Crackers'. The following year their cars sometimes appeared with low-pressure superchargers, which made them perform even better. Painted in M.G.'s competition colours—light cream bodies and chocolate-brown mudguards—the three P-types attracted much attention and won many awards.

It was natural for the M.G. Car Company to take an interest in such a popular sport, as other sports car manufacturers also did, and in the 1935 Land's End Trial three Magnettes were driven by Lewis Welch and two M.G. employees, Freddie Kindell and Sam Nash. Their cars were three NE models with ordinary K.2 bodies —one of them, indeed, the actual 1934 T.T. race winner—and they were dubbed the 'Three Musketeers'. Before long they scored their first major success by taking the Team Prize in the Welsh Rally, which Sam Nash won outright. The same trio competed in the Torquay Rally, using the three P-types that had run at Le Mans shortly before, but Abingdon then evolved three new cars from a remarkable assortment of Midget and Magnette components. The basically NE-type engines were opened out to PB (60 mm) bore size, giving a capacity of 1408 c.c., and sometimes fitted with Marshall superchargers. Alec Hounslow of M.G. was also tried out as one of the team's drivers, but he indicated with some disgust that, for a man who had acted as riding mechanic to Tazio Nuvolari in the 1933 T.T., messing about in mud held no attraction whatsoever. . . .

There was some ill-feeling about the number of factory entries in trials about this time, and by the end of 1935 M.G. had to be a little more unobtrusive in their methods. The Musketeer Magnettes were taken over by Bastock, Macdermid and an ex-Singer driver, Archie Langley. To perpetuate the Cream Cracker team M.G. built three new supercharged PB Midgets for Maurice

Toulmin, J. E. S. ('Jesus') Jones and a Midlands M.G. Car Club member named Ken Crawford. The first appearance of the two new M.G. teams, in the Exeter Trial on 27th December, proved almost embarrassingly successful, for they tied for the Team Prize. Throughout 1936 the Crackers and Musketeers dominated the trials scene and were virtually unbeatable.

This caused even more resentment among private owners, one trials organizer even going so far as to introduce a selling-plate clause in the regulations. Moreover, success with o.h.c. cars was clearly of limited publicity value to M.G. when the P-types and N-types went out of production during the year. For 1937, then, M.G. produced six modified TA two-seaters, the Crackers in their familiar cream and brown finish, the Musketeer cars painted red. These were 'sold' to the team drivers on the understanding that M.G. would repurchase them for an agreed figure at the end of the year. Maintenance was to be paid for out of an agreed allowance, and hotel expenses, etc., were also covered by the Company. Although the 1937 cars differed comparatively little from standard TA specification, both teams had a good year and the Cream Crackers won the coveted M.C.C. Team Championship Trophy.

Growing opposition from other makes called for more extensively modified cars in 1938. The Musketeer TAs had very special engines with Marshall superchargers, and gave almost 50 per cent more power than the standard unit. An interesting experiment was the fitting of VA engines to the Cream Cracker TAs, but these gave such disappointing results that they were bored out to WA (73 mm) size, making the capacity 1708 c.c. This recipe proved very effective, for once again the Cream Crackers won the Team Championship, although the trials world was being invaded by many specially-built cars, some of them with large-capacity V.8 engines. A third works-supported M.G. team in 1938, now almost forgotten, was the 'Highlanders'. They used two of the 1937 Cream Cracker cars and another Midget formerly driven by 'Goff' Imhof. The two regular team members were Keith Elliott and Norman Gibson, the third car being driven by Murray Frame, Watson, MacDonald or Weir. All three cars were painted in the dark blue favoured by Scottish drivers.

The Cream Crackers unfortunately lost their captain when Maurice Toulmin succumbed to matrimony in January 1939, and the team was disbanded. The Musketeers also suffered a blow when Macdermid decided to build himself a rear-engined trials car, but his place was taken by Dickie Green with another modified TA, and until the outbreak of war the Three Musketeers continued to win many awards. It was clear, however, that the days of standard or near-standard trials cars were limited, and mud-plugging eventually became the exclusive preserve of freak vehicles, specially built for the purpose and towed on trailers to the start of each event.

With trials cars and record-breakers, M.G. thus contrived to keep their name in front of the sporting enthusiast even under Cowley management. As Cousins says, 'They kept the pot boiling—or at least simmering slowly. So long as we had a little of that we could keep the old atmosphere going.' On the commercial side, too, the situation was quite good. After a very bad year in 1935, when production fell by more than 40 per cent, things picked up again considerably in 1936, and this was followed by a record production year in 1937. There was a slight recession in 1938, when the Munich crisis had its effect on trade in Britain, but it was satisfying to note that export sales accounted for 15 per cent of total production, M.G.s going to no less than twenty-eight different countries.

Rising costs caused a general price increase in May 1939. The SA saloon went up to £398, the coupé to £425. The VA tourer now cost £295, the saloon £335 and the coupé £360. The WA went up to £450 as a saloon, £475 as a coupé. The TA price increases were very small: £3 more for the two-seater, and a mere 10s. more for the coupé.

What very few people realized, because it was not revealed until September, was that the TA had turned into the TB with the fitting of a new engine. This was a modified version of the new Morris M.10 unit, with a dry clutch and the much closer gearbox ratios of the VA model. Although the engine capacity went down from 1292 to 1250 c.c., its taxation class went up from 10 to 11 h.p. because the bore had increased in size, such being the effect of the absurd British horsepower formula. This may explain M.G.'s reticence in announcing the change, for a substantial increase in horsepower tax was foreshadowed in the April parliamentary budget.

Despite its lower capacity the new engine was a much better one, giving slightly more power throughout the r.p.m. range and a promise of greater reliability because of its shorter stroke—its dimensions were 66.5 × 90 mm instead of 63.5 × 102 mm. But M.G. could scarcely have foreseen that they would still be using the same engine fifteen years later and extracting the most remarkable power output from it in supercharged form; that it would drive the Gardner-M.G. at well over 200 m.p.h.; that it would be used, too, in then-unknown racing cars with names like Kieft, Lister, Cooper and Lotus.

The TB Midget enjoyed only a brief life, for when war broke out in September 1939 Kimber decided to discontinue car production immediately so that the factory could be turned over to munitions work as soon as possible. When the last few cars had been completed they brought the total number of M.G.s built, from the marque's earliest days, to approximately 22,500, and many must have wondered what the future held for Abingdon in a very uncertain world. Before two decades had passed, however, that same factory was to produce more sports cars in six months than M.G. had built in its first seventeen years.

As soon as the last cars had been assembled all the equipment that M.G. had gathered together in their ten years at Abingdon was ruthlessly cleared away, and hundreds of tons of car parts moved to a disused factory elsewhere in the town. George Propert has written, 'This was rather a sad job. . . . It seemed that we were destroying any possibilities of making M.G. cars again . . .' And then, 'At the end of 1939 we found ourselves with a completely empty factory and no work to do.' Cowley passed on no wartime contracts to M.G. at this time, says Cousins. 'They completely ignored us—just left us with nothing.'

Kimber and Propert went cap-in-hand around the Ministries begging for work—any work, so long as it contributed to the war effort. The press shop started making shell racks and a variety of other light pressings. A small contract was secured for overhauling Carden-Lloyd tanks, which led to a similar job on the heavier Matilda tanks. Then came great excitement: an order to recondition Browning machine-guns for Spitfires. This seemed a real 'front line' job at last, and M.G. spent three months equipping a complete department for this work, only to be told that as they had no firing range for testing machine-guns, the contract would be placed elsewhere.

However, other contracts were soon found. They started collecting and assembling army trucks, which were sent over from America in huge packing-cases. This proved a blessing in disguise. The factory had by this time taken on so much tank and aircraft press-work that the press shop was crowded out, but building materials were unobtainable. M.G.'s maintenance men broke up the packing-cases and used them to build an extension on the press shop. Then M.G. began repairing armoured cars, which they tested on the Berkshire Downs. The sight of so many fighting vehicles disporting themselves over open country was too much for the boys of the nearby Abingdon aerodrome to resist, and M.G.'s testers were regularly subjected to low-level bombing attacks with bags of flour. They had never had *that* experience when testing sports cars.

All this time preparations were going steadily ahead for M.G.'s biggest wartime task. An aircraft known as the Albemarle, Britain's first nosewheel bomber, had been so designed that it could be built in sections by different factories, and Kimber had sent Propert and Cousins to examine the prototype of the main frontal section, G.1. They were more than a little startled, for this proved to be a stainless steel tubular structure housing pilot, co-pilot and observer, and packed with complicated control gear— the very nerve centre of the whole aircraft. 'The first sight of the intricate maze of bits and pieces filled us with alarm, and it did not appear that it was the sort of job we could ever hope to handle' (Propert). 'It seemed like asking someone to build a radiogram in the garden' (Cousins). However, M.G. took a deep breath and said they *could* build the G.1 section of the Albemarle. It was this decision that led to the subsequent dismissal of Cecil Kimber, as related in Chapter 1.

M.G. might have felt less confident about the 'Marble', as they called it, had they realized that three other concerns—one of them actually an aircraft company—had been scratching their heads over this complicated structure for a very long time without making any progress at all. The Abingdon men are to this day immensely proud of the fact that M.G. succeeded where others failed; indeed, they took over all the partially built sections from the other contractors and became sole suppliers of this vital assembly, building a total of 653 themselves and completing a further 285.

This was not achieved quickly or easily. Special tools had to be designed and made, and the factory equipped with suitable jigs and fixtures. Sufficient labour had to be found—the job totalled 3,500 hours per complete section—and the current man shortage led to the employment of women, who had to be taught welding and other specialized work. A training school was established, a bus service instituted, even a girls' hostel opened, complete with sewing room and laundry. A complete new inspection department had to be set up to enforce the very strict requirements of the

Aeronautical Inspection Directorate as well as the Inspectorate of Fighting Vehicles. Some two million small components had to be made for the main G.1 structure. Test rigs were devised for the oxygen system, the pneumatic, hydraulic and mechanical control gear. Two of M.G.'s inspectors, Giles Hoyle and Bill Bulcock, produced a most complex test rig so that all the electrical controls of the Albemarle could be checked under operational conditions. They were more than a little thrilled to find it was the only test equipment of its type being operated in the entire aircraft industry, and it was subsequently purchased by a leading aeroplane manufacturer.

Another big aircraft job was to produce Lancaster bomber engine mountings, and assemble interchangeable 'power units' which incorporated Rolls-Royce Merlin engines. Many other components were made for the Lancaster and Typhoon, followed by the highly specialized task of making complete wing spars for the Tempest II, with leading and trailing edges in dural. Meanwhile the work on weapons expanded steadily: building the Crusader tank, Oerlikon and Bofors gun turrets, and finally the Neptune amphibious tank. Sherman, Churchill and Centaur tanks were converted for special purposes, and in five weeks—despite a fire that almost destroyed the department concerned—M.G. produced 3000 sets of 'wading equipment' which allowed tanks to be landed from seaborne tank-carriers in the D-day invasion of Europe.

Hardly any job was considered too big or too small; one part of the factory would resound to the riveting-up of 16-ton tanks, another produce thousands of intricate little blood-centrifuging attachments for the Admiralty. One department spent the whole war making fuel dipsticks for tanks—so many, indeed, that Propert decided every British tank in existence must have had at least a dozen M.G. dipsticks before the war ended.

Eventually the wartime contracts were cancelled one by one, for reasons obvious to everyone who read the newspapers. The Tempest spar shop was cleared and car assembly lines laid down where, a few weeks before, aircraft wings had been built. If the M.G. men looked forward joyfully to the future, they also looked with some satisfaction on their immediate past. 'What we did before the war,' says Cousins with understandable pride, 'was nothing to what we achieved during the war.'

Chapter 6

Post-War Expansion (1945–1954)

During the six wartime years the British motoring press, having little else to write about, had filled many columns with surmise over the post-war motoring scene. There were some who saw it as a new era of supercharged production cars with sophisticated chassis and futuristic bodywork, speeding over a nationwide network of magnificent motorways; very few realized, as the war drew to a close, that new cars were going to be extremely scarce in Britain. But nobody doubted that petrol would soon be freely available to all.

Before Cecil Kimber left Abingdon he had placed a clever series of advertisements in which members of the armed forces commented, as they looked at their corvettes, fighter aircraft and the like, 'It reminds me of my M.G.' This epitomized the widespread feeling of nostalgia during the war, when private motorists had only a small ration of petrol for three years and none at all for the remaining three. Kimber understood—none better—how they longed for the time when they could again use their cars for pleasure, while a new generation (the present writer among them) eagerly awaited their first opportunity to drive, and if possible to drive a sports car.

Had he survived, Kimber would have been appalled by the conditions that British motorists actually encountered. A new government took office before the war ended and quickly displayed a deliberately restrictive attitude, as much from political expediency as economic necessity, towards all forms of private motoring. Time has laid a benevolent veil over the memory that petrol remained strictly rationed for a further five years—longer than during the war itself—except for a period of eight months in 1947/8 when it was again withdrawn completely. Even when a 'basic ration' was restored, it was so meagre that it allowed less than 100 miles a month of pleasure motoring, and the joys of long-distance touring or unrestricted fast driving remained out of reach. The only fuel that could be bought in those austere days was a dreadful mixture of low-octane grades known as 'Pool', on which no engine of more than the most modest compression ratio would run efficiently. Petrol rationing was at last discontinued in June 1950, but not until February 1953 were better-quality fuels available once more.

For much of that dismal post-war period the government permitted motor manufacturers to have supplies of steel only in strict proportion to the number of cars they exported, and new cars became virtually unobtainable in Britain. Anyone lucky enough to acquire one could sell it immediately for twice as much—until fresh legislation compelled the buyer to sign a 'covenant' not to resell within two years. Such was the shortage that pre-war cars changed hands for fantastic sums; in 1946 a nine-year-old VA tourer was advertised for £530 when the list price of a brand-new M.G. was £375. Not until well into the 'fifties did the market even begin to approach normal conditions. By that time, rising costs and heavy taxation had combined to force new car prices up to three times their pre-war level. Even then it was customary to wait six months or more for delivery, and some cars were still almost impossible to buy on the home market. In 1952, for example, forty-two M.G. Midgets were sent overseas for every one that stayed behind in Britain.

This long spell of unnatural conditions and severe restrictions, extending as it did for almost fifteen years, had a far-reaching effect on the British motor industry. Its effect upon the M.G. Car Company was totally unexpected and in many ways altered that concern out of all recognition.

M.G. had made their name with a series of fairly specialized models designed precisely to meet the needs of the typical sports car enthusiast of modest means. However they might be despised by superior beings who preferred their cars to be large, expensive and preferably hyphenated, these little M.G.s had achieved their purpose admirably and become immensely popular; they had sold well in Britain, by the standards of the times, and even found a small but enthusiastic following overseas. Abingdon's policy had been modified considerably by the new management of 1935, but the founder of the marque still played some part in guiding its destiny, and it was never completely submerged by commercialism.

Now, however, M.G. faced the unknown, and did so without the guiding hand of Cecil Kimber. In the years that followed, Abingdon was to become more and more the Cinderella of a large and ever-expanding organization, denied the capital investment that the factory needed for proper development, yet called upon to produce relatively enormous numbers of sports cars to meet a demand that nobody had—or could have—foreseen. M.G. design was to be dictated more and more by the requirements of overseas customers, whose demands had to be satisfied however mysterious or even incomprehensible they might seem. This had to be achieved with minimum expenditure, and without losing the basic home market that protects every British motor manufacturer from the vagaries of taste or legislation that can close an export outlet almost overnight.

But all this still lay in the future when, late in 1945, Abingdon returned to car manufacture. Before the war, M.G.s had sold mainly on the home market, and only four models had exceeded a production rate of 1000 cars a year: the J.2 Midget, the PA/PB Midgets, the TA/TB Midgets and the original M-type Midget, in that order. The obvious choice was to concentrate on building one model only, and that a Midget two-seater. By making use of a pre-war design, as most other manufacturers had to do, M.G. could get production under way quickly to meet the pressing needs of the British motorist. It didn't matter that the design was out of date because he would take anything he could get, and nobody outside Britain would want the thing anyway.

So the Cowley design staff made the bare minimum of alteration to the pre-war TB Midget. The sliding-trunnion suspension, one of the few remaining legacies of original Abingdon design, was abandoned as a needless complication and replaced by conventional shackled springs, together with different shock-absorbers. The two-seater sports body, which had proved its worth beyond doubt, was retained but made four inches wider across the cockpit. Within five weeks of the war's official conclusion M.G. were able to announce, in October 1945, their TC Midget, and by the end of the year they had built eighty-one of them. 'We did it up in a corner, sort of thing,' says Cousins. 'And it wasn't nearly as good in its day as the PB was in *its* day. The PB was a gorgeous little motor-car; the TC was a lash-up by comparison.'

Lash-up or not, more than 1500 TCs were built the following year, and over one-third of them went overseas. Of those that stayed at home, one was bought by a young naval officer—it was his first new car—and naturally he often took his girl-friend out for a ride in it. This caused some misgivings at her family home; an M.G. two-seater, especially when driven with naval enthusiasm, was not considered an ideal conveyance for the future Queen of England. Twenty-two years later, their eldest son bought *his* first car: an M.G. two-seater.

The performance of the TC must be measured against that of the TA, since the TB had too short a life to be fully road-tested for any magazine. As might be expected, there was little to choose between the two. *The Autocar* gave both models a maximum speed of around 74/75 m.p.h. with windscreen up, and a small difference in the 0–60 m.p.h. acceleration figure (22.7 secs. for the TC, 23.1 for the TA) may have been accounted for by the TC's dry clutch and closer-ratio gearbox. *The Motor* reduced the TC's acceleration time to 21.1 secs. and managed a one-way 77.6 m.p.h. All the TC figures would undoubtedly have been better still had the car not been tested, of necessity, on Pool petrol.

Although the price went up in mid-1946 from £375 to £412, which purchase tax raised to £528, home sales increased slightly in 1947. What was more remarkable, however, was that more TCs were sold abroad than in Britain that year. People in the most unlikely parts of the world had begun to display an interest in this funny little two-seater which, for most of them, was just about the most unsuitable vehicle that could be imagined. In its own native land it was something of an anachronism, heaven knows, and *The Autocar* said: 'In a motoring world in which ... cars tend more and more to resemble one another . . . the M.G. Midget stands unique.' But overseas, most post-war cars were developing into monocoque saloons with soft but well-controlled springing, independent front suspension, small-diameter pressed-steel wheels, unobtrusive, low-revving but powerful engines—with, in some countries, fully automatic transmission—and extremely roomy bodies which provided every conceivable comfort. It seemed extraordinary that anyone should want a stiffly sprung sports car, angular as a matchbox, with enormous wire wheels and a high-revving engine that was far from quiet—especially when any modern large-capacity car could beat it for acceleration or speed on the straight.

But people overseas were discovering something the British had known about for quite a long time: the sheer joy of driving a taut and responsive little car and flinging it through the curves just as fast as it would go. They found the sensation all the more intoxicating because it was so unfamiliar to them. As one American writer has said: 'It was a way of life. A wildly different car that you jazzed around in on weekdays and raced on weekends. . . . A moving spot of color on a still-drab post-war landscape.'

So for a time they forgot that the M.G. TC made not the slightest concession to the requirements of other countries; that it had no heater, no bumpers, could not be bought with left-hand drive; that scarcely anyone knew how to service or even maintain it; that comparatively few, indeed, really knew how to drive it. And the M.G. Car Company found themselves in a very enviable position when the British Chancellor of the Exchequer, Sir Stafford Cripps, virtually closed the home market late in 1947. M.G. could sell ten of their cars abroad for every one sold in Britain, and in 1948 alone brought in a cool £1m. worth of sorely needed foreign currency. By the time TC production ceased, at the end of the following year, no less than 10,000 had been built—more than three times the total production of any previous M.G. model.

We have read so often that the vast majority of TCs were sold in America (and the present writer, alas, is among those who have written it) that it comes as a distinct surprise to find this is completely untrue. The number sold in Britain was 3408; overseas, 6592. Of the latter, exactly 2001 cars went to the U.S.A. Yet the effect the TC had upon that country is beyond question. It introduced the pleasures of sports car ownership to a land that had never known them before, and blazed the trail for the multitude of other imported cars that followed. It transformed American motor racing from a little-known professional sport into an activity within everyone's reach. Even the Sports Car Club of America sprang from one small U.S. branch of the international M.G. Car Club. One can scarcely believe that a couple of thousand little old-fashioned two-seaters could so influence the tastes of an entire nation.

If people like Clark Gable bought a TC because it amused them, there were others—Briggs Cunningham, John Fitch, Phil Hill and many more—who saw it as a passport to the delights of motor racing, and the awards won by M.G.s almost began to rival the great days of the mid-'thirties. Successes were gained in America, Africa, Australia, Spain, Portugal, Singapore, Switzerland—even in England and Ireland. They brought, as racing always does, a demand for more power, and in 1949 Abingdon produced an admirable manual of tuning recommendations, every step of which had first been tried out at the factory. By following these the standard engine's 54.4 b.h.p. could be raised through various stages to a maximum of 97.5 b.h.p. in supercharged form, and all the necessary 'hot bits' were put on the market for those who wanted them. This was a completely new departure for a British production car factory, and the fact that it was done revealed a slight relaxation in Cowley's attitude to motor sport. Rather surreptitiously—for Nuffield policy had not changed all that much—Abingdon also started to give a little solid assistance to some of those who raced TCs in Britain.

When Kimber cleared the factory for wartime work in 1939, the cars and material that went into storage included the record-breaking Gardner-M.G., fresh from its 200 m.p.h. triumph in Germany, together with a special 750 c.c. six-cylinder engine that M.G. had built for an attack on Kohlrausch's 1936 record. The war had put paid to that idea, and a few years later a fire had destroyed the 1100 c.c. engine and most of the spares, but the car itself and the 750 c.c. engine had been saved.

On Kimber's dismissal late in 1941, 'Pop' Propert had remained as M.G.'s general manager but under strict direction from Cowley, where one of the Nuffield directors would hold the responsibility for controlling M.G. affairs. For several years the man in charge was H. A. Ryder, who kept a tight rein on Abingdon and particularly disapproved of sporting activities. When Lt.-Colonel Goldie Gardner (as he now was) reappeared on the scene at the end of the war, eager to make his long-postponed attempt on the 750 c.c. record, there could be no question of preparing the car at the M.G. factory. It was therefore made ready elsewhere, and Jackson and Enever were rather grudgingly released from their other duties occasionally to advise on its preparation.

The special engine that Enever had designed had an N-type Magnette block with the bore reduced to 53 mm and the stroke to 56 mm, giving 741 c.c. As the original supercharger had been lost in the fire, Chris Shorrock designed a new one. Everything was ready by the summer of 1946, and Jackson and Enever took the record car across war-shattered Europe into Italy, where there was a happy reunion with Count Lurani at a restaurant owned by Nuvolari's great rival of earlier days, Achille Varzi. The record attempt was not so happy, mainly because the chosen stretch of autostrada was unsuitable. In October a second attempt was made at Jabbeke on what is now the Ostend/Brussels motorway, and Gardner succeeded in breaking Kohlrausch's ten-year-old record with a speed of 159.15 m.p.h. over the flying mile. The following year the engine was reduced to 500 c.c. capacity by putting two cylinders out of action, and in this form the car recorded 118.06 m.p.h.

Understandably dissatisfied with the very limited assistance provided by the Nuffield Organization, Gardner had by this time ceased to refer to his car as an M.G. He emphasized this in 1948 by having the M.G. engine replaced by a two-litre Jaguar unit (actually a smaller-capacity prototype of the twin-o.h.c. XK.120 engine), with which he achieved a mean speed of 176.69 m.p.h. at Jabbeke in September. This was rather a slap in the face for M.G., though they had the consolation of remembering that the car had travelled at over 200 m.p.h. with an M.G. engine of only 1100 c.c. back in 1939.

Meanwhile, however, there had been another palace revolution at Cowley. No less than nine directors had left the Nuffield board, and the new man in control of M.G. was S. V. Smith. While 'S.V.' was just as strict as his predecessor, he had a somewhat more understanding attitude towards motor sport, and eventually sanctioned M.G.'s participation in record attempts. This became all the more desirable when Taruffi broke M.G.'s 500 c.c. record in November 1948.

Enever therefore redesigned the Magnette engine, going back to the original bore size of 57 mm but using a special three-throw crankshaft of 64.5 mm stroke, which made the engine a 497 c.c. unit with only three of its six cylinders operative. The Gardner car thus became an M.G. once again and celebrated this metamorphosis with a rousing 154.23 m.p.h. at Jabbeke in September 1949. Gardner had beaten Taruffi's highest speed by almost 26 m.p.h. to regain Class I supremacy. After appearing at the New York Auto Show early in the New Year, the record car was then prepared for an attempt on Class J (350 c.c.), using only *two* of the six cylinders. In July 1950 Gardner achieved 121.09 m.p.h. at Jabbeke, easily breaking the previous record held by Johnny Lurani.

This meant that the Gardner-M.G. was now the world's fastest car in five of the ten recognized international capacity classes, from 350 to 1500 c.c. Such an accomplishment was unique, and very nice for M.G. prestige in a general sort of way, but some hypercritical individual was liable to point out that neither the car nor its engine bore the slightest resemblance to current production M.G.s—which, in any case, belonged in only one of those five capacity classes. While the ageing Gardner-M.G. could undoubtedly be used to good effect again, there would have to be some new thinking if it were to provide really worthwhile publicity for the marque.

The M.G. TC had not been in production for eighteen months

when it was joined by another M.G. that had been designed before the war, although it had a much more up-to-date specification. This was a compact little saloon, the Y-type or 1¼-Litre, which used a single-carburetter version of the 1250 c.c. TC engine in a welded, box-section chassis that was underslung at the rear, had rack-and-pinion steering, and independent front suspension by coil springs and wishbones. The four-door saloon body was closely related to that of the Morris Eight. The chassis was both sturdy and sound but the complete car, like so many pre-war Cowley designs, was far too heavy for its engine, weighing almost 5 cwt. more than the TC two-seater.

However, the little Y-type was extremely well received when it was announced in the spring of 1947 at £575 (£672 with tax), for i.f.s. was still something of a rarity in Britain at that time and it was judged exceptionally comfortable by contemporary standards. The M.G. 1¼-Litre sold quite well, not only at home but also overseas. It was capable of higher cruising speeds than most small British saloons of its day and the engine could readily be given the full TC tuning treatment, so some owners entered their Y-types for major events such as the Monte Carlo Rally. One privately owned example was fitted with a low-pressure Shorrock supercharger and taken to Jabbeke at the time of Gardner's 1950 record attempt, for its owner, Dick Benn, had a fancy to see it timed at 100 m.p.h. Gardner obliged with a run at 104.7 m.p.h. before loud noises came from under the Y-type's stubby little bonnet.

In October 1948 the 1¼-Litre also appeared as an open four-seater, the YT, at the same price as the saloon but reserved for export only. It had two carburetters and weighed 1½ cwt. less than the saloon, but this still left it a long way behind the TC two-seater in performance, while the bodywork was about as sporting in appearance as the average Victorian bathtub. The YT tourer met with little success and was withdrawn early in 1950, its demise mourned by few.

A sharp reminder that the M.G. Car Company was now just part of a large organization came in May 1949, for the new Nuffield board decided to transfer production of Rileys—M.G.'s old competitors of the showrooms and the racing circuits—to Abingdon. 'Pop' Propert, general manager for almost twenty years and associated with M.G. since the Bainton Road days of 1925, retired in July, and was succeeded by one of the influx of Riley men, Jack Tatlow. Every morning Tatlow would drive the sixty miles from Coventry to Abingdon, and if the M.G. staff at first felt wary of this Midlander in their midst, they soon learned to respect him. 'He was as straight as a gun-barrel,' says Cousins, '—the best man I ever worked for. He had an honesty of purpose that instilled loyalty into people.' And Tatlow in turn found much to respect at Abingdon, notably a knowledge of production planning and parts control that made Riley methods look extremely happy-go-lucky. Before very long the men of the octagon and the men of the blue diamond had settled down to work very contentedly together, and old rivalry was forgotten.

By the early summer of 1949 there was a demand from overseas for something a little more comfortable, a bit more civilized than the spartan TC two-seater—without, of course, being as gutless as the YT tourer had proved. The disappointing sales of the YT may have influenced S. V. Smith to look towards Abingdon for suggestions. Inside a fortnight M.G. had 'designed' a new model without ever putting pencil to paper, simply by chopping five inches out of a Y-type chassis (making the wheelbase that of the TC) and plonking a TC body on top. It must have looked most peculiar, but it served to indicate the lines on which a new Midget could be produced without protracted development work.

In due course Cowley brought out the finished TD design on this basis. The box-section chassis was similar to that of the Y-type, except that it passed over the rear axle instead of beneath. The same type of i.f.s. was used, and the excellent rack-and-pinion steering not only provided more precise control than any TC had ever enjoyed, it could easily be transposed for left-hand steering. The i.f.s. made it necessary to fit disc wheels similar to those of the Y-type, but slightly smaller. Much more powerful two-leading-shoe brakes were fitted at the front, and a hypoid rear axle lowered the transmission line slightly. The final-drive ratio was that of the TC, but the overall gearing was reduced by the smaller wheels. At first the engine was almost identical to that of the TC, although later it was much improved in detail; the gearbox employed the wider ratios of the Y-type model.

The body, while retaining the two-seater layout exactly, somehow looked entirely different. Being four inches wider than the TC it appeared lower and more squat, although the hood-up height was unchanged. The small disc wheels, of course, played a major part in the transformation. Mudguarding was more generous, the lines of the body less angular, and the presence of bumpers, front and rear, also helped to alter the appearance. Inevitably the weight had gone up by 1½ cwt.

The new TD Midget was an excellent compromise between old and new, a knockabout two-seater that handled well and cruised at high speed without the discomfort experienced in its predecessor. When it was announced early in 1950 at £445 (£569 with tax), the motoring press did not hesitate to acclaim it as a considerable improvement on the TC: '. . . the famous "Midge" has really gone ahead by a large stride,' said *The Autocar*. And *The Motor* called it 'a car which, like its forerunners, one took to with enthusiasm and parted from with reluctance, the only difference being that both the enthusiasm and the reluctance were greater than before'. Roadholding was considered as good as that of the TC, if not better, and certainly improved on bumpy surfaces. The greater weight was countered by the lower overall gear ratio, so the acceleration was unchanged. As for maximum speed, both magazines recorded higher figures than they had with the TC—and they were still using Pool petrol.

But traditions die hard, and the approval of the motoring press was certainly not shared by all M.G. enthusiasts, the disc wheels arousing particular contempt. The Midget had undoubtedly lost a certain lithe quality, a coltishness that had been part of its charm, and by comparison with the TC the TD could only be described as matronly—or, at best, wifely. Though a woman of *savoir-faire* may provide all that the heart desires, it's the young dolly-bird that gets into the advertisements in this imperfect world.

So the TC owners were as loud in their disdain for the TD as, fourteen years earlier, the PB owners had been in their scorn for the TA. In terms of sales, however, the TD proceeded to knock the TC into a cocked hat, and exports soared almost out of sight. In 1950 Abingdon's total production for the year, counting the Rileys which were also being built there, exceeded 10,000 for the first time. Two years later the total was 11,560 in M.G.s alone, and 10,621 of these were sold overseas.

These figures included an improved version of the 1¼-Litre saloon which had appeared at the end of 1951, priced at £565 (£880 with the much-increased tax of that time). The YB used the hypoid axle, smaller wheels and two-leading-shoe brakes of the TD, while larger shock-absorbers were fitted together with a front anti-roll bar. This made a desirable improvement in handling characteristics, and although the YB was made in comparatively small quantities—because Abingdon was bulging at the seams with TD production—it was a better car than its predecessor in this respect. One YB saloon, in the hands of Dick Jacobs, achieved the unparalleled feat of winning its class three years running, 1952–1954, in the Silverstone Production Touring Car Race.

During this time substantial purchase tax increases, coming on top of small increases in the basic price, had put the TD two-seater up to more than £825 on the home market. This could have had an unfortunate effect on sales if M.G. had had any significant number of cars available for the home market—but they hadn't. In one year alone they sent 10,592 two-seaters overseas, and managed to retain just 246 for British sports car enthusiasts. The fairly widespread criticism of the TD in England may to some extent have been a simple matter of sour grapes.

It was also during the early life of the TD Midget that new ideas on the Gardner-M.G. record car crystallized into a decision to fit the car with a supercharged TD engine, just to show the world what the current power unit could do when fully developed. By the time Enever had finished with that 1250 c.c. pushrod engine it was giving 213 b.h.p. at 7000 r.p.m., an output that was downright indecent for such a simple and unsophisticated design. It was quite sufficient to propel the Gardner-M.G. at something over 210 m.p.h. and show that the pushrod engine had just as much potential as its more complicated o.h.c. predecessor..

Two attempts were made on the Bonneville Salt Flats at Utah, in 1951 and 1952. Unfortunately both were bedevilled with problems—failure of the timing apparatus, bad weather conditions and considerable wheelspin among them—so that the promised goal was never attained, although several records were broken on both occasions and a speed of 202.14 m.p.h. was officially achieved, one-way. During the second Utah attempt, however, Gardner spun on the wet salt and suffered a sharp blow on the head from a marker post. He seemed all right at the time, but this was to prove the last appearance of the Gardner-M.G. and its gallant driver in record-breaking.

If the two Utah record attempts were not as successful as M.G. had hoped, they were by no means complete failures; the new international figures (one of them 189.5 m.p.h.) were quite impressive enough and the American National records even more so, since a one-way timing was accepted for these and speeds of over 200 m.p.h. had been reached. The first Sebring 12 Hours Race in Florida, held in 1952, had brought another boost for M.G. prestige when three TDs won the Team Prize, one car finishing sixth overall, and this was backed up by a fine array of racing and rallying successes in many other parts of the world that same year.

It was, indeed, a highly significant year for M.G. all round. Abingdon production had risen steadily to reach a peak of 13,669 cars in one year, Rileys included. Towards the end of 1952 Jack Tatlow was succeeded as M.G.'s general manager by John Thornley, a super-enthusiast with the boundless energy of a Fred Astaire—whom, indeed, he closely resembled; a man, too, who had been the first honorary secretary of the M.G. Car Club, had driven on occasions for the pre-war trials teams, and written a splendid book on M.G.'s racing days.

Commercially, M.G.s had never known greater success. On the race-tracks, too, they were more than a match for other production sports cars of similar size and price, while the ever-willing M.G. engine was used by all the more successful builders of specialized sports-racing cars, Cooper and Lotus included. And behind the scenes Syd Enever was standing by with the complete prototype of a beautiful new M.G. two-seater, capable of being put into production within twelve months at the most. At that stage in the history of M.G., Abingdon could so easily have moved into the very forefront of the sports world.

It did not, for 1952 was also the year when the Nuffield Group was amalgamated with the Austin Motor Company to form the third largest motor manufacturing business in the world, the British Motor Corporation. Lord Nuffield relinquished all but nominal control of his organization, leaving Sir Leonard Lord very firmly in charge of policy. In the period immediately following this uneasy alliance of two concerns that had cordially detested each other for years, nobody had either the time or the inclination to listen sympathetically to the yearnings of a tuppenny-ha'penny little sports car factory.

Back in 1949, when a TC was *the* car for the amateur racing enthusiast, a home-brewed version with very light bodywork had appeared in several major events—including Le Mans and even the French Grand Prix, run as a sports car race that year—in the hands of a tough individual named George Phillips, known to his friends as 'Phil' because he didn't much care for his Christian name ('Good enough for a king, I s'pose . . .', he would say grudgingly). In earlier days as a Fleet Street despatch-rider Phil had learned to cover the ground fast, whatever the conditions of traffic or weather, and in later years he was to become famous as chief photographer of a new weekly magazine, *Autosport*. He was one of three drivers (the others were Dick Jacobs and Ted Lund) provided with works-prepared TCs for some English races in 1949, and these had been replaced by modified TDs for 1950 and 1951. They had achieved a class 1-2-3 in the 1950 T.T. in appalling weather, winning the Team Prize, and although an H.R.G. had pipped them for a class win at Silverstone in 1950, the Jacobs TD had beaten the H.R.G.s the following year.

In 1950, too, Phil had entered his rebodied TC for Le Mans again, and finished second in the 1½-litre class behind a works-entered Jowett Jupiter. Suitably impressed, M.G. had agreed to build him a car for the next Le Mans race. Basically this was a tuned TD, but provided with an exceptionally good-looking body on modern lines which Syd Enever had designed with the Gardner-M.G. at the back of his mind. The effect of this sleek *carrosserie* was startling. Although the TD engine could not be drastically tuned for a twenty-four-hour race, the car had a maximum speed of almost 120 m.p.h.—a 50 per cent increase on that of the standard TD two-seater, mainly achieved just by fitting bodywork with a fairly small frontal area and a low drag factor.

Phil was understandably thrilled with his Le Mans car, UMG.400, but engine trouble led to its early retirement from the 1951 race. It has never been clearly established whether this resulted from over-enthusiasm or the very low-quality fuel provided for competitors that year. However, the car's appearance had excited everyone who saw it. The one problem was that the driver sat absurdly high because of the TD chassis layout. This shortcoming so irritated Enever that he designed a new frame with its side-members spaced well apart so that driver and passenger could sit low between them, one each side of the transmission line. He had a couple of these frames made, and on one of them he fitted a body almost identical to that of UMG.400, but with full road equipment in the way of bumpers, sidescreens, hood, windscreen and so on. The high T-series engine made rather a bulge in the bonnet top, but apart from that it was a handsome and practical car with very definite possibilities as a new production M.G. two-seater.

This prototype, EX.175, was completed late in 1952 and duly shown to M.G.'s new masters, the management of BMC, with a request for permission to go into production with it as the successor to the TD Midget. The project was turned down flat. At the 1952 Motor Show, Donald Healey had unveiled a new Austin-based sports car with a 2660 c.c. A.90 engine and equally attractive bodywork, and Sir Leonard Lord had arranged for this to be built in the Austin factory at Longbridge, calling it the Austin-Healey 100. He saw no need for BMC to manufacture two new sports cars, so M.G. were told to continue making their now rather old-fashioned TD.

The disappointment at Abingdon was intense, and as 1953 went by it soon became apparent that for M.G., at least, BMC's decision was a calamity. Export sales of the TD fell to almost half the previous year's level and although a few hundred more were sold on the home market, helped by a reduction in purchase tax, total production for the year dropped by 40 per cent. If the TD was considerably cheaper than the new Austin-Healey, and still scored a few class wins here and there, it certainly looked out of date beside Donald Healey's pretty little two-seater. Sales of the 1¼-Litre saloon also fell drastically, for it, too, was now outmoded both in appearance and performance. People began to talk of M.G. as a marque that had had its day.

All that BMC would sanction was a 'facelift', as the motor industry calls it, on the TD. From the scuttle forwards the bonnet line was dropped to a sloping imitation radiator, the headlamps faired into the front mudguards, and the tail end raked to match the new front. Bucket seats replaced the one-piece squab of the TD, and new hubs were designed so that wire wheels could be offered as an option. The engine was the slightly-tuned unit of the TD Mark II, the so-called 'competition' model which gave three or four b.h.p. more than the standard car. At the 1953 Motor Show the TF Midget made its first appearance. its price £20 more than that of the TD at £550 (£780 with tax).

If BMC thought the TF was going to fool anybody they clearly knew little about sports car enthusiasts, for the new M.G. was greeted with derision. British pressmen merely damned it with faint praise, but elsewhere the comments were more forthright. Tom McCahill of the American *Mechanix Illustrated* wrote: 'I feel the new TF is a big disappointment . . . Mrs Casey's dead cat slightly warmed over. To get down to facts, the new M.G. TF is a dyspeptic Mark II imitation that falls short of being as good as the Mark II. . . . Only out of supreme arrogance would the manufacturers attempt to keep ramming this old teapot down the throats of American buyers. . . . I personally feel the current management of M.G. has let me and hundreds of other American M.G. fans down pretty hard.'

Every knowledgeable enthusiast recognized the truth of this.

The 'new model' was not helped by a BMC catalogue that contained the following howler: 'Remember how, way back in 1935, George Eyston's team of women drivers in M.G.s won the Le Mans 24 Hours race?' Faced with that sort of thing, many of M.G.'s most ardent admirers began to feel their intelligence was being insulted.

The announcement at the same Motor Show of two other new models made the situation even worse. One was Triumph's latest two-litre sports car, with a low-revving 90 b.h.p. engine and, originally, a basic price only £5 above that of the TF Midget. Its handling at the limit was more than a little doubtful and it was downright ugly by comparison with the M.G., but these faults were forgotten when it proved to be the cheapest 100 m.p.h. sports car in the world, and before long the TR.2 began to reap a rich harvest of rally successes which made a considerable impression on all.

The other car that upset M.G. enthusiasts at the 1953 Show actually shared the M.G. stand with the TF. The previous year Gerry Palmer, designer of the much-praised Jowett Javelin (and, later, the not-so-praised Riley Pathfinder), had produced a new saloon body shell on very similar lines to that of the contemporary Lancia Aurelia. This had been fitted with the 1250 c.c. M.G. engine and was, in fact, intended as a new M.G. saloon, but a last-minute change of policy had turned it into the Wolseley 4/44, in which guise it appeared at the 1952 Show. But Y-type sales had fallen so badly by this time that a new M.G. saloon was obviously overdue, so the car was given an imitation M.G. radiator and fitted with a new 1489 c.c. engine. This, the first new power unit to be produced under BMC aegis, traced its ancestry back to Austin's A.40 engine, and it is an intriguing coincidence that one of the men responsible for it was M.G.'s old chief designer, H. N. Charles, who had joined Austin as development engineer towards the end of the war. H. N. Charles describes it as 'a horrible engine, but free from bugs'. Horrible or not, it was to prove as responsive to tuning as M.G.'s version of the old Morris M.10 unit had done.

So the new TF was accompanied at the 1953 Motor Show by the new ZA Magnette saloon. M.G. fans could scarcely decide which aspect of this situation offended them most: the fact that an obvious Wolseley was being presented as an M.G.; that the sacred name of Magnette should be revived for a *saloon* (quite forgetting that the first Magnettes of all had been saloons); that a closed

M.G. should be given a 1½-litre engine when the sports car, which so urgently needed one, still had to make do with its 1¼-litre. The correspondence columns of the motor magazines were filled for quite a few weeks after the doors closed at Earls Court.

Luckily, Sir Leonard Lord had a visit round about this time from one of the very few people whose opinions he admired and respected: Captain George Eyston. While Eyston had had no direct connection with M.G. after the Nuffield takeover of 1935, he had never lost his affection for the marque. Moreover, his wife was of American birth and he spent much of his time in that country, where he saw at first hand what was happening in the sports car world.

After the 1952 record attempt Goldie Gardner, then in his middle sixties, had become bedridden with a serious illness, and it was clear that his record-breaking days were over. Eyston now urged Lord to let M.G. make another record run at Utah, and as a Castrol director he was able to promise some backing for such a venture.

However, the Gardner-M.G. was the personal property of its driver and had always been backed by the rival Duckham's Oil Company. The only solution was to build another car. The EX.175 prototype was brought out from under its dust-sheets and fitted with a cockpit cover, undershield and other fairings, but a few tests sufficed to show that it was too close to a production car to make a successful record-breaker. Fortunately the spare chassis frame was still there. It was fitted with a new body, almost identical to that of the Gardner-M.G., and so a new M.G. record car, EX. 179, emerged.

For Gardner's two attempts with the T-type or XPAG series engine, the capacity had remained at 1250 c.c. but the engine had been supercharged. The new record car, it was decided, would run unsupercharged but with the capacity increased to 1466 c.c. Experiments had been made by many private owners in over-boring the 1250 c.c. engine, a risky procedure which had led to the development of a re-cored 72 mm-bore engine known as the XPEG. This had existed for some time, but BMC had so far refused to put it into production.

In August 1954 the new M.G. record car appeared at Utah, driven by George Eyston and Ken Miles, a well-known figure in American sports car racing. They secured a batch of longer-distance records at speeds up to 153.69 m.p.h. and maintained just over 120 m.p.h. for twelve hours.

This allowed M.G. to fit the XPEG engine into the TF Midget and market it as 'the new TF 1500 with the record-breaking 1½-litre engine'. It was only another stopgap exercise, of course, but it renewed M.G.'s sporting image and allowed the TF to be kept in production a little longer with this small shot in the arm. Although *Road and Track* commented, 'So the M.G. has a full 1.5 liter engine at last—too little, too late, so what?', they admitted that it boosted the performance a good deal. Several of these larger-engined TFs subsequently did quite well in competitions: one driven by Denny Hulme over in Australia, another in British events by Pat Moss, sister of Stirling.

However, the TF 1500 had no great significance in the scheme of things; what really mattered was the motive that lay behind its introduction—buying time to prepare a new M.G. that *would* be new. When the EX.179 record car crossed the Atlantic on its way to Utah, the man who had created it stayed behind in Abingdon. Syd Enever had been appointed chief designer of M.G. and told to turn his EX.175 prototype into a production car as soon as possible. The BMC management had at last realized that the old square-rigged M.G.s were finished. They had also realized, by some heaven-sent stroke of inspiration, that the best way to produce a good M.G. was to reopen a full design office at Abingdon. The effect of these two decisions was soon to startle even the M.G. men themselves.

Chapter 7

Modern Idiom (1955–1962)

The early part of 1955 saw great activity at Abingdon. BMC had approved the establishment of a competitions department to help publicize the entire group, and it was being set up within the M.G. factory by a well-known figure in pre-war motor racing, Marcus Chambers. The ZA Magnette was now far outselling the TF Midget, aided by a class 1-2-3 in the Silverstone Production Car Race (it was the fifth successive year that Dick Jacobs had won the class with an M.G.), and M.G. had to build six saloons for every two-seater in an attempt to satisfy the demand. Syd Enever and his drawing-office staff were putting the final touches to their design for the TF's successor, which would go into production just as soon as bodies were available.

Originally, the intention was to announce the new car at the beginning of June and then run three of them in the 24-hour race at Le Mans—a Thornley inspiration that, for sheer boldness, rivalled the most audacious feats of the good old days. Looking back, it was perhaps fortunate that a delay in the supply of bodies caused the new M.G. to be revealed to the public only a week or two before the race, and not as a production model but a racing prototype so fresh from the development shop that it was simply called EX.182.

After all, M.G.s had been known affectionately for a very long time as narrow-bodied and rather angular little cars with separate mudguards and exposed fuel tanks, and M.G. enthusiasts are ever resistant to change. In the world of sports car racing, however, the full-width streamlined bodywork of the contemporary Mercedes-Benz, Ferrari, Maserati, Jaguar and Aston Martin had come to be accepted as a necessity inspired by the needs of high performance, not the influence of mere stylists. It seems likely that the storm of protest at such a radical change in the beloved M.G. shape was much abated—though not completely prevented—by its direct association with Le Mans, and the general feeling of delight that M.G. were returning to racing after a lapse of exactly twenty years. How could one criticize such a purposeful device that was known to all as 'the Le Mans M.G.'?

And the new car certainly had a sporting pedigree. The chassis had already exceeded 150 m.p.h. at Utah the previous year, and the body shape could be traced back through the 1951 Le Mans car to the 200 m.p.h. Gardner-M.G. If the 1489 c.c. BMC engine was still unproved, the competition successes of the ZA Magnette had revealed something of its potential; besides, a hint had been dropped here and there that a more powerful engine had been under development since 1953, and might be fitted at some time in the future.

Glistening in their British Racing Green paintwork, the three aluminium-bodied M.G.s made a tremendous impression on arrival at Le Mans, and ran beautifully throughout the practice periods. The Abingdon contingent felt quietly confident about their prospects of finishing the race at a respectable average speed, which was their declared aim. But in the early stages of the event there occurred the most appalling tragedy in the history of motor sport when a Mercedes-Benz ran into the tightly-packed crowd opposite the pits, with horrifying results. Almost simultaneously one of the M.G.s crashed at White House, gravely injuring its driver, Dick Jacobs. However, the race continued, and the remaining two M.G.s accomplished more than was expected of them by averaging 86.17 and 81.97 m.p.h. for the twenty-four hours to finish fifth and sixth in their class behind three very fast Porsches (one of which came fourth overall in the race) and an Osca.

In September a three-car team was entered for the Ulster T.T. —two of them, as part of the planned development programme, now being fitted with experimental twin-o.h.c. engines. The push-rod o.h.v. car finished fourth in class, again behind the Porsches, and the two experimental cars retired. By a cruel coincidence, the T.T. was the scene of another dreadful accident involving seven cars and causing a horrifying outbreak of fire. Two drivers died in this, and another was killed later in the race, as a result of which the Dundrod course was never again used for car events.

Although the M.G.s had not been in any way involved, BMC were naturally shocked by these occurrences, together with the fact that Dick Jacobs's recovery was a slow and painful affair. The M.G. Car Company's long-awaited re-entry into the sport there-fore came to an end after only two races.

After the T.T. the production version of EX.182 was at last unveiled and at last acquired a model designation, if not a name— for the term 'Midget' was dropped as being obviously inappropriate. Having run right through the alphabet M.G. returned to the beginning, added in their own famous initials, and called the new model the MGA. Its price was £595 (£844 with tax), and it bore a close resemblance to the racing cars. The bodywork was mostly of steel, of course, and there was a full-width screen complete with full weather equipment. Naturally there was no metal cover over the passenger's seat, and the luggage space was no longer occupied by an enormous fuel tank. The cooling system was slightly different, wider ratios were used in the gearbox, and there was no oil-cooler (although this later became a standard fitting). There was a choice of disc or wire wheels. In production form the engine gave 68 b.h.p. at 5500 r.p.m.; this was soon raised to 72 b.h.p. and the bottom-end bearings improved.

In a thoroughly well-planned 'launch' the MGA went straight to the Frankfurt, Paris and London Motor Shows. During the latter, Marcus Chambers took five BMC production cars to Montlhéry, where each put more than 100 miles into the hour in frightful weather. Ken Wharton completed 102.54 in a near-standard MGA, and John Gott drove one of the Le Mans cars, achieving 112.36 miles in the hour.

Every magazine that tested the MGA emphasized its competition background, and the new model earned unstinted praise. *The Autocar* recorded a top speed of 96 m.p.h. in full road trim, *Autosport* 96.7 m.p.h., and the 0–60 m.p.h. acceleration figure was a mere 15 seconds. This considerable improvement on the performance of its predecessors was accompanied by improved fuel economy, close on 30 m.p.g. The brakes, the steering, the road-holding—all were equally approved.

In its handling, indeed, the MGA was almost certainly the safest M.G. ever produced. By the standards of today it would break away quite early, but it did so in the most gentle and predictable manner, always under the full control of the driver. This made it sheer joy to drive over narrow, twisting roads, while to 'lose' an MGA on a corner called for the most outrageous lack of discretion.

The success of the MGA was immediate and spectacular. In its first full year of production, 1956, more than 13,000 were built—far exceeding the entire production of the TC Midget in over four years. Together with the popular Magnette (which, with higher-output engine and higher final drive, had now turned into the ZB) M.G. production comfortably exceeded 20,000 for the year. Taking in the Rileys as well, Abingdon's 1956 output almost equalled the entire production of M.G.s, all models, from 1923 to 1929. And the number of M.G.s exported exceeded 15,000.

Most of them went to America. John Christy of *Sports Cars Illustrated*, giving advice to buyers of secondhand sports cars about this time, was able to write: '. . . the M.G. in its various forms is probably the best known and probably has the best service availability of any foreign car made, except possibly the Volkswagen. . . . Virtually unbreakable and infinitely modifiable, the M.G. forms the backbone of the sports car market in the United States. It has a further point in its favor in that it's known to the trade as a "forgiving" automobile, which means that it can be driven execrably and still carry its driver safely while he learns how to handle a sports car without killing himself.' M.G.'s old slogan, Safety Fast, really meant something at Abingdon, where good handling always took precedence over sheer performance.

The higher cruising speed of the MGA and other mid-'fifties sports cars revealed the shortcomings of the traditional hood, which came in for a good deal of development work, while a detachable hard-top was also marketed and widely used in rallies. At the 1956 Show M.G. brought out an additional version of the MGA with a closed coupé body and glass side windows—the modern equivalent of the 1925 Sporting Salonette, and a further indication that the GT era was just around the corner. It cost £699 (£1050 with tax), and its smoother lines gave it the edge over the open model in top speed, *Autosport* easily obtaining 102 m.p.h. The same Show brought a slightly modified ZB Magnette called the Varitone, with two-tone colour scheme and larger back window.

Unable to go racing, the Competitions Department concentrated on rallies with a single-mindedness that was eventually to make it the most successful organization of its kind in the world. Nancy Mitchell drove MGAs and Magnettes to win the ladies' championship of Europe in 1956, and again in 1957. It was left to others to race the MGA, which they did to good effect. *Autosport* recognized the increased specialization of the sports-racing car by offering a trophy for series-production sports cars, and in its first year this was most appropriately won by a privately owned MGA. Three MGAs won the Team Award in the Sebring 12 Hours of 1956 and 1957, finishing first and second in class on the second occasion. When the last Mille Miglia was held, in 1957, two private MGAs came second and third in their class behind an Austin-Healey. Dick Jacobs, having retired from driving after his

Le Mans crash, ran a team of Magnettes which scored many successes, including an outright win in the Six-Hour Relay Race of 1956.

Two different types of twin-o.h.c. engine had been fitted to the MGAs in the 1955 T.T. One was a completely new design, the other an adaptation of the BMC B-type engine used in the MGA and Z-series Magnette. One of the latter was fitted to the EX.179 record car; it was unsupercharged, had a compression ratio of only 9.3 : 1 and ran on ordinary pump fuel, making it an extraordinarily inoffensive unit to use in a record-breaker. As EX.179 had one of the prototype MGA chassis, BMC's publicity department felt justified in calling it a two-seater MGA with a special body and a modified B-type engine. The two most successful members of the Le Mans team, Ken Miles and Johnny Lockett, drove the car at Utah in August 1956 and took no less than sixteen international 1500 c.c. class records, covering ten miles at 170.15 m.p.h. and maintaining 141.71 m.p.h. for twelve hours. This must have been a little embarrassing for Donald Healey, whose Warwick-built car managed only 152.32 m.p.h. over 500 kilometres the same month; it was fitted with a tuned 2639 c.c. six-cylinder engine, prototype of the Austin-Healey 100-Six unit.

In 1957, EX.179 reappeared at Utah with yet another engine, a 948 c.c. pushrod o.h.v. unit similar to that used in BMC's Austin A.35 and Morris Minor saloon; the reason for this choice was to become apparent the following year. Driven by David Ash and Tommy Wisdom, it maintained 118.13 m.p.h. for twelve hours and startled everyone by returning 49.8 m.p.g. while doing so. Then a similar engine was installed with a low-boost Shorrock supercharger, and in this form, driven by Phil Hill, the record car achieved 143.47 m.p.h. over the flying mile. The grand total with the two engines was nine International and fifty-six American National records.

All this, however, was no more than a curtain-raiser. Syd Enever had built a highly exciting new M.G. record car, EX.181, which *Sports Car Illustrated* called 'a ground missile of the most advanced type'. It had a single-seater tubular chassis with the now familiar M.G. front suspension and rack-and-pinion steering, and de Dion rear axle with quarter-elliptic springing. There was only one brake, and that at the rear, an ingenious arrangement opening an air flap for cooling when the brake pedal was operated. The driver sat well forward and the engine was in the middle, so the chassis layout recalled the pre-war Grand Prix Auto Union—and, for that matter, anticipated the Grand Prix car of today. The wheels were the smallest that had ever been used on a really high-speed car, and Dunlop had had to undertake a special research programme to develop tyres for them.

The chassis layout allowed a 'teardrop' body of almost ideal streamlined form to be fitted, giving about 30 per cent less drag than the Gardner-M.G. or EX.179 body. It, too, had been designed by Enever and it was the sleekest shape imaginable, only 38¼ inches to the very top of the cockpit cowling.

The aim was to attack a record that had stood to M.G.'s credit since 1939. The day after Gardner's 203.5 m.p.h. flying kilometre in Class G (1100 c.c.), Jackson and Enever had bored out the Magnette engine to 1106 c.c. so that Gardner could take the equivalent Class F (1500 c.c.) record with a run at 204.2 m.p.h. Nobody had ever bettered that figure. M.G. had now decided to do so; decided, moreover, to raise it to 250 m.p.h. if possible—or cetainly four miles a minute, 240 m.p.h. They proposed doing it with a supercharged version of the twin-o.h.c. 1½-litre engine used in the 1956 Utah run.

This called for an output of 280 b.h.p. By the time development work had been completed, 290 b.h.p. had been achieved at 7300 r.p.m., with 32 p.s.i. boost from a Shorrock supercharger originally designed for use on commercial diesel engines, and the spare engine had shown a reading equivalent to 300 b.h.p.—a specific output of 200 b.h.p./litre.

On the evening of 23rd August 1957, after waiting impatiently for suitable surface conditions on the always-tricky Salt Flats, Stirling Moss climbed into EX.181 and broke five International Class F records with a top speed of 245.64 m.p.h., two-way average. The mission had been accomplished. It was quite an experience for Moss, too, being some 50 m.p.h. faster than he himself had ever driven a car at that time.

M.G. now went right ahead with their plans for the higher-performance version of the MGA, and in July 1958 announced the new Twin Cam. The most significant alteration to the MGA chassis was the fitting of Dunlop disc brakes all round, and unusual centre-lock disc wheels similar to those on the all-conquering D-type Jaguar. The twin-o.h.c. engine had a cross-flow cylinder head in aluminium alloy, larger SU carburetters were used, and the bottom end was generally sturdier than on the pushrod unit. Although the 88.9 mm stroke of the experimental 1489 c.c. engine had been retained, the bore was increased to 75.4 mm to give a capacity of 1588 c.c., thus making better use of the 1600 c.c. class that had now become popular in competition, and the power output was 108 b.h.p. at 6700 r.p.m. At a basic price of £854 10s. (£1283 with tax) the Twin Cam cost about £180 more than the ordinary MGA at that time.

The effect of the new engine was impressive. To quote one magazine: '. . . of all the cars so far tested by *The Motor* only machines built specifically for sports-car racing would keep pace with this 1600 c.c. touring two-seater in a standing-start match to speeds of 60, 70 or 80 m.p.h.' In a trial that extended over 1500 miles they found much to praise and only minor disadvantages, such as increased noise and heavier oil and fuel consumption. The 0–60 m.p.h. acceleration time had gone down from 15 to 9.1 seconds, the one-way maximum from about 100 to an easy 115 m.p.h. These tests, moreover, were conducted on 97-octane German pump fuel, which was not really good enough for the 9.9 : 1 compression ratio of the Twin Cam engine.

M.G.'s original intention in returning to an o.h.c. engine had been to offer a car that could be used successfully in competitions, but they had reckoned without the intensive development of sports-racing machinery. When Dick Jacobs entered a lone Twin Cam for the 1958 T.T. (now transferred to Goodwood), Gregor Grant of *Autosport* called it 'probably the only genuine production car in the race'. The following week, John Bolster reminded his readers that 'T.T.' meant Tourist Trophy, and commented, 'Most of us are getting heartily sick of the modern competition sports car, which has now become an extremely expensive white elephant.' So it is not surprising that the Twin Cam, driven by Tom Bridger and Alan Foster, managed only third place in the 2-litre class behind two Porsches.

Over the next two seasons, however, Dick Jacobs's two Twin Cams secured thirty 'places' in thirty-two events, and won their class of the *Autosport* Championship both in 1959 and in 1960, when one of the cars again took a class third in the T.T. The Silverstone GT Race of 1959 saw an impressive 1-2-3-4 class victory by privately owned Twin Cams, and at a record 82.97 m.p.h. average that was not beaten for two years. In the Sebring 12 Hours, two Twin Cam coupés came second and third in their class in 1959, third and fourth in 1960; these were prepared at Abingdon for the American M.G. importers, who did not share BMC's official disapproval of racing.

In the same way, the Abingdon development shop quietly built a special 1762 c.c. Twin Cam coupé for a syndicate of M.G. Car Club North-Western Centre members who had arranged an independent entry for Le Mans. In 1959 the car ran well for nineteen hours, but a collision with a dog on the Mulsanne Straight damaged the bodywork, and this caused gearbox overheating which led to the car's retirement. In 1960, however, the same car completed the twenty-four hours at an excellent 91.12 m.p.h. average to win the 2-litre class, driven by Ted Lund and Colin Escott. It was a measure of how sports car racing had changed in just ten years that the distance covered by the M.G. would have given it outright victory in 1950, ahead of the winning $4\frac{1}{2}$-litre Lago Talbot of Louis Rosier. After the 1960 race, Ted Lund drove the Twin Cam all the way back to his home in Lancashire.

Abingdon built an even more specialized car for the 1961 race, then had cold feet at the thought of BMC's possible reaction and kept it under a dust-sheet. In any case the situation had altered even before the previous event. The Twin Cam, in sympathetic hands, displayed both speed and stamina in races and in rallies, too. As a production car, unfortunately, it was a different story. The very high compression ratio called for a fuel of at least 100 octane rating, which was not generally available at that time—especially overseas. The mixture strength, and even the ignition timing, had to be exactly right. Above all, the Twin Cam was such a willing performer that the incompetent driver could break it with his right foot; it was all too easy to damage the engine by over-revving in the indirect gears. The result was a crop of service complaints, and Marcus Chambers returned from the 1960 Sebring race with the news that Twin Cam problems were earning M.G. a bad name in the U.S.A. In April it was discontinued, after 2111 cars had been built.

Many new developments had taken place at Abingdon before Twin Cam production came to an end. The staff under John Thornley had shown BMC how well they could face up to a new challenge: Cec Cousins as works manager, Syd Enever as chief designer, Reg Jackson as chief inspector, Gordon Phillips as service manager, and many others who had served the Company for thirty or forty years without becoming unduly set in their ways. The factory had succeeded in building cars in large numbers, of doubling its output in little over two years, while maintaining its high standard of assembly. So BMC decided to transfer Austin-Healey production from Longbridge to Abingdon, for there were developments on that side which made increased output desirable. The Austin-Healey was now fitted with BMC's C-type six-cylinder engine and selling steadily. Donald Healey had started designing a new small sports car for the BMC A-type engine—the 948 c.c. unit fitted to EX.179 for the 1957 Utah attempt.

During 1957 the M.G. development staff worked on the 'Buzz-box', as they called it, while the production departments arranged the changeover from Riley to Austin-Healey production. Total production for the year was almost 28,500 cars, of which well over 20,000 were pushrod MGAs. In May 1958 the new small sports car was announced; to the disgust of old-time Riley enthusiasts, it was called the Austin-Healey Sprite. It proved an immediate success and Abingdon production soared to unprecedented heights—over 41,000 cars, of which some 26,000 were M.G.s, 15,000 Austin-Healeys.

One big disappointment for M.G. men, though, was BMC's decision to discontinue the very popular ZB Magnette, which had just won its class in the BRSCC saloon racing championship and sold better in 1958 than ever before. Insult was added to injury when BMC presented one of their very undistinguished 1½-litre saloons as the M.G. Magnette Mark III. It was the first car bearing the name of M.G. to be built outside Abingdon in nearly thirty years. Worse still, it was by M.G. standards an overbodied beast of a thing with poor performance and very doubtful road-holding. From BMC's point of view this 'badge engineering', as it was called at the time, was perfectly permissible; a mediocre car could be sold in larger quantities if it borrowed the reputation of a good one. In seeking short-term advantage they ignored the long-term effect on the name of M.G., and the fact that the marque thus lost for all time a respected position in the sports saloon market.

However, the transfer of Riley production elsewhere and the cessation of the ZB Magnette meant that Abingdon were now building sports cars only, and they celebrated this with an output of no less than 52,785 cars—47,000 of which were exported—in 1959.

This was really amazing for a small factory whose production floor-space had not changed since the days of a couple of thousand cars a year; when they were simply pushed along the lines by hand; where every single car was tested on the road before final inspection. By comparison with other BMC factories, Abingdon had virtually no mechanization and only a tiny labour force. This caused BMC's chief planning engineer, Frank Ford, to draw a disparaging contrast between the complexity of Longbridge and the simplicity of Abingdon, where, as he said, '. . . they build one car per week per man, from John Thornley down to the office-boy, and all *they've* got in the way of mechanical equipment is a wheelbarrow!'

The increased demand during 1959 was due to two new models in addition to the tremendously successful Sprite. In July the MGA, after four years of production, had its engine capacity increased to that of the Twin Cam and Lockheed disc brakes fitted at the front. This combination of disc front brakes and drum rear was better for normal traffic conditions than the all-round discs of the Twin Cam, besides making it easier to provide an efficient handbrake. The remodelled engine gave a useful power increase of some 6 b.h.p. and, more important, a valuable increase in low-speed torque. The MGA 1600 was accompanied by a new Austin-Healey with 3-litre engine and, again, disc front brakes.

In 1959, too, the EX.181 record car returned to Utah with the 1489 c.c. twin-o.h.c. engine opened out to 1506 c.c. so that it could run in International Class E (2000 c.c.). In this form it gained M.G.'s fastest-ever record—254.91 m.p.h.—driven by Phil Hill, who had started his racing career with a TC and, in 1961, was to become the first American-born world champion driver.

He had previously driven the record car on test runs in 1957, and subsequently described the experience to the writer: 'That was really thrilling. I never thought it would be, just going in a straight line, but it was terrific. Really frightening, too—I can't remember any time I've been more frightened, because it lasts so long. I was a little bit uncertain about the directional stability of the car, sitting up so far forward and not being able to see anything but the ground in front, but it was so beautifully made compared to that other one [EX.179], which seemed sort of truck-like. Everything about it looked like it was thought out, and after a while I had a lot of confidence in it. . . . And then, when I started to ease off, nothing happened—it just went on and on—so I kept lifting my foot off, and this terrific volume of fuel came into the cockpit and I got one good lungful of it, just enough to really paralyse my breathing, and I suddenly realized I might not be able to last out until the darn thing stopped. All I could do was exhale and wait. . . . It took about four or five kilometres to get the blessed thing stopped with just one puny little brake, and by that time I was *very* woozy.'

For a long time BMC, as a welcome change from mere badge engineering, had been developing something really new that was known within the organization as the Sputnik. It was unveiled in August 1959 as the Austin Seven or Morris Mini-Minor, but before long nobody thought of it as anything but 'the Mini'. The announcement of this small saloon was to have a far-reaching effect on the sports car world, for it set new standards in road-holding that conventional sports cars found hard to match, while its light construction brought quite startling power/weight ratios within easy reach.

M.G.'s development staff were naturally excited by the possibilities of this car as the basis for a new Midget—just as Kimber, thirty-one years before, had seen the sporting potential of the original Morris Minor. The talk was all of front-wheel drive, and during 1960 Abingdon built an attractive little open 2/4-seater using the front end of the Mini. But this project, ADO.34, was never to see the light of day. BMC considered that tooling-up for a sports body would be much too expensive. Besides, the single-seater Coopers were doing very well with tuned A-type engines in Formula Junior at this time, and it was decided to build a disc-braked Mini with much-modified engine which would be called the Mini-Cooper. This was announced in September 1961.

Meanwhile Abingdon had designed a completely new body to replace the original frog-eyed Sprite, with conventional bonnet and luggage boot, and a much-improved engine (giving 46.4 b.h.p. at 5500 r.p.m.) mated to the close-ratio gearbox that had been developed for use by the Competitions Department. This came out in May 1961. One month later it was followed by the announcement of a new M.G. Midget—but not the front-wheel-drive car that Abingdon had hoped for. It was simply the Austin-Healey Sprite Mark II with a few very transparent attempts at disguise. While M.G. enthusiasts were glad to have a Midget once again—it was the first of under one litre capacity since the PB had gone out of production in 1936—this car left them with mixed feelings, for it was not generally known that most of the design had been done at Abingdon and they found it hard to accept it as a genuine M.G. However, *The Autocar* called it 'a thoroughly well-planned and soundly constructed little car . . . easy and safe to drive', and *The Motor* agreed that it was 'indisputably a sports car, fun to drive and responsive to good driving'. *The Autocar* road test came first, a top speed of 86 m.p.h. being recorded with 0–60 m.p.h. acceleration in 20.2 seconds, but the Midget that *The Motor* tested several months later was clearly a more loosened-up example. They achieved a mean 87.9 m.p.h. on a banked circuit, with a one-way 90 m.p.h., and clipped almost two seconds off the 0–60 m.p.h. acceleration time.

The new Midget was accompanied by a revised MGA, which had only the most minor styling changes—including a not very inspired radiator grille—to the bodywork. The engine, however, had been redesigned completely; not only had the capacity gone up to 1622 c.c., the whole unit had been greatly improved in detail. The power output was increased by more than 10 b.h.p. and the engine now peaked at only 4500 r.p.m., while the torque also went up by 10 lb. ft, allowing the final-drive ratio to be raised from 4.3 to 4.1 : 1. This provided quieter high-speed cruising but rather concealed the extent to which the engine had been improved, acceleration being only marginally better than before. It did, however, ensure that the 100 m.p.h. maximum, previously very dependent on 'favourable conditions', could now be reached with relative ease.

In its latest guise the MGA was given the somewhat clumsy label of 1600 Mark II. There was also a little-known model called the MGA 1600 Mark II De Luxe, which made use of the discontinued Twin Cam chassis with Dunlop disc brakes all round. Waste not, want not, was ever the motto at Abingdon.

But face-lifts, even quite good ones, can only go so far to prolong the life of a model once buyers begin to consider it old-fashioned. MGA sales dropped considerably in 1960, again in 1961, yet again in 1962. The fact that two works-built 1600 coupés came first and second in their class at the 1961 Sebring 12 Hours, that a Competitions Department 1622 c.c. coupé won its class in both the Monte Carlo Rally and the Tulip Rally of 1962, meant comparatively little measured against the indisputable fact that the MGA was, by 1962, in its seventh year of production at a time when car design generally was beginning to make rapid strides forward.

The new Midget, too, though popular enough, was scarcely attaining the highest sales of the TD in its palmy days of ten years before. There were two good reasons for this: one was the almost identical Sprite at a basic price £27 below the Midget's £472; the other was the Mini-Cooper, which offered better all-round per-

69. Goldie Gardner climbs into his Railton-bodied Gardner-M.G. while Syd Enever (*right*) holds the unusual steering-wheel. This car broke records from 1938 until 1952, becoming the world's fastest in five of the ten international classes with various M.G. engines.

70, 71. Private owners modified their M.G.s extensively after the factory's withdrawal from racing: (*opposite*) Harvey Noble's single-seater Q-type raised the Brooklands Outer Circuit 750 c.c. record to 122.4 m.p.h. in 1937; (*above*) Reg Parnell successfully raced Hamilton's old K.3, eventually fitted with i.f.s. as well as new bodywork.

72. The short-lived TB Midget appeared only a few months before war broke out. The Hartley headlamp mask and white mudguard flashes recall the problems of blackout motoring.

73. Abingdon's wartime products were a far cry from two-seater sports cars, though some would have made short work of a trials hill.

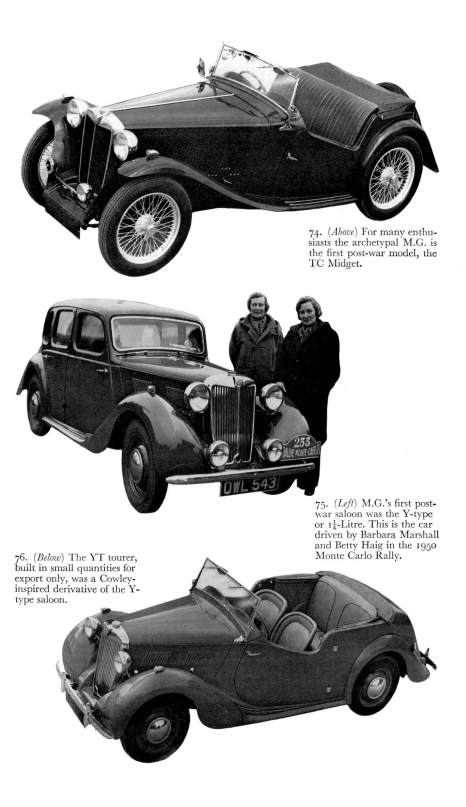

74. (*Above*) For many enthusiasts the archetypal M.G. is the first post-war model, the TC Midget.

75. (*Left*) M.G.'s first post-war saloon was the Y-type or 1¼-Litre. This is the car driven by Barbara Marshall and Betty Haig in the 1950 Monte Carlo Rally.

76. (*Below*) The YT tourer, built in small quantities for export only, was a Cowley-inspired derivative of the Y-type saloon.

77. TD with a difference: the 1951 Le Mans car which became the first prototype of the later MGA model.

78. Peter Thornley and his father, John Thornley, enjoy a mid-'sixties gymkhana at Beaulieu with a standard TD Midget.

79. The last of the traditional Midgets, the TF, was intended mainly for overseas markets.

80. One of the new MGA team cars is tailed through the Esses by a Ferrari at Le Mans, June 1955. It is driven by Johnny Lockett, the racing motorcyclist.

81. The Z-type Magnette, last of the Abingdon-built M.G. saloons. Ron Flockhart is seen here with his ZB in 1957, the year he won the Le Mans 24 Hours—with a Jaguar—for the second time.

82. Ken Miles and Johnny Lockett exceeded 170 m.p.h. at Utah in 1956, the EX.179 record car powered by a prototype Twin Cam engine.

83, 84. M.G.'s last record-breaker, EX. 181, had a rear-mounted Twin Cam engine with supercharger. With it Stirling Moss (*left*) exceeded 245 m.p.h. in 1957, and Phil Hill (*below*) topped 254 m.p.h. two years later.

85. John Gott and Ray Brookes at the finish of the 1958 Liège–Rome–Liège marathon, in which their hardtop Twin Cam was placed ninth overall.

86. In this special Twin Cam coupé, Ted Lund and Colin Escott won the 2-litre class at Le Mans in 1960 with an average speed of 91.12 m.p.h. for the 24 hours.

87. Badge engineering: B.M.C.'s version of the Magnette was based on the contemporary Morris Oxford and could scarcely be described as a sports saloon. This is the Mark IV model, announced late in 1961.

88. The M.G. Midget of 1961, the first of under 1000 c.c. to appear in 25 years, was based on the Austin-Healey Sprite. Unlike the Magnette, the Midget was built at Abingdon.

89. Don Morley wins his class in the 1962 Monte Carlo Rally with an MGA 1600 Mk. II coupé. This car, a class-winner again in the 1962 Tulip Rally, is one of the rare De Luxe models built on the Twin Cam chassis.

90. M.G. designers: H. N. Charles (*right*) discusses old times with his successor, Sydney Enever, during a visit to Abingdon in 1963.

91. In March 1962, a few months before MGA production ended, the 100,000th example of this model came off the lines at Abingdon.

92. Raymond Baxter and Ernie McMillen used a works-prepared M.G. 1100 in the 1963 Monte Carlo Rally, finishing fourth in their class.

93. With a hardtop MGB the Morley brothers not only won their class in the 1964 Monte Carlo Rally, but beat all the other sports cars to gain the Grand Touring category award.

94. The Brands Hatch 1000 Miles of 1965, the longest race held in Britain since pre-war days, was won at 75.23 m.p.h. average by another hardtop MGB driven by Warwick Banks and John Rhodes.

95. These two special Midgets, built for Dick Jacobs in 1962, were raced successfully for several years, usually driven by Andrew Hedges and Alan Foster.

96. The Mark II version of the production Midget, announced early in 1964, featured wind-up windows, semi-elliptic rear suspension and an improved engine.

97. The 3-litre MGC was introduced at the 1967 Motor Show, but discontinued after two years' production.

98. In the 1964 Le Mans race, Paddy Hopkirk and Andrew Hedges averaged 99.9 m.p.h. with this extended-nose MGB to win the *Motor* Trophy for the highest-placed British car.

99. The special lightweight MGC coupé, last of the racing M.G.s, being tested at Silverstone before winning its class in the Sebring 12 Hours of 1968.

100. The two 1972 versions of the MGB: the GT coupé and open two-seater. Well over 250,000 have been built since the model first appeared at the 1962 Motor Show.

formance *and* four seats for a basic price of £465. However uncomfortable the Mini, it was more acceptable to the family than a two-seater open sports car. Then, at the 1962 Show, Triumph brought out their Spitfire. It cost more than the Sprite or Midget but it had swing-axle i.r.s., which gave a smoother ride than Abingdon's quarter-elliptic rear springs. There were many seekers after comfort who failed to appreciate that, in the Spitfire, it had been achieved at the expense of predictable high-speed cornering behaviour.

Several factors therefore combined to reduce the demand for Abingdon products, and from 1960 the factory was quite glad to have the job of assembling Morris Minor vans and estate cars on the side. It is a measure of their increased efficiency that the output of this small 'sideline', 20,000 in five years, exceeded the total Riley production in ten years.

In fact the sports car market had gradually altered to a very considerable extent. There had been a time when the sports car enthusiast gladly accepted inconveniences of one sort or another— limited space for passengers or luggage, a harsh and uncomfortable ride, poor wet-weather protection, a noisy and probably rather thirsty engine which might demand frequent attention to keep it in tune, the necessity for a fair degree of driving skill—in exchange for a performance well above that of the ordinary saloon. Once the saloon started to catch up with the sports car in performance, it was inevitable that fewer buyers would put up with inconvenience in order to run a sports car. And sports cars *had* to be made less uninhabitable in any case when their performance reached the stage where people were cruising at 90 instead of 60 m.p.h. Which, in turn, attracted a new type of customer who demanded still more comfort and convenience. A perfect illustration of this was provided by the MGA, which had far more luggage space than any T-series car. T-types were seldom criticized on this point, but MGA owners continually complained that they had insufficient space for luggage. Again, nobody seemed to mind the highly inconvenient sidescreens of earlier cars—not surprisingly, for it was considered 'correct' to drive with the hood down in anything short of a snowstorm. But hood-down motoring at 90-plus is too fatiguing altogether, so the hood and sidescreens of the MGA had to be modified repeatedly during production.

In the spring of 1962 the 100,000th MGA rolled off the assembly line, establishing a record that was unique at that time; no other sports car manufacturer had built and sold so many examples of one model. A further 1081 cars followed before production came to an end in June, and there were many who regretted the passing of this exceptional M.G., which had weaned all but the most obstinate Abingdonians away from the virtues—and vices—of the traditional M.G. shape.

It was obvious that the MGA's successor would have to be very good indeed, and development work had gone on for a long time. First thoughts were in the direction of a new body on the same chassis, and a very sleek-looking car was built for M.G. by an Italian specialist, Frua. But it was realized that a separate chassis and body construction would still impose limitations on output, so a completely new monocoque body was designed at Abingdon, with final detail work by Farina, and the MGB was born. Once again Syd Enever turned to an M.G. record car for inspiration: 'The MGB shape, though you might not realise it, was basically borrowed from EX.181. . . . When we started the MGB we took this shell and developed it into a passenger car.'

Announced at the 1962 Motor Show, the MGB cost £690 (£950 with tax). The new body provided an enormous increase in interior space, yet its exterior dimensions were for the most part less than those of the MGA; the wheelbase had been reduced by 3 inches, the overall length by 5 inches, the overall height by 1 inch; only the width had increased, and that by just 2 inches. Visibility was much improved, with a wide, deep windscreen and glass side-windows. The doors were wider than before, and now had interior and exterior handles, complete with locks. The instruments were grouped in front of the driver, the driving position was admirable, and the seats were adjustable for rake— but traditionalists noted with a twinge of regret that the hand-brake was no longer of the fly-off type. It had been abandoned because the new generation of M.G. owners found it incomprehensible.

The long-suffering BMC B-type engine had been remodelled once again, giving a capacity of 1798 c.c. The power output— 95 b.h.p. at 5400 r.p.m.—was not a great deal higher than that of the 1622 c.c. engine, but the torque had gone up yet again, this time to 107 lb. ft at 3500 r.p.m. There was a larger starter motor, a larger water-pump and a completely new clutch. The bottom end of the engine had been redesigned, as had the gearbox. The final drive ratio was very much higher but the wheels were a little smaller than on the MGA, so the overall gearing went up only slightly. Steering, suspension and brakes followed MGA design with a number of modifications. Taking the car as a whole, the full list of improvements made one realize with some surprise how many minor shortcomings the MGA had possessed by the standards of the early 'sixties.

So once again M.G. had adapted to the changing needs of the sports car buyer—and done so, some would say, rather tardily. It remained to be seen if the MGB would do as much for M.G. sales as the TC, TD and MGA had each done in their turn.

Chapter 8

Half-a-Million M.G.s (1962 onwards)

The comments of the motoring press suggested that Abingdon had made a good job of designing the MGB. *Autocar* (which dropped its definite article early in 1962) hailed it as 'an altogether superior car to its predecessor', and *The Motor* called it 'a delightful modern sports car . . . a pleasure to drive'. *Sports Car* said it was 'unquestionably the best sports car ever made at Abingdon', and *Motoring News* judged it 'undoubtedly the best all-round conventional sports car on the market . . . extraordinarily good value'. Perhaps more important for M.G., equal approval was voiced on the other side of the Atlantic: 'Bound to be a success . . . a rugged, comfortable sports car at a reasonable price,' said *Canada Track and Traffic*, who later voted the MGB their Car of the Year for 'Excellence of Design, Performance and Consumer Value'. And *Road and Track* said the MGB was simply 'the best engineered, the best put together M.G. we've ever seen'.

In terms of performance the improvement over the MGA was not great: a top speed of around 105 m.p.h. and 0–60 m.p.h. acceleration in 12.2 seconds represented only slightly better performance than the MGA had provided in its final 1622 c.c. guise. And to MGA owners the MGB's handling seemed 'soft'—but in this respect the new model was a very deceptive car; although it did roll somewhat, it was actually capable of far higher cornering speeds, and very few drivers ever reached the breakaway point.

Where the MGB really scored over other cars in the same price bracket was in the way it offered genuine sports car performance which the ordinary man could enjoy without risk, discomfort, fatigue, or even the mildest inconvenience. This rather lifted M.G.s out of the minority market, and output began to soar. The first full year of MGB production, 1963, saw a 75 per cent increase in the number of M.G.s built—well above the previous record. In 1964 this was bettered again with a total of almost 38,000, more than 30,000 of which were exported, and Abingdon's total output—despite much lower Austin-Healey production—exceeded 55,000 cars. Of these, over 44,000 were exported, more than 34,000 of them to the USA. This was a considerable relief to

BMC, who had invested heavily in a new American import organization with a ten million dollar stock of spares, not long before Ford brought out their new Mustang in 1964. Though the Mustang sold extremely well, it apparently did so without detriment to M.G. sales.

The 1962 Motor Show had brought another example of BMC 'badge engineering' in the shape of the M.G. 1100, an octagon-wearing version of the ADO.16, BMC's front-wheel-drive saloon with Hydrolastic suspension. It cost £590, or £812 with tax. At the same time the Sprite and Midget—known collectively at Abingdon as the 'Spridget'—were given a 1098 c.c. engine and disc front brakes. No new type designation was announced for these models, which caused a certain amount of confusion, but within the factory they were known as AN.7 (Sprite) and GAN.2 (Midget). The improved specification had little effect on demand for the Midget, which seldom exceeded one-third of MGB sales. Better results were achieved when, in the spring of 1964, the Spridget was completely remodelled as Sprite Mark III (Type AN.8) and Midget Mark II (Type GAN.3), with a new windscreen, glass windows instead of sidescreens, semi-elliptic instead of quarter-elliptic rear springs, and an improved engine giving 59 instead of 55 b.h.p.

There were many who regretted that the Spridget was 'growing up'—that it was no longer just a cheap and simple sports car for the youngsters—but sales immediately rose by 20 per cent although the price had been increased by more than £20. It is more intriguing to note that although the two cars were virtually identical and the Midget cost about £12 more than the Sprite, from 1964 onwards the M.G. always outsold the Austin-Healey—a state of affairs that could only be explained by the better reputation of M.G.

BMC again attempted to cash in on the Abingdon charisma by marketing their 1100 saloon exclusively as an M.G. in America, but this effort misfired badly. The saloon lacked the stamina that enabled the sports cars to withstand being driven by people reared on big-engined cars with automatic transmission, and there were continual service problems. There was no real improvement in the situation when a 1275 c.c. engine was fitted in 1967, and the following year BMC produced a special 'Austin America' version with automatic transmission.

Another special problem on the US market concerned the MGB overdrive, which had been available from early 1963 but for some time was withheld from America—where it was most needed—because it might adversely affect the already dwindling sale of the big Austin-Healey. Eventually commonsense prevailed, and American drivers who chose to ignore speed limits could savour the delights of 100 m.p.h. cruising at a mere 4484 r.p.m.

While Abingdon thus enjoyed the commercial success of their new models, things began to look no less exciting on the sporting side. Marcus Chambers had made the BMC competitions department a force to be reckoned with in international rallying, especially with the highly-developed 'big Healey', which had been turned into one of the most successful rally cars of all time. His retirement late in 1961 coincided with the announcement of the Mini-Cooper, which soon began to oust the Austin-Healey from its commanding position under the forceful guidance of the new competitions manager, Stuart Turner. This in itself added nothing to M.G. prestige—except that the more knowledgeable enthusiasts knew these cars were prepared at Abingdon—but the Mini-Cooper also became prominent in motor racing, which encouraged BMC's management to view that sport in a rather different light. Thus M.G. were able, eventually, to return to the racing circuits once more.

Ever since the Le Mans and Ulster T.T. disasters of 1955, Abingdon's racing activities had been officially restricted to building a team of cars each year for the American M.G. importers to enter in the Sebring 12 Hours. This was done jointly by the development and competitions departments, and the work paid for by the American organization. The Donald Healey Motor Co. at Warwick enjoyed a BMC allocation to finance an annual racing programme, and BMC support was also given to the 'Cooper Car Co. to race the Mini-Cooper and BMC-engined Formula Junior Coopers, but Abingdon could lend only surreptitious support to racing—which, of course, they did, being the enthusiasts they were.

Early in 1962 the Abingdon development department built three very attractive little cars on this under-the-counter basis: Midget coupés with hand-beaten aluminium bodywork mounted on the standard steel chassis platform by a combination of rivets and epoxy-resin adhesive. The body shape was wind-tunnel tested and the complete cars weighed 1242 lbs.—324 lbs. less than a standard Midget. The suspension was a modified version of the standard design and there were disc front brakes, as fitted to production Midgets later in the year. The engine was at first a tuned 75 b.h.p. 972 c.c. unit, progressively enlarged to 995, 1139, and eventually 1293 c.c. (the maximum permitted enlargement of the 948, 1098 and 1275 c.c. engines under racing regulations).

One of the cars went to a Scottish racing enthusiast, John Milne, and the other two were handed over to Dick Jacobs. The two Jacobs cars competed mainly in the more important British races, driven by Alan Foster and Andrew Hedges, and earned a fine reputation for speed and reliability. Their many successes included a class win and third overall in the 1963 *Autosport* Championship, while in 1964 they gained a class 1-2 in the 1000-kilometre race at the Nürburgring, the highest-placed British cars in the event. At the end of the 1964 season they were returned to the factory, but their racing career had by no means ended.

Dick Jacobs had also run an M.G. 1100 saloon in the Six-Hour Saloon Race at Brands Hatch in October 1962, just four days after that model was announced. Hedges and Foster scored a comfortable class win, after which the M.G., like its fellow class-winners, was loaned to *The Motor* for a road-test. Some surprise was expressed that, unlike the others, it did not feel at all 'racer' ('Put back a few bits of minor trim that had been removed, and Auntie could have driven it to the shops herself . . .'), and *The Motor* also commented favourably on the state of the engine compartment: 'So clean that it was difficult to imagine that it had run at all, let alone been raced.'

After Christmas a bitterly cold winter clamped down on Britain, making it impossible for the Abingdon competitions department to carry out full tests on two MGBs they had prepared for the 1963 Sebring 12 Hours. The result was unfortunate. In this first major race for the MGB, unexpected oil surge was encountered and both cars ran their bottom-end bearings. However, Alan Hutcheson drove one of the Sebring cars in the Silverstone GT race and succeeded in winning his class (at 87.25 m.p.h.), as he had earlier done (at 85.71 m.p.h.) at Goodwood with another MGB, a car built by the development department as a general hack.

Another of the successful competitors at this 1963 Silverstone meeting, driving a Mini-Cooper 'S' in its racing debut, was Paddy Hopkirk, who had joined the BMC rally team the previous October and was limbering up with a season of circuit racing. Somehow Stuart Turner persuaded BMC that it would be a good idea to enter an MGB for Hopkirk and Hutcheson to drive at Le Mans. The car Abingdon built for them was a steel-bodied open MGB with fibreglass hardtop. It had an extended nose to improve air penetration, enabling the fairly mildly tuned engine (fitted

with a single twin-choke Weber carburetter to suit the siamesed
inlet ports of the B-type cylinder head) to pull a final drive ratio
of no less than 3.307 : 1. On this gearing, more than 130 m.p.h.
was available at just over 6000 r.p.m. BMC were still a little coy
about M.G.'s return to racing, insisting that the car should
officially be 'privately owned'. Right at the start of Le Mans it
looked as if their doubts might be justified, for Hutcheson ran into
the sand at Mulsanne and had to spend almost 1½ hours digging
the M.G. out again. However, despite this long delay they won
their class at an average of 92 m.p.h. for the 24 hours, giving M.G.
their fifth (and, as it turned out, their last) class win at Le Mans.

The Le Mans car was then entered for Andrew Hedges to drive
in the Tour de France, a ten-day affair which Hedges's co-driver,
John Sprinzel, described enthusiastically as 'the world's most
complete motoring event'. There was a rally-style set route of
3600 miles interspersed with speed events, and the M.G. was
lying fourth overall after the first three stages when Hedges hit a
rock face on the Col de Jau, bringing his drive to an abrupt halt.
But another MGB—a genuine private car which the driver,
Patrick Vanson, had bought the very day before the start—completed the Tour to finish seventh in the GT category.

In 1964 Paddy Hopkirk achieved BMC's first Monte Carlo
Rally victory, driving a Mini-Cooper 'S', and the jubilation that
attended this remarkable accomplishment quite obscured the fact
that the Morley brothers, in the same event, had won the GT
category in an MGB. Next on the list came the Sebring 12 Hours,
and a class third for one of the works MGBs. By this time the BMC
main distributor for the West Coast, Kjell Quale, had started
taking a keen interest in racing and decided to build three cars for
Indianapolis. They had the Offenhauser engine at the rear of the
chassis—something unusual for American-entered Indy cars in
those days—and a little ingenious faking of the suspension system
made it resemble the Hydrolastic design of the M.G. 1100 saloon.
One of the three 'M.G. Liquid Suspension Specials' was to be
driven by A. J. Foyt, but he changed his mind and drove a conventional front-engined car, with which he won America's classic
500-mile race. Pedro Rodriguez crashed one of the cars in practice
and therefore non-started, and Bob Veith failed to reach the
finish. The third car was driven by Walt Hansgen. He spent 27
minutes at the pits with a faulty fuel pump, but the 'M.G. Special'
eventually finished twelfth and last—one of the two rear-engined
cars that completed the 1964 race. The following year Jim Clark

won Indianapolis with a rear-engined Lotus-Ford, but all three of the 'M.G. Specials'—driven by Hansgen, Veith and Jerry Grant —retired.

In 1964 a lone MGB was again entered for Le Mans. It was similar to the previous year's car but driven by Hopkirk and Hedges, Paddy finding that by a happy coincidence it bore Number 37, the same as his Monte-winning Mini. The M.G. lapped steadily at just under 105 m.p.h., recording 139 m.p.h. over the flying kilometre on the Mulsanne straight, and completed the race at an average of exactly 99.9 m.p.h. As John Thornley remarked, it made better publicity than the even 100, and if it was not fast enough to catch the lightweight Alfa Romeos and 904GT Porsches in the same class, there was satisfaction in winning the *Motor* Trophy for the highest-placed British car. In twenty-four hours the only drama occurred when one of the *plombeurs* snapped off the M.G.'s filler-cap, which would have meant disqualification if the tank could not be sealed. The M.G. mechanics solved this problem very simply by walking along to Marcus Chambers at the Sunbeam Tiger pit and scrounging a complete filler-cap assembly from their erstwhile competitions manager.

A third season of limited participation in racing opened with the Sebring 12 Hours of 1965, for which Abingdon prepared the two ex-Jacobs Midgets and a pair of hardtop MGBs, one entered in the GT class, the other in the prototype class. Before the race was two-thirds run a fantastic tropical storm burst over the Florida circuit, flooding it hub-deep in a matter of minutes and giving rise to the most extraordinary scenes. The open sports-racing cars almost filled up with water and crept around at about 20 m.p.h., the drivers soaked from head to foot. Timo Makinen, who drove an open Sprite, said afterwards: 'When I accelerate, the water rushes up around my shoulders; when I brake it runs down to my toes. To empty the car I go fast around a corner and open the door at the right moment.' These conditions handicapped the special-ized machinery much more than the M.G.s, which seized the opportunity to improve their positions. One of the Midgets had dropped out early with engine trouble, but its sister car beat the Triumph Spitfires to win its class. One of the MGBs had battery trouble after an off-course excursion, though it finished, and the other came second in its class.

One of the Midgets was then entered for that classic Sicilian road race, the 447-mile Targa Florio, and Hopkirk and Hedges finished eleventh overall out of twenty-eight finishers—less than half of the original field—to take second in their class behind an Abarth Simca. The same pair went on to drive an MGB at Le Mans; once again a lone entry; once again a car modified but little from standard specification. By coincidence they again finished eleventh overall and second in their class, averaging 98.26 m.p.h for the twenty-four hours but completely outpaced by a Porsche 904GTS. Beaten to the post by the Rover-BRM gas-turbine car, they also failed to retain the *Motor* Trophy as highest-placed British finisher.

This was the third successive occasion that a single M.G. had been entered for the race and finished at a very respectable average for a modified production sports car. While this was an impressive demonstration of reliability, Abingdon had to accept the fact that the MGB was far slower than its competitors on the Sarthe circuit; it was, indeed, becoming increasingly difficult even to meet the class qualifying speed during practice. So this, sadly, was the last Le Mans for M.G.—the last marque to enter a car in keeping with the original spirit of the race.

Shortly before Le Mans, on 22nd May, a 1000-mile race was held at Brands Hatch. It was the longest race to be run in England since pre-war days and rather a reminder of the old Brooklands Double Twelve, for it was split into two 500-mile heats—though work on the cars was permitted during the intervening night. BMC being still somewhat opposed to Abingdon's participation in racing, Abingdon's hardtop MGB was entered by Don Moore, who had raced M.G.s successfully some ten years earlier. Driven by two well-known Mini racing men, John Rhodes and Warwick Banks, it won the first 500-mile heat outright at 75.33 m.p.h. ahead of a Le Mans Sprite and a 4.2-litre E-type Jaguar—and this was no handicap event. On the second day it was delayed by an oil leak from the filter bowl and therefore came fourth behind a Morgan, an Austin-Healey 3000 and another E-type, but the aggregate results gave it outright victory. Indeed, there were five MGBs among the first twelve finishers, and they scored a class 1-2-3. One of these MGBs was driven by Trevor and Anita Taylor, the other by J. F. ('Baggy') Sach and Roger Enever, son of M.G.'s chief designer.

Three Abingdon-prepared M.G.s—a hardtop MGB and two hardtop Midgets—then crossed the Atlantic for the Bridge-hampton 500, one of the major East Coast events. With the MGB, Paddy Hopkirk finished fourth overall behind the inevitable Porsche 904 and two Lotuses. Timo Makinen, who had followed

Paddy's example by winning the 1965 Monte with a Mini, had to have his Midget's exhaust system welded up at the pits but still finished eleventh overall, third in his class, while his BMC team-mate and fellow-Finn, Rauno Aaltonen, brought the other Midget home sixth overall to win the class.

At the end of the year Abingdon were somewhat surprised to find that their MGB model had been placed third in class behind Porsche and Alfa Romeo in the GT Constructors' Championship, although entered in only two of the twelve qualifying races, and the Midget was second in class behind Abarth Simca, although entered in only four out of nine qualifying events. The big Austin-Healey had also been well placed in the Championship, and BMC gained a special award from the SMMT for the racing performances of their sports cars. This possibly encouraged them to adopt a slightly more sympathetic attitude towards M.G.'s racing activities in 1966.

There was one other notable race result for M.G. during 1965. In Phoenix Park, Dublin, where the C-types had won the Irish Grand Prix in faraway 1931, an event known as the Kingway Trophy Race finished with the first five places occupied by M.G.s. They were led by a rapid Midget driven by Alec Poole, son of the M.G. importer for Ireland.

Most of the racing MGBs had used the original three-bearing engine, though a new engine with five main bearings had been developed for the ADO.17, BMC's new front-wheel-drive 1800 saloon, and fitted to the MGB since the 1964 Motor Show. This was partly because a nitrided three-bearing crankshaft was available, partly because the five-bearing engine had recalled the problems that arose when the three-bearing P-type replaced the two-bearing J.2. The power output was at first a little disappointing, and it was not improved until the optional oil-cooler was made a standard component.

During 1965 the demand for Abingdon's sports cars had slackened somewhat after the record sales of the previous year, but in October a new version of the MGB was announced: a GT coupé of very sleek appearance. At £825 (£998 with tax) it was the realization of John Thornley's long-cherished ambition to build 'a poor man's Aston Martin', and as he commented in *Motor* (so-called since March 1964) a few months later, 'We've produced a motor-car now in which no managing director would be ashamed to turn up at the office.' And so it proved. If the MGB had enlarged Abingdon's potential market considerably, the GT attracted people who would never have dreamt of buying an open sports car. Moreover, road tests soon revealed that although the GT was almost 2 cwt. heavier than the open MGB, its acceleration was little inferior, its maximum speed higher because of the better shape, and the roadholding definitely improved by stiffer suspension and a greater proportion of weight in the tail.

One mistake made by BMC's sales and publicity people was to present the GT as a '2 + 2'. Since it was obviously no such thing, this merely encouraged criticism at first, but before long this quite unsuitable tag was dropped and the GT accepted as an excellent closed two-seater with very adequate space for luggage—or two extremely small children—in the back. M.G. sales rose again during 1966 and a new assembly line had to be laid down at the factory, making a total of seven. By the end of the year a new record had been established with a production of almost 40,000 M.G.s in twelve months. M.G. exports to the USA also represented a new record, and BMC ranked second only to Volkswagen in American sales of imported cars. Total Abingdon production for the year was below the 1964 record, however, because of the fall in demand for Austin-Healeys.

Only the most minor changes were made to the MGB for the 1966 Show, but the Sprite and Midget were given a new folding hood and a 1275 c.c. engine, similar to that of the latest Mini-Cooper 'S', providing 65 b.h.p. at 6000 r.p.m. Unfortunately the opportunity was taken to increase the prices of all the Abingdon-built cars apart from the slow-selling Austin-Healey 3000. The Midget went up to £555 (£684 with tax) in its Mark III guise, the open M.G.B. to £746 10s. (£919), and the GT to £865 (£1065). Of the two BMC-built M.G. saloons, the Magnette Mark IV was unchanged in price but £27 was added to that of the M.G. 1100. Thereafter, price increases occurred with such dismal regularity that the Midget eventually cost more than an MGB would have done some five years earlier.

The 1966 competitions season started badly for BMC when three Minis scored a 1-2-3 victory in the Monte Carlo Rally only to be disqualified for using tungsten-halogen headlamps. In that same event Tony Fall drove an MGB and had to retire when the steering chafed through an oil-cooler pipe. Two hardtop MGBs ran at Sebring, one in the GT category, the other with its engine opened out to 2004 c.c. and entered in the prototype category. The larger-engined car, which was giving 138 b.h.p., threw a connecting-rod after ten hours' racing, but the remaining MGB won the 2-litre class, came third overall in the GT category, and was the highest-placed British car to finish.

For 1966 the Brands Hatch organizers decided to reduce their long-distance race to 500 miles and throw it open to the more specialized Group 4 cars in order to attract more spectators. This suggested that M.G.s would be completely outclassed. But most of the race was run in heavy rain—so heavy that its length was further reduced to six hours' duration—and the Enever/Poole MGB, all 1798 c.c. of it, kept within 3 seconds of the lap time that Piper and Bondurant were maintaining in their 7-litre Shelby American Cobra. The big Cobra averaged 77.11 m.p.h. to win the race, followed by a 4.7-litre Ford GT40, and the sprat-like MGB kept plugging along at a 73.38 m.p.h. average to finish third. Of the nineteen survivors seven were M.G.s: a solitary Midget which won its class ahead of a Sprite and a Spitfire, and six MGBs, of which the Nicholson/Bunce car came third in the 2½-litre class behind the Enever/Poole MGB and a Lotus Elan. On the very same day, over in sunny Sicily, two works MGBs were taking part in the 50th Targa Florio. Driving the car that had retired from the Monte, Makinen and Rhodes finished a most impressive ninth overall among the fiercer machinery to win not only the 2-litre GT class but the entire GT category, irrespective of engine capacity, and the Hedges/Handley MGB came second in the class. That the two M.G.s thus outpaced—as well as outlasted—many Porsches, Fords and Ferraris was remarkable, for they had standard open bodies with hardtops, were even fitted with bumpers front and rear, and had Stage 6 engines giving no more than 107 b.h.p. Yet the results emphasized the rapid progress that had been made in the development of sports-racing cars; the leading M.G.'s race average would have given it outright victory in the Targa Florio some seven years earlier.

A couple of weeks later Hedges took his Targa Florio MGB on to the Spa 1000 Kilometres in Belgium, where, partnered by Julien Vernaeve, he won his class and the GT category. A week after that they ran in the Nürburgring 1000 Kilometres, where the long-suffering MGB burst a water hose and blew a gasket. However, Hedges then raced the other Targa Florio car in the Circuit of Mugello, a little-known Italian road race similar to the Sicilian classic, and with Robin Widdows came third in the GT category behind two Ferraris.

Two of the MGBs were entered for an unusual event in August.

Half-a-Million M.G.s (1962 onwards)

The famous four-day 'Marathon de la Route' or Spa–Sofia–Liège Rally, which was really a long-distance road race although listed in the rally calendar, had recently been replaced by a seventy-two-hour endurance run on the Nürburgring. Competitors were required to maintain a set average speed on every lap for three days and nights, so it was not strictly a race, the emphasis being on regularity and reliability, but in some ways it was more difficult; the pressure was maintained throughout and there was no chance of easing back after achieving a commanding lead. The 1965 event had proved a little too easy, so for 1966 the scheduled speeds were increased and the length increased to eighty-four hours. Abingdon entered Hedges and Vernaeve with the MGB which had already run in the Monte, the Targa Florio and at Mugello; Roger Enever and Alec Poole had a development department car which had already done 10,000 miles at 100 m.p.h. in a Shell publicity stunt.

The start of the eighty-four-hour Marathon was not very promising, for Enever crashed on his first lap and Hedges on his second, both on a corner which had been resurfaced after official practice had ended. While Enever's car went into a ditch, Hedges's cleared the ditch and bounded into a field, so it was even more extensively damaged than the former. However, both M.G.s were repaired and put back in the running, though heavily penalized for delay. Slowly they climbed up the leader-board, and by the second morning they lay third and fourth overall, after which the leading Volvo retired and moved them up another place. On the third morning a Ford Cortina came between the M.G.s until Alec Poole applied some pressure to this Dagenham intruder, speeding it up until it had to retire. Then came a sudden thunderstorm in which the leading Ferrari crashed, and the M.G.s were first and second—until Enever crashed too, after aquaplaning on a sheet of water near the pits. Poole regained second place, only to have a half-shaft break after seventy-nine hours of racing, but Hedges and Vernaeve continued with the remaining MGB to cover a total of 5620 miles and win the Marathon outright. Of the fourteen survivors, it was the only GT car to finish the event.

This was to be M.G.'s last major victory on a racing circuit, although many more awards were gained in lesser events. The Marathon quartet took the same two cars to Montlhéry in October for the 1000-kilometre race there, coming second and third in the 2½-litre class to a Porsche Carrera. Over in Australia, in a twelve-hour race at Surfers' Paradise, Queensland, Holden and Underwood won their class with an MGB which they had driven 650 miles from Sydney—and which they drove back to Sydney after the race. The third of the special Midget coupés which had been built in 1962 did a full season's racing to gain John Milne the Scottish National Speed Championship of 1966, and in America another Midget driver, Carson Baird, won the Class G National Championship.

While M.G. thus enjoyed no small measure of success on the racing circuits, Abingdon had been faced with some serious problems on the commercial side. An American lawyer, Ralph Nader, had attacked certain US-built cars as basically unsafe, and the resultant outcry had eventually led to the so-called Safety Act being approved by President Johnson in September 1966. Another new piece of American legislation, the Clean Air Act, called for certain standards in relation to the carbon monoxide and unburned hydrocarbons in exhaust gases. Heavy penalties were laid down for failure to meet stipulated standards by a deadline on 1st January 1968, and the onus of doing so was placed squarely on the manufacturer.

For Abingdon, which was now sending more M.G.s to America than ever before, this meant a full-scale test and development programme to review the design of all their sports cars. Brand-new cars had to be crashed under strictly controlled conditions to ensure that the effect on various components lay within approved limits. A fully-equipped laboratory had to be erected so that cars could be tested for exhaust pollution; this alone cost almost £60,000. The drawing office had to draw up specifications for padded facias, special switches, new brake gear, special tyres, collapsible steering-columns, new door locks, and a host of other new components to meet twenty-two specified safety requirements, while inlet and exhaust systems had to be extensively modified to meet the air pollution regulations.

There was difficulty in obtaining supplies of all these new components, and during 1967 production fell to its lowest level for five years, the open MGB suffering particularly badly. Austin-Healey production also fell; it was decided that the big Healey should be discontinued at the end of the year, partly because a new BMC engine was being designed for a new 3-litre saloon, partly because the Austin-Healey 3000 would have needed a complete redesign to meet the safety requirements. There were other developments which added to the generally unsettled atmosphere at this time. John Thornley became gravely ill following an operation in September 1966, and recovered only very slowly. Stuart Turner decided to leave the competitions department in the spring of 1967. Then came the retirement of Cec Cousins, who had spent nearly half-a-century with the organization and been involved in building M.G.s since the earliest days of the marque. BMC merged with Jaguar to form a new controlling body known as British Motor Holdings, and the M.G. Car Company was renamed the M.G. Division—a change which had little effect in practice, but did suggest a slight loss of identity.

It was also decided that the new 3-litre engine would be used for a new version of the MGB to replace the big Austin-Healey, an idea which seemed reasonable but soon led to complications. First, the sturdy front cross-member of the well-tested MGB front suspension had to be removed to make room for a larger engine, and this meant that the coil-spring layout had to be replaced by torsion bars. Initial development work was done with an Australian-designed engine, actually an 1800 c.c. unit with two additional cylinders which had given good results overseas. When the new six-cylinder engine eventually appeared from Longbridge, it was found to be 70 lbs. heavier than expected, which called for a hurried redesign of the whole suspension system to cope with the altered weight distribution. Moreover, the new engine had poor manifolding and an unsatisfactory design of cylinder head. At the bottom end, no less than seven main bearings had been squeezed into a rather inadequate length of crankshaft. It was not one of Longbridge's cleverer designs, and Michael Scarlett of *Autocar* later remarked that 'it appears to have been drawn up by an ex-marine diesel designer who was transferred against his wishes to the tractor engine department'.

The new MGC was announced at the 1967 Show and cost £895 (£1102 with tax) as an open two-seater, £1015 (£1249) as a GT coupé. It looked almost identical to the MGB apart from a bulge in the bonnet (the new engine had also proved taller than M.G. expected) and slightly larger wheels. The gearbox was an all-synchromesh unit, with automatic transmission as an option. At the same Show the MGB also had an all-synchromesh gearbox, with optional automatic transmission, and minor modifications included an alternator instead of a dynamo.

Though the MGC weighed about 3 cwt more than the MGB, it had almost 50 per cent more power available—145 b.h.p. was claimed at 5250 r.p.m.—so everyone expected the performance to be really impressive. At the top end of the scale this was so, the maximum speed being slightly over 120 m.p.h., but at lower speeds the MGC proved very disappointing, the engine completely lacking the low-speed torque that one expected from a 3-litre six-cylinder. Both *Autocar* and *Motor* commented on this in their very unenthusiastic road-test reports. *Motor* said the MGC was 'much more of a high-speed touring vehicle than a sports car', and *Autocar* remarked sagely, 'somewhere in the large BMC complex it has lost the "Abingdon touch"'. Both magazines also found the handling inferior to that of the MGB, with steering that seemed vague by comparison and a strong tendency to understeer.

If the production version of the MGC was thoroughly disappointing, it fathered an exciting new racing M.G. The last event that Stuart Turner attended as competitions manager, after shepherding the Mini through its fourth successive Monte victory, was the 1967 Sebring race. This was the first major event in which the MGB GT had been entered, although the hardtop MGBs had usually run in the GT category. Rather confusingly, the GT was not yet homologated for racing and therefore had to be entered in the prototype category, while a hardtop MGB (actually the well-used 1966 Marathon winner) was entered in the GT category. The hardtop car, its engine enlarged to 1824 c.c., was driven by Makinen, Rhodes and Baird; the GT, opened right out to 2004 c.c., by the successful Hopkirk/Hedges partnership. Each car finished third overall in its category, the GT winning its class and outpaced by only two other prototype cars, the 7-litre Ford Mark IVs which came first and second in the race.

After Sebring, the competitions department had six lightweight MGC GT bodies made in aluminium. As the MGC had not yet been announced, one car was assembled with a 2004 c.c. MGB engine, this time with oversize SU carburetters instead of the usual competition Weber. In this form, giving 150 b.h.p. at 6000 r.p.m., it was raced in the Targa Florio by Hopkirk and Makinen, who finished ninth overall and third in the unlimited-capacity prototype class behind two 910-8 Porsches. A hardtop 1824 c.c. MGB for Hedges and Poole ended its race when Hedges hit a tree; Sicily's so-called Short Madonie Circuit is forty-five miles long and consists mainly of mountains, so Hedges was glad to thumb a lift back to the pits by helicopter.

The competitions department was then instructed to concentrate on the new Austin 1800, but some M.G.s enjoyed a particularly full season of sports car racing in Britain. At Sebring one of the classes had been won by two keen USAF men with a 'Sprite' which was actually a Mark II Midget with a frog-eyed Mark I Sprite body. A reverse metamorphosis was arranged in England when a Sprite which had been raced successfully for nine years was resurrected as a lightweight Midget coupé by John Britten, and with 1148 c.c. engine it proved capable of about 120 m.p.h. at 8000 r.p.m.—for competition work had developed BMC's smallest pushrod o.h.v. engine to the point where it revved like an o.h.c. racing unit of pre-war days. Another very fast Midget, built by the development department at Abingdon, was Roger Enever's hardtop car of fairly unassuming appearance, which had a 1293 c.c. fuel-injection engine. These two Midgets set up class records at Crystal Palace, Snetterton, Brands Hatch, Cadwell Park, Croft, Mallory Park, Oulton Park, Rufforth and Silverstone, often outpacing 2-litre or even 3-litre sports cars. Enever lapped the Brands Hatch G.P. circuit at an average of 83.68 m.p.h., the Silverstone G.P. circuit at no less than 93.25 m.p.h. As for John Britten, he won so many events during the year that he was awarded the 1967 Amasco Championship.

For the 1968 Sebring race the lightweight MGC coupé was able to assume its proper identity, with an MGC engine giving over 200 b.h.p. in modified form. This made a rapid motor-car in which Hopkirk and Hedges finished tenth overall—one place higher than with the steel-bodied MGB GT the previous year—winning their class and coming third overall in the prototype category behind the winning Porsches. For two American drivers, Jerry Truitt and Randy Canfield, a Group 4 hardtop Midget had been prepared by Geoff Healey at Warwick, instead of by the Abingdon competitions department. With this they won not only their class but the entire sports car category.

In the 1968 Targa Florio, Hopkirk and Hedges drove a steel-bodied MGB GT instead of the lightweight MGC, the complexities of race regulations putting them in the sports car category along with the twin-o.h.c., fibreglass-bodied Porsche Carrera Sixes. Though the GT's overall placing was lower than the lightweight car had gained the previous year, the M.G. beat all but one of the Porsches to finish second in the sports category, the highest-placed British car in the event. Tony Fall and Peter Brown had a hectic race in a privately owned open MGB, for they crashed, found the gear-lever disappearing through the floor, because the gearbox cross-member had broken, kept going, crashed a second time, and still contrived to finish twenty-fourth overall.

Privately owned MGBs also ran in the Nürburgring 1000 Kilometres and the Circuit of Mugello, without achieving any success. A second lightweight MGC was completed in time for the eighty-four-hour Marathon. It was to be shared by Enever, Poole and Clive Baker, but overheated and retired in the early stages of the event, while a privately owned MGB retired after 3000 miles because of transmission trouble. After sixty-seven hours the original lightweight MGC was lying third overall, driven by Hedges, Vernaeve and Fall, but the disc pads had worn right through. When Hedges braked for his next pit-stop the backing-plates welded themselves to the discs, and a satisfactory repair was impossible within the permitted servicing time. The race ended with the MGC in sixth place.

This was in fact M.G.'s last official race entry, for by this time drastic changes had occurred back in England. In May 1968 the still-young British Motor Holdings organization had joined forces with Leyland, an old-established manufacturer of commercial vehicles, in a 'merger' which was soon revealed as a Leyland takeover in which that company's chief, Sir Donald Stokes, gained complete control. This put Abingdon in the curious situation of coming under the authority of their main rivals in the sports car market, for Leyland had previously taken over Standard-Triumph, whose sports cars M.G. viewed with contempt.

It was not a very happy position to be in, and those at Abingdon felt distinctly uncomfortable as the months went by without any announcement being made about future policy on the sports car side. A BBC features producer, Rayner Heppenstall, has de-scribed the atmosphere at Broadcasting House shortly after a change of management which eventually led to his department being closed down: 'A sense of insecurity gnawed at us all, together with a feeling of diminished status, a loosening of interest in what we were doing and a lack of that forward-looking optimism which is itself creative. The demolition squad, we felt, had moved in.' These were precisely the sensations experienced at Abingdon during 1968, when there was considerable uncertainty about the future of the competitions department and, far more important, the entire Abingdon factory.

On 15th October 1968 a statement on competitions policy was at last made by Sir Donald Stokes, who said the department would continue its activities but added, '. . . I can assure you we have no intention of participating in any competitions where we do not have a chance of winning.' He also said there would be increased emphasis on racing saloon cars.

Before this statement was made it had been decided that all BMC's magazines, including the Abingdon-produced sports car monthly, *Safety Fast*, would be discontinued. Support was also withdrawn from the BMC car clubs, including the M.G. Car Club, which, after a happy association with the M.G. manufacturers that had lasted for almost forty years, now had to be reorganized as a completely independent body. The next move by the new British Leyland Motor Corporation was to sub-divide its empire into seven groups, and when Abingdon heard that one of these was to be known as the Specialist Car Division, it was naturally assumed that this would incorporate M.G. Instead, it was made up of Standard-Triumph, Rover and Jaguar, and M.G. were lumped anonymously into the Austin-Morris Division. This was indeed a slap in the face, which did nothing to improve the Abingdon atmosphere. Many of the older employees now decided to accept early retirement. In July 1969, John Thornley retired from his position as general manager, at the age of sixty.

Meanwhile the two lightweight racing MGCs had been sold together with a competitions MGB GT to the American M.G. importers, who ran them in the 1969 Sebring 12 Hours, the three cars finishing fifteenth, twenty-fourth and twenty-eighth overall. The remaining body shells, still unused, were sold privately. The Abingdon competitions department turned its attention to Triumphs and other British Leyland makes until, in August 1970, an abrupt decision was made to close down what had become the most consistently successful organization of its type in the world.

There is a certain aura that surrounds a community of people engaged in work they enjoy, and for some forty years this had been particularly true of Abingdon; the place had an ethos of its own. It survived the Nuffield takeover, the cessation of sports car production during the war, and the increasing influence of Long-bridge under the BMC regime, but after the Leyland takeover many people remarked on a change. 'They've killed it now, the atmosphere,' said Cec Cousins. 'I didn't think anyone could, but they have. I thought the roots went too deep to get rid of it.'

One might imagine that such a change would be reflected in falling production figures, but on the contrary, they rose steadily. Despite it, and despite the fact that the big Austin-Healey had been discontinued, total production rose in 1968 and again in

1969—when the MGC was also discontinued and Sprite production greatly reduced. Indeed, the MGB and Midget were built in such quantity that more M.G.s were produced than in any previous year. M.G. exports to the USA increased by 40 per cent over the 1968 figure, which had itself been a new record. And although nobody noticed it at the time, the grand total of M.G.s exceeded half-a-million that year.

For the 1969 Motor Show the cars were merely 'face-lifted' by fitting new wheels, new seats and a new front grille. Even fewer changes were made for the 1970 Show, but they included a redesigned hood for the open MGB and some much-needed improvements to the heater on all models. Although total production dropped slightly in 1970, it was only because the Sprite programme had been drastically reduced; M.G. production went up yet again to exceed 50,000 for the first time, with a new record of almost 41,000 M.G.s exported, 36,500 of them to America.

In May 1971 it was Syd Enever's turn to retire, just too soon to see the 250,000th MGB come off the assembly line. The following month the Austin-Healey Sprite (which from the beginning of the year had been renamed the Austin Sprite) was dropped, and for the first time in twenty-two years Abingdon reverted to building M.G.s exclusively. Then British Leyland stopped producing the M.G.1300 saloon at the end of August; as the Magnette Mark IV had been discontinued in the spring of 1968, the marque thus became associated solely with sports cars.

For quite a long time before this the prototypes of two completely new but very different M.G.s had been undergoing tests at Abingdon. One, Project EX.234, was a front-engined car with independent (Hydrolastic) suspension all round. The other, new from stem to stern apart from the power unit, was ADO.21, an exciting mid-engined sports car with de Dion rear suspension. However, both remained in the prototype stage, and in October 1971 the MGB appeared for its tenth Motor Show, the Midget for its eleventh, with only minor modifications. The Midget had a fuel tank of larger capacity, but otherwise there were no significant mechanical changes except to cars intended for the American market. These had the effect of detuning the engines slightly in order to meet the latest air-pollution regulations. One project that seemed more likely to reach production was the installation of a Rover V.8 engine in the MGB, an experiment which gave promising results during early tests.

The mixture-as-before specification of the 1972 models naturally disappointed many M.G. fans, but it serves to emphasize the problems that the specialist car manufacturer of today has to face. The ultra-specialist manufacturer who sells a few hundred exotic sports cars in America each year is excused from compliance with current regulations; the manufacturer who sells in thousands is not. On the one hand he must meet the ever-growing host of new regulations arising out of the original Nader-inspired Safety Act of 1966 *and* the later Clean Air Act; on the other, he must recover his tooling and development costs—the former a major item at all times, the latter continually inflated by the requirements of new legislation.

To quote M.G.'s new chief designer, Roy Brocklehurst: 'The regulations are getting more stringent all the time, not only in America but also in Europe. Nowadays you don't design a motor-car any more—you just throw up all the regulations and draw a line around them. It's certainly taken the glamour out of the job. Our main concern nowadays is to provide a sort of instant padded cell—crash resistance, passive restraint and all the rest of it.

'Moreover, in the automobile industry tool amortisation is the name of the game. The production life of a new model is decided entirely by how long it takes to recoup tooling costs, and if production is relatively low it can take a long time. That's really what has stopped so many of our prototypes from seeing the light of day. And the cost of compliance with all the regulations is astronomical —it just isn't on to recover tooling and development costs with an output of less than 50,000 cars a year.'

In such circumstances as these it does seem unrealistic to dream, as M.G. enthusiasts do, of a really advanced sports car design receiving British Leyland approval for the fairly small-scale production of Abingdon. Commercialism, alas, seldom encourages individualism, as Kimber himself discovered many years ago. It is not difficult to predict that the near future will bring more and more 'rationalization' of the entire British Leyland range of models, sports cars included.

Yet the M.G. marque has weathered many storms and has never been more popular. It is the world's best-selling sports car at the time of writing. The demand in America has reached its highest level so far. At the Abingdon factory, more cars are being built now than ever before. Even the hucksters of the motor industry would hesitate to extinguish such a successful name.

Acknowledgments

In preparing a book such as this one inevitably consults many different individuals and publications, and some may well have been forgotten because the research has extended over a period of twelve years. To those I have inadvertently omitted I offer my apologies, and to all I want to express my heartfelt thanks.

Some of the most valuable material on M.G.'s early days was contained in a collection that passed into my keeping many years ago; I believe, but cannot be sure, that it was originally collected about 1937 by George Tuck, then publicity manager of M.G., with a view to preparing a history which was never written. I loaned the greater part of it to Lytton Jarman and Robin Barraclough for their book, *The Bullnose Morris* (Macdonald), and I have in turn drawn upon that to some extent. Similarly, Kenneth Ullyett expanded considerably the information I gave him for his *M.G. Companion* (Stanley Paul), which offered useful guidelines for further research. Two admirable books that have been in constant use are G. N. Georgano's *Complete Encyclopedia of the Motorcar* (Rainbird) and *The Life of Lord Nuffield* (Blackwell) by P. W. S. Andrews and Elizabeth Brunner. And it goes without saying that anyone who writes of M.G.'s racing activities in the early 'thirties, or record-breaking up to 1954, must be indebted to John Thornley for his splendid *Maintaining the Breed* (Motor Racing Publications). I am indebted to him in any case because he employed me at Abingdon twelve years ago and thus set the ball rolling.

Special mention should be made of certain people who provided particular assistance. Mrs Jean McGavin, the younger daughter of Cecil Kimber; Cec Cousins, former works manager and deputy general manager of M.G.; Reg Jackson, former chief inspector; Charlie Martin, former production manager; and H. N. Charles, former chief designer—these five have been more helpful than I can say, dealing patiently with literally hundreds of questions from me even when they had more pressing problems confronting them. Three people were good enough to read portions of the original typescript and offer extremely useful comments: they were Russell Lowry, former general secretary of the M.G. Car

Acknowledgments

Club; the late Dr Stuart Milton, who made a special study of early racing Midgets; and Martin Brent, honorary secretary of the MGCC SVW Register. I am especially grateful to my former colleague, Cyril Posthumus, the well-known motoring historian, who kindly read through the entire book in typescript. Others who have helped in many ways include: Mike Allison, Oliver Arkell, Mrs J. Armstrong, Scott Bailey, Chris Barker, Syd Beer, Eric Bellamy, John Bibbing, William Boddy, John Bolster, Arnold Bolton, Ken Bowsher, Roy Brocklehurst, Bill Burrows, Harold Connolly, Billy Cooper, Tom Crolius, Ronald Davidson, Sammy Davis, Tony Day, Steve Dear, Mrs Lisa Delamont (née Kimber), Syd Enever, Capt. George Eyston, Arnold Farrar, Rivers Fletcher, Hubert Fossett, Ron Gammons, G. S. ('Jack') Gardiner, Doug Gardner, Eddy Gosling, Mrs Eric Graham (formerly Mrs Cecil Kimber), Anthony Harding, Harold Hastings, Terry Hemmings, Norman Higgins, Phil Hill, Fred Horner, Alec Hounslow, Peter Hull, Barré Jackson, Mike Jennings, Vernon Kimber, Carl Kingerlee, Henry Kyle, Les Lambourne, the late Jack Lowndes, the late Wilfrid Mathews, Reg Miles, Mrs W. Munnoch, Sam Nash, Mrs M. O'Brien, the Oxford Motor Licensing Office, Gordon Phillips, the late Laurence Pomeroy, Mrs Doreen Price, Ron Riegelhuth, R. W. Savage, Stuart Seager, Michael Sedgwick, Miss Mary Smith, Miss Heather Stratton, Vic Vines, Rodney Walkerley and Michael Ware.

Charles Carter, Dennis Lowe and Mrs Vickridge of the former Nuffield Photographic Department have spared no pains to fill in the gaps in my collection of M.G. photographs, as have several of those already named.

Considerable recourse has been made to M.G. Car Company records of all kinds. While it is scarcely feasible to draw up a complete bibliography, in addition to books mentioned specifically above I have referred to: *A History of Coachbuilding*, by George Oliver (Cassell), *A Little Learning*, by Evelyn Waugh (Chapman & Hall), *Aston Martin* by Dudley Coram (Motor Racing Publications), *Brooklands to Goodwood*, by Rodney Walkerley (Foulis), *Full Throttle*, by Sir Henry Birkin (Foulis), *Grand Prix Racing Facts and Figures*, by George Monkhouse and Roland King-Farlow (Foulis), *How to Buy a Used Sports Car*, by John Christy (Sports Car Press), *Jaguar*, by Lord Montagu (Cassell), *Lost Causes of Motoring*, by Lord Montagu (Cassell), *Out on a Wing*, by Sir Miles Thomas (Michael Joseph), *Portrait of the Artist as a Professional Man*, by Rayner Heppenstall (Peter Owen), *Seven Year*

Twitch, by Marcus Chambers (Foulis), *The Austin Seven*, by R. J. Wyatt (Macdonald), *The Grand Prix Car*, by Laurence Pomeroy (Motor Racing Publications), *The History of Brooklands*, by William Boddy (Grenville), *The Rolls-Royce Motor Car*, by Anthony Bird and Ian Hallows (Batsford), *Wheelspin* and *More Wheelspin*, by C. A. N. May (Foulis), and *Wheels to Fortune*, by James Leasor (Bodley Head).

The periodicals used most extensively for reference were *Autocar* (formerly *The Autocar*), *Autosport*, *Motor* (formerly *The Motor*), *Motor Sport* and its predecessor, *The Brooklands Gazette*, and *Safety Fast*; not the present M.G. Car Club magazine of the same name, but the M.G. Car Company publication that appeared monthly from 1959 to 1968. Others include: *Canada Track and Traffic*, *Mechanix Illustrated*, *Motoring News*, *Proceedings of the Institute of Automobile Engineers*, *Road and Track*, *Sports Car*, *Sports Cars Illustrated*, *The Automobile Engineer*, *The Light Car and Cyclecar*, *The M.G. Magazine* (1933–1935), *The Morris Owner*, *The Railway Gazette* and *The Sports Car* (1935–1939). Special references to sources of information are detailed at intervals in the notes that follow.

Notes

Chapter 1: In preparing this brief biography of Cecil Kimber I enjoyed the fullest co-operation from his daughters, Mrs Lisa Delamont and Mrs Jean McGavin, and his brother, Vernon Kimber, all of whom consented to tape-recorded interviews. Mrs McGavin's assistance went far beyond that; she obtained useful information from Cecil Kimber's widow, Mrs Eric Graham, provided material on Kimber family history back to the seventeenth century, and allowed me to examine many family papers and photographs from their private collection.

H. N. Charles, Carl Kingerlee, Cec Cousins and Reg Jackson provided many memories of their former chief. Harold Hastings gave me copies of his correspondence with Cecil Kimber. Michael Sedgwick helped me to identify the hitherto mysterious rebodied Singer that Kimber drove about 1915. The files of local Oxford papers provided background information on Edward Armstead's suicide. Harold Connolly allowed me a lengthy taped interview, and the extent to which I am indebted to him is obvious from the text.

Out on a Wing (Michael Joseph), the autobiography of Sir Miles

Notes

Thomas (now Lord Thomas), has been invaluable as a source of material for this and other chapters. Martin Brent kindly obtained for me a copy of *The Railway Gazette* of 10th August 1945, in which the King's Cross accident was reviewed in great detail.

There are several curious gaps in the life story of Cecil Kimber which his family were unable to fill in—mainly, I think, because of the quarrel with his father which led to his leaving home. It is certainly remarkable that he was twenty-seven before entering the motor industry, that he did so during the First World War, and therefore had comparatively little experience of actual car manufacture before coming to Oxford. I have been unable to determine if Kimber may be considered a practical engineer: his family regard him as such, but former employees do not. Car design is usually a team effort, with a few notable exceptions, and it is fairly clear that Kimber relied heavily on H. N. Charles, Cec Cousins, Reg Jackson and others for mechanical details, while I have been told that the detailed design of M. G. bodywork owed much to a man named Cannell (whom I have been unable to trace) employed at Abingdon in pre-war days. H. N. Charles says that he was 'Sullivan to Kimber's Gilbert'. In all matters, the final decision rested with Kimber himself.

Cyril Posthumus has told me how the famous George Lanchester, rather against his will, was compelled to make use of a worm-drive rear axle made by E. G. Wrigley Ltd. When it was eventually replaced by a better design he remarked that in future, 'The only use I'll have for a Wrigley worm is on the end of a fishing-line.' It is a story that, I feel sure, Kimber himself would have appreciated.

Chapter 2: The collection of early reference material previously mentioned included reminiscences by some of the older employees which I have expanded by interviewing as many of them as possible before (and in some cases after) their retirement. It also included estimates of production figures based on information provided by Ernest Jones Ltd, later Carbodies Ltd, now BSA-Carbodies Ltd; some of these have been modified slightly because other coachbuilders were also employed. I have tried to avoid dogmatism where reference material is incomplete or nonexistent. I think the conflict between previously published accounts of the earliest M.G. days may be partly explained by the fact that Morris Garages activities were so divided up between Longwall, Queen Street, Alfred Lane and other depots; employees working at one might have no idea what was occurring elsewhere in Oxford. It is hard to decide if the 'telescoping' of the 1923 and 1925 Land's End Trials for publicity purposes, in later years, was done deliberately or accidentally.

Three of the earliest M.G. owners, Oliver Arkell, Jack Gardiner and Billy Cooper, all gave me taped interviews. It has been said that the Arkell car was bought in June 1923, but reference to Mr Arkell's personal diary and bank-book confirms the dates now quoted. The late Harry Charnock's comments on his Bullnose M.G. are extracted from an article he wrote for *Safety Fast* a few weeks before his death.

Many different sources were consulted in the attempt to disentangle the history of the Kimber Special, FC.7900, starting with an approach to the Oxford Motor Licensing Office, to Kimber's passenger in the 1925 Land's End, the late Wilfrid Mathews, and ranging far and wide thereafter, including a trip to Manchester to trace the first private owners of the car. The fact that the car should be dark grey, not red, is confirmed by the original registration details and the *Motor* report (14th April 1925) of the Trial. The cost of building FC.7900 was given by Kimber as £279 in *The Sports Car* of December 1936, £285 in *The Motor* of 5th October 1937. The Trial was on 10/11th April 1925, and it was very soon afterwards (one account says 'immediately') that Kimber sold the car to a friend, the late Harry Turner of C. H. Turner Ltd, Stockport, for £300, a price quoted by Kimber in 1937 and confirmed to me by Wilfrid Knight, managing director of that company. He recalls frequent bearing trouble due to oil starvation and a tendency to burst into flames—which may account for the body having been repainted in black and maroon before the car was sold on 10th November 1930 to Ronald Davidson, who paid £50 for it.

Cecil Kimber revealed very little interest in the car when Mr Davidson wrote to him about it early in 1931, but a year later he said—in response to another letter—that he might buy it if the original body was still fitted. He was just a couple of days too late; despairing of finding spares to repair the engine, Mr Davidson had sold it *via* a Manchester auctioneer for eleven guineas to, he thinks, a butcher in Birmingham, and was unable to trace it. Later, Mr Knight saw it being used to tow a trailer of pig-food.

It is then said to have been found in a Manchester scrapyard by an M.G. employee and bought for either £12 or £15. This must have been soon afterwards, for M.G. records indicate that the car was running again and involved in a crash in December 1932 when being driven by the late Douglas Clease of *The Autocar*; he was unable to recall this when I asked him about it in 1960. It may have been at this point that a new front axle was fitted, with smaller brake-drums than used originally. What looks like an M-type windscreen was also fitted according to a photograph taken about 1934.

I have been told that the car was stored at Cowley during the Second World War and narrowly escaped damage when a building was bombed, also that for a time it was in the hands of Cockshoot's, the Manchester M.G. distributors. Then it seems to have been rebuilt at Cowley, after which the Nuffield Organization had it reregistered to use for publicity purposes. They advised the Oxford authorities that it had 'not been previously registered', and the number FMO.842 was therefore allocated on 15th March 1950. By this time the body had been painted red all over and the car differed in many minor respects from its original appearance as revealed by contemporary photographs. Publicity material invariably referred to the car as 'The first M.G., built in 1923', and it was sometimes said to have 'won the Land's End Trial'.

In 1959 I was astonished to find that the original registration number had become void (because the car had not been licensed for at least five years) some time after transfer to Stockport on 25th June 1925. Being void it was still available, and I asked John Thornley's approval to change back to the original; it was *not* done, as has been stated, 'as the result of representations by the Bullnose Morris Club'. In 1962 the car crossed the Atlantic for exhibition at the New York Auto Show. Several years later it was unfortunately 'restored' almost beyond recognition for use on the M.G. stand at the 1969 London Motor Show.

When dating early leaflets and catalogues I had considerable assistance from Lytton Jarman, whose knowledge of Bullnose Morris components must be unrivalled. He takes into consideration every visible part of a car, and some (grease-nipples, for example) that would be invisible to ordinary mortals.

While refraining from mentioning the name of the artist who illustrated the dreadful M.G. catalogue of late 1926, it is only fair to say that it was neither Leslie Grimes nor Harold Connolly.

Throughout this book I have used the term 'bulkhead' for the partition between engine and driver (in America, the 'firewall') in preference to the contemporary 'dashboard', which eventually became synonymous with 'instrument panel'. For no good reason the latter subsequently turned into 'facia' or 'fascia', scarcely justified unless it is made of wood (now uncommon) or stone (never a popular material on motor-cars).

Chapter 3: When records are incomplete and memories hazy, one must indulge in some surmise. My most reliable source of information on early M.G. days, Cec Cousins, has been good enough to admit frankly that he cannot remember the exact specifications of all the side-valve models, though his memory is phenomenal. It is illogical, in any case, to talk of standard specifications when a car is still under development and production has scarcely reached double figures. There can also be confusion because a 1928 model, for example, means a car built any time from shortly before the 1927 Show to shortly before the 1928 Show.

I believe that the *production* side-valve M.G.s probably followed this sequence:

14/28 Mark I: The 1924/5 Bullnose M.G. with modified Morris Oxford chassis (three-quarter elliptic rear springs), four-wheel brakes, artillery wheels with Ace discs, beaded-edge tyres, and optional two-tone finish to all-aluminium body.

14/28 Mark II: The 1925/6 Bullnose, similar to the above but with servo-assisted brakes, wire-spoked (open-hub) wheels, Barker headlamp dippers, and wider body in aluminium and steel.

14/28 Mark III: The first (1926/7) flat-radiator car on the new (semi-elliptic rear springs) Morris Oxford chassis, Marles steering, smaller brake servo, sheet-steel bulkhead, balloon tyres, and with false piece soldered to bottom of radiator.

14/40 Mark IV: The similar but 'cleaned up' 1927/8 car with redesigned braking system (no servo), finned brake-drums, cast-aluminium bulkhead, metal front apron, new exhaust manifold with forward outlet, and other modifications.

14/40 Mark V: The last of the side-valve cars, mostly built 1928/9 (some may have been completed after the move to Abingdon; some were not registered until mid-1930, but a long delay between completion and registration was not uncommon when cars sold slowly). The specification may have evolved only gradually; it included new wheels with smaller hubs (often carrying an M.G. motif as on the M-type Midget), cellulose paintwork, electric wiper and vacuum headlamp dippers.

The first three of these models were normally referred to simply as 'M.G. Super Sports', so I am not strictly correct in using '14/40' as the generic term for flat-radiator cars, even if it does

Notes

avoid confusion. 'Mark V' was never used—it is adopted here merely for convenience in classification.

Though the 1927 San Martin event is almost unquestionably M.G.'s first racing victory, it is not M.G.'s first success on a racing circuit. On 17th October 1925 the MCC held their first High-Speed Trial at Brooklands and Billy Cooper won a gold medal with his first M.G. tourer, MF.8068, while another was awarded to Cecil Kimber who drove a 'Morris saloon', which must surely have been an M.G. Super Sports Salonette. To gain such an award they had to average about 45 m.p.h. for one hour. In the similar event held the following year, Cooper gained another 'gold' with his second Bullnose M.G., which—by that time—was actually referred to as an M.G. in the report in *The Autocar*.

The extensive modifications made to the Morris chassis at Edmund Road are given in great detail in *The Automobile Engineer* of March 1928.

Chapter 4: Initial research on the vertical-drive o.h.c. cars was undertaken towards the end of 1960 for a series entitled 'Portrait Gallery' published in *Safety Fast* and subsequently reprinted in poster form as 'M.G.s Through the Ages', but I later realized that the sources I had used then were not wholly reliable. In referring back to original M.G. drawing-office records, some discrepancies could not be completely explained, and I remain very suspicious of dogmatic assertions about certain features. H. N. Charles, Cec Cousins, Reg Jackson (in particular), Alec Hounslow and others supplemented the admirable account of M.G.'s racing years contained in John Thornley's *Maintaining the Breed*, while race reports were double-checked by reference to contemporary periodicals, and Gordon Phillips kindly allowed me to copy his personal collection of cuttings (the source of which was sometimes unidentifiable). Lack of space has forced me to condense my accounts of the races considerably, and the reader cannot do better than turn to *Maintaining the Breed*, or to two series of articles by William Boddy and Cyril Posthumus in early issues of *Safety Fast*, for the anecdotes I have regretfully had to omit.

Henry Kyle provided copies of Shell power curves and experimental data on the 18/100 Mark III, which is referred to therein as the 'Tiger'. This was also chalked under the seat-cushion of one of Chris Barker's two cars, and the same word appears in Carbodies's production records, which seems to support the use of this name in preference to the female Tigress (or even a Gallic

Tigresse which has appeared occasionally). Yet at least one other car manufacturer had a Tiger model, as Syd Enever pointed out to me. And I have also found that older M.G. employees tended to refer indiscriminately to *any* of the old o.h.c. Sixes as a Tiger. Hence my preference for the unequivocal but unglamorous '18/100 Mark III'.

It may or may not be significant that the 'Safety Fast' slogan came into use the year after *The Motor* commented, in their 12th March 1929 road test of the 18/80 Mark I saloon, that: '"Safety with speed" might well be a slogan for the manufacturers, for this feeling above all is impressed upon one. . . .'

It is a moot point whether the 1933 Mille Miglia should be regarded as the K.3's first race or first *major* race. Robin Jackson drove the ex-Monte car in the first Donington Park meeting, held on 25th March, but this was of course a short-chassis prototype, not a true K.3. Incidentally, the very first Donington race was won by an M.G.—E. R. Hall's C-type Midget.

Sir Henry Birkin's rude remarks about M.G.s appear in his famous *Full Throttle*, originally published by Foulis in 1932. His comments on Brooklands were no less scathing, and strangely at variance with the reverential awe accorded to that circuit today.

The production totals of various K-series models differ considerably in different M.G. factory records. Mine are deduced from a combination of allocated chassis numbers, coachbuilders' records, and the known total production each year.

The correct engine capacity of the KD and N-type Magnettes came to light when double-checking specifications against contemporary press reports. I could not confirm it from drawing-office records because of a discrepancy there, and could locate one crankshaft drawing (to check the stroke) but not the other. Two Magnette owners, Syd Beer and Mike Allison, kindly checked the stroke on several engines and found it to be 83 mm in each case. Finally Cec Cousins confirmed this figure and explained how the imaginary 84 mm stroke had arisen, saying that, 'H. N. Charles was hopping mad about it'. An engineer would scarcely appreciate falsification of technical records.

Some of the figures quoted in the comparison of M.G., Auto Union and Mercedes-Benz power outputs come from an article that the late Laurence Pomeroy wrote for the first issue of *Safety Fast*, others from his magnificent book, *The Grand Prix Car, 1906–1939*. Charles and Cousins have both reminded me that M.G. were much indebted to Hubert Fossett, assistant to Air Commodore 'Rod' Banks, who had developed a special fuel for Rolls-Royce to use in the Schneider Trophy Race. Fossett came to Abingdon frequently to (as he put it to me) 'make cocktail mixes—bloody dangerous, really'. He was responsible for the development of several special sprint and racing fuels, among them the widely used MG.1 and MG.2. Later he assisted in the development of Jaguar engines.

Regrettably, there are no photographs of the all-independent car built by Syd Enever and Reg Jackson, but they provided me with a sketch of the chassis layout and described the car in detail. Reg Jackson recalls that Cecil Kimber's comment was, 'This is the way our future lies.' Nor was this Abingdon's only all-independent two-seater, by any means—indeed, for the past twelve years or so there has scarcely been a time when the development department did *not* have at least one prototype under test.

After the Nuffield takeover H. N. Charles returned to Morris Motors at Cowley, as mentioned in Chapter 5. He sees the R-type as the basis of the post-war Morris Minor, which used torsion-bar independent suspension at the front end. Certainly the last R-type built was modified in its suspension and sent to Cowley, where it remained until sent to a scrapyard years later and eventually rescued for restoration. There is evidence that it had never been driven after modification.

It seems not unlikely that Kimber would have attempted to enter the Grand Prix field if the Nuffield takeover had not occurred. The S-type single-seater was already projected, its engine could well have been enlarged from 1100 c.c., and Kimber waged a vigorous press campaign for a $1\frac{1}{2}$-litre Grand Prix formula at this time. If this came to Lord Nuffield's attention, it provides yet another reason for the takeover. In any case a major reorganization of the Nuffield empire had been advised after two court actions were fought (both successfully) against supertax demands in the late 'twenties, while Nuffield was also open to adverse comment because the company of which he was chairman bought most of its supplies from concerns that he, personally, controlled. An improvement on the stock market early in 1935 made this a suitable time to embark on the reorganization.

Chapter 5: The M.G. drawing office existed in a sort of limbo for nearly twenty years after the Nuffield takeover, and models produced during that time are not at all well documented. Martin Brent disinterred much information on the SVW models (which he does not allow me to call the WVS range) by investigating Cowley records when he was working for my department at Abingdon, but the most painstaking efforts still left a number of gaps.

In regard to the vertical-drive o.h.c. engines, it does not seem to be generally realized that these will run *apparently* satisfactorily (but greatly lacking in power) when the valve timing is at least three teeth out of adjustment, while it is easy to turn the eccentric rocker-bushes 'over-centre' when adjusting clearances, or to misalign the vertical drive when refitting the cylinder head; hence the comment made by Reg Jackson. I am convinced that these common mistakes (some of which I have made myself) are responsible for the poor reputation that these engines have earned in some quarters, together with the widely held notion that racing M.G.s were ultra-special by comparison with the production models. They were not (although certain special components were used), but they *were* properly assembled. Gordon Phillips commonly devoted at least a week to preparing the top end of a racing engine, and no-one considered that he was wasting his time.

For information on the trials cars I have drawn on factory records and the two pre-war M.G. magazines, *The M.G. Magazine* and *The Sports Car*, together with C. A. N. May's two classics, *Wheelspin* and *More Wheelspin*. Some additional information was provided by Steve Dear, chairman of the MGCC Triple-M Register, and by Martin Brent. Enlarged VA engines of the type used in the 1938 Cream Cracker TAs were also fitted to VA tourers supplied to the police. Many years later it was the special needs of the police that led to an alternator being developed for the MGB.

As originally pointed out to me by Ron Gammons, former honorary secretary of the MGCC T Register, great care is needed when using T-type catalogues for reference purposes because most TB catalogues are illustrated by TA photographs. Indeed, pre-war illustrations were used in some TC literature. M.G. publicity material possibly reached its lowest level under the influence of Cowley in the late T-type period, with pictures of M.G.s 'racing' complete with hub-caps, full-width windscreens, bumpers and everything else—but not a club badge in sight. However, it was rivalled in the early 'sixties by advertisements for the Magnette Mark III saloon in which people were shown hotly disputing for the 'privilege' of driving that dismal motor-car.

Most of the information on wartime activities came from an

admirable little booklet by George Propert entitled *Abingdon in Wartime*, kindly loaned to me by Charlie Martin, who, together with Cec Cousins and Reg Jackson, told me even more from their recollections of the period. I believe that George Propert also wrote an article that appeared in *The Autocar* of 26th June 1942; the name of the factory is withheld for security reasons, but everything points to its being Abingdon.

Chapter 6: Except in regard to record-breaking, this period has not really been covered at all in book form, so it relies on factory records, contemporary periodicals, and one or two articles written subsequently for *Safety Fast*, together with the usual stout assistance from Cousins, Jackson, and one of the 'Riley men' who came to Abingdon in 1949, Arnold Farrar. Charlie Martin has gone to endless trouble to provide production figures. The reader may well be as surprised as I was to find how few TCs were sold in the USA, but the records are quite clear on this point. Indeed, no M.G.s went to America at all in 1945 or 1946, only six in 1947. It was the TD, not the TC, that accounted for most American sales until the MGA arrived on the scene.

There has been insufficient space to record all the many changes in specification—often unimportant—made during the life of the post-war T-type cars, but further mention of the TD Mark II should perhaps be made. This model has since acquired a quite unjustified reputation as a fire-eater; it was really quite mildly tuned, although the water passages were different and the cylinder head was not at first interchangeable to ordinary TDs. Nor does an engine number prefixed XPAG.TD2 indicate a TD Mark II. It denotes a standard unit with the larger (8-inch diameter) clutch and flywheel that were fitted during the production run.

In writing of this period I have also been able to draw on personal recollections to a greater extent, since by this time I was on the staff of *Autosport* and much concerned with developments in the sports car world. Present-day admirers of the 1250 c.c. TF may be shocked to read contemporary opinions of the car, but it aroused little enthusiasm when announced at the 1953 Motor Show; one fellow-journalist called it 'a TD that's been kicked in the face'.

Chapter 7: For the first four years of this period I used much the same sources as for the previous chapter, with additional reference to Marcus Chambers's book, *Seven Year Twitch* (Foulis), on the early days of the BMC competitions department. From early 1959 onwards I was myself employed at Abingdon and therefore able to keep in close touch with competitions activities as well as the development of production sports cars. Dick Jacobs, at the end of each season, would send me a very lucid summary of the results he had achieved with his cars.

John Christy's remarks about M.G.s are taken from *How to Buy a Used Sports Car* (Sports Car Press), published in 1957 but written, I think, early in 1956.

In considering Abingdon's continual increase in production, it is noteworthy that this was achieved without recourse to a night shift at the factory. There has never been night shift working at Abingdon except during the Second World War.

My assessment of the MGA is derived partly from contemporary road tests, partly from personal experience of driving these cars on the road, and partly from racing one in minor club events —not a factory car, but an oldish one loaned to me by Gordon Cobban, the present general secretary of the M.G. Car Club. Road-test cars were definitely not 'tweaked' during my time at Abingdon, and I believe that this was never done after the war. From about 1950 onwards, press road tests have become very much more thorough and accurate than they were in earlier days.

Phil Hill's description of driving the EX.181 record car is taken from a taped interview I carried out in 1960 when he was staying at the house of a friend, Derek Dunt. This part of the interview has not been previously published. The flow of fuel vapour into the cockpit was attributed to a pressure drop, due to the boxed-in wheels pumping air out of the body, and modifications were made to prevent a recurrence of it.

The excitement aroused in the Abingdon design department by the advent of the Mini was intense, as was the disappointment when they were not allowed to proceed with an M.G. version of it. I once asked Sir Alec Issigonis why the Cooper variant had been chosen in preference to ADO.34, and he replied, 'Oh, ADO.34 was a dreadful thing; you just think it's good because it was designed at Abingdon.' He may have been right, at that.

Syd Enever's comment on the derivation of the MGB body shape is taken from an article published in *Motor* of 4th June 1966.

Chapter 8: On the whole, the motoring press have continued to express approval of the MGB throughout that model's lengthy production life, but with increasing reference to its 'vintage' character. *Motor* of 27th December 1969 said: 'There is no doubt

that for a substantial proportion of motoring enthusiasts throughout the world the letters MG are almost synonymous with the
term sports car. What an MG is and does, therefore, has a good
deal of influence on the popular idea of the sports car. And its high
export sales make the MG to some extent an ambassador for
Britain. . . . Before our retest of the open MG B we expected to find
this ageing design, first introduced in 1962, to be completely outclassed by subsequent progress and perhaps no better than any of
several lively but quite ordinary family saloons. We are happy to
report that our expectations were, for all the important things,
largely confounded. The MG B is still a fast and satisfactory sports
car.'

Since riding comfort is a relative quality, it is not illogical to call
MGB suspension soft in 1962, comparatively hard a few years
later. The TA Midget was thought softly sprung in 1936 but (as the
TC) distinctly uncomfortable by the late 'forties.

The story of the M.G.1100 and its successors is a little bewildering. The 1275 c.c. engine was offered as an option in the summer
of 1967, apparently for the home market, but standardized for the
American market about this time. It was stated that the final drive
had gone up from 4.13 to 3.65 : 1, a considerable jump, but there
are grounds for believing that it was even higher—3.44 : 1, in
fact, which was pleasant for touring but ruined the acceleration.
At the 1967 Motor Show the 1100 was to be discontinued in favour
of the 1300, with 1275 c.c. engine, new seats, new wipers, a remodelled tail end, etc., but the larger-capacity engine was in short
supply, so the new body was fitted with the 1100 engine and this
car was produced for a few weeks as the M.G.1100 Mark II. It was
also announced that the 1100 and 1300 would be fitted with an
all-synchromesh gearbox, but this does not actually seem to have
been available until early in 1968, by which time the short-lived
1100 Mark II had been discontinued.

Also at the 1967 Show, automatic transmission was offered as
an option, but when this was fitted, only one carburetter was used.
The power output of the 1275 c.c. engine in this form was quoted
as 58 b.h.p. at 5250 r.p.m. (later amended to 60 b.h.p.). The
1100 engine had given 55 b.h.p. at 5500 r.p.m.

Examples of the M.G.1300 built until April 1968, whether
with manual or automatic transmission, had only one carburetter.
Two were fitted thereafter, giving 65 b.h.p. at 5750 r.p.m. At about
the same time the car seems to have been withdrawn from the
American market and replaced by the automatic-transmission

Austin America. This, too, seems to have been withdrawn, and for a time the Vanden Plas version of the ADO.16 was marketed in the USA. with an M.G. badge.

At the 1968 Show the M.G.1300 Mark II was announced, with uprated engine giving 70 b.h.p. at 6000 r.p.m. It may have been at this stage, or earlier (the records are somewhat confusing), that the final drive became 3.65:1. Some of these cars were produced with automatic transmission, but I understand that the engines were all detuned to 65 or even 60 b.h.p. form. Not long after, the automatic transmission was discontinued.

H. N. Charles, in a paper read to the Institute of Automobile Engineers in February 1935, quoted three main reasons justifying participation in motor racing. The first two were the publicity and development value of such activities, the third that: 'A fine spirit is created amongst all those responsible for the effort, and all concerned come away from the contest more capable and self-reliant because of what they have seen and done.' While most of the BMC competitions department's successes were gained with Minis and Austin-Healeys, they certainly aroused considerable pride at Abingdon.

M.G.'s racing activities between 1963 and 1968 have been covered at some length because they were mentioned but little in contemporary periodicals (apart from *Safety Fast*). Present-day races are given a fraction of the coverage accorded to pre-war events and reporters must concentrate on the outright winners, often ignoring praiseworthy achievements lower down the field. I feel that M.G.'s accomplishments with near-standard sports cars, running in scratch events against ever more specialized (and expensive) lightweight, low-profile machinery, were remarkable, and bear favourable comparison with pre-war successes in events where the opposition was often less intense.

Those who have attended a Sebring race will know that it is always difficult, and sometimes impossible, to obtain accurate results. Some results sheets subsequently issued indicated that there was no 3-litre prototype class in 1967 or 1968, but the organizers had awarded cash prizes to Hopkirk and Hedges for winning it on each occasion!

For the 1967 Targa Florio a new regulation called for a car to cover at least 90 per cent of the distance completed *by its class-winner*, with the ludicrous result that those who finished from seventh to tenth overall were unclassified while slower cars were rated as official finishers. The new lightweight M.G. ran in the same class as the winning 910-8 Porsche and finished third in that class, ninth overall, but officially it was a non-finisher, ninth place being awarded to a privately owned Austin-Healey that finished thirteenth. This occurred because the Austin-Healey's class was won by a Ford GT40 that had made several pit-stops and completed a shorter distance than the winning Porsche.

The Indianapolis cars were designed by Joe Huffaker of San Francisco. I am not suggesting that they can really be considered as M.G.s; it is just an interesting—if somewhat tenuous—association between M.G. and America's leading race. Actually an M.G. won the American Grand Prix in the mid-'thirties, but this was a very minor affair.

The incident with the broken filler-cap at Le Mans in 1963 recalls a similar one in 1937 related to me by Betty Haig. It happened when Dorothy Stanley-Turner and Enid Riddell were driving a privately entered PB Midget, and they overcame it by persuading the *plombeur* to wire an orange into the filler orifice and affix the usual official seal.

Although Michael Scarlett is a member of the *Autocar* staff, his comments on the MGC engine were made in an article published in *Farmer and Stockbreeder* of 17th December 1968. Hence, no doubt, the reference to tractors.

The description of the change in atmosphere at Broadcasting House is taken from *Portrait of the Artist as a Professional Man*, by Rayner Heppenstall, published by Peter Owen at £1.90.

I would like to draw a distinction between the various British Leyland decisions in regard to Abingdon (which they were entitled to make, and which seem to be justified by commercial considerations) and the way such decisions were promulgated (which aroused widespread and, I think, well-merited resentment). The steady rise in production after the bad year of 1967 is admirable, but the sacrifice of a contented atmosphere suggests planning for immediate advantage rather than the ultimate good of this small community.

Roy Brocklehurst's views are not those of a greybeard who is naturally opposed to sports cars. He was thirty-seven when he took over as M.G.'s chief designer, and has spent his entire working life at Abingdon. There can be few in this country more qualified to comment on American safety regulations, for at the time of writing he has paid twenty-one visits to the USA to study this important question.

Appendices

Appendix I
Specifications of all M.G. models

Note: These specifications, being necessarily condensed, are intended to be read in conjunction with the text. Power outputs are not quoted in the case of certain racing models, for example, where results varied with compression ratio, fuel used, boost pressures, etc., but fuller details will be found in the text.

Model:	11.9 h.p. 'Raworth'	14/28 Super Sports	'Flat' 14/28 & 14/40 Mk. IV
Approx. production period	Mid-1923 to late 1924	Late 1924 to late 1926	Late 1926 to late 1929
Number produced	6	Approx. 400	Approx. 900
No. of cylinders Bore & stroke Capacity	Four 69.5 × 102 mm 1548 c.c.	Four 75 × 102 mm 1802 c.c.	Four 75 × 102 mm 1802 c.c.
Valve location & operation	Side-valve Mushroom tappets	Side-valve Mushroom tappets	Side-valve Mushroom tappets
No. and type of carburetters	Believed 1 hor. SU	Smith, SU or Solex (1)	1 hor. Solex
Power output	Not known precisely	Not known precisely	Believed 35 b.h.p. @ 4000 r.p.m.
Clutch & Gearbox	Wet cork clutch Manual 'crash' (3-sp.)	Wet cork clutch Manual 'crash' (3-sp.)	Wet cork clutch Manual 'crash' (3-sp.)
Type of suspension	½-elliptic (F) ¾-elliptic (R) (shackled)	½-elliptic (F) ¾-elliptic (R) (shackled)	½-elliptic F+R (shackled)
Type of road wheels	Bolt-on artillery	1924/5: bolt-on artillery with Ace discs 1925/6: bolt-on wire spoke	Bolt-on wire spoke. (Smaller hub in 1929)
Brake type & drum diam.	9″ drum rear only	12″ drum F+R (servo-assisted in 1925/6)	12″ drum F+R (servo-assisted in 1926/7)
Wheelbase Track	8′ 6″ 4′ 0″ F+R	8′ 6″ and 9′ 0″ 4′ 0″ F+R	8′ 10½″ 4′ 0″ F+R
Available coachwork	2/S only	2/S, 4/S & various closed	2/S, 4/S & various closed

18/80 Six Marks I & II	M-type Midget	18/100 Six Mark III	C-type Midget
Mk I: late 1928 to mid-1931 Mk II: late 1929 to mid-1933	Late 1928 to mid-1932	Early to late 1930	Mid-1931 to mid-1932
Mk I: 500 Mk II: 236	3235	5	44
Six 69 × 110 mm 2468 c.c.	Four 57 × 83 mm 847 c.c.	Six 69 × 110 mm 2468 c.c.	Four 57 × 73 mm 746 c.c.
Chain-driven overhead camshaft	O.h.c. driven through vertical dynamo	Chain-driven overhead camshaft	O.h.c. driven through vertical dynamo
2 hor. SU (1 float-chamber Mk. I)	1 hor. SU	2 hor. SU (special)	Various, also Powerplus supercharger
Believed abt. 60 b.h.p @ 3200 r.p.m.	Early: 20 b.h.p. @ 4000 r.p.m. Later: 27 b.h.p. @ 4500 r.p.m.	Depending on state of tune	Depending on state of tune
Wet cork clutch Manual 'crash' 3-sp. (Mk. I) 4-sp. (Mk. II)	Dry clutch Manual 'crash' (3-sp.)	Dry clutch Manual 'crash' (4-sp.)	Dry clutch Manual 'crash' (4-sp.)
$\frac{1}{2}$-elliptic F+R (shackled)	$\frac{1}{2}$-elliptic F+R (shackled)	$\frac{1}{2}$-elliptic F+R (shackled)	$\frac{1}{2}$-elliptic F+R (sliding trunnion)
Centre-lock wire spoke	Bolt-on wire spoke	Centre-lock wire spoke	Centre-lock wire spoke
12″ drum (Mk. I) 14″ drum (Mk. II) Some models with servo	8″ drums Cable-operated	14″ drums Cable & rod	8″ drums Cable-operated
9′ 6″ 4′ 0″ (Mk. I) 4′ 4″ (Mk. II)	6′ 6″ 3′ 6″ F+R	9′ 6″ 4′ 4″ F+R	6′ 9″ 3′ 6″ F+R
2/S, 4/S & various closed	2/S, closed, & Double Twelve Replica	4/S only	2/S only

Model:	D-type Midget	F-type Magna	J.1 & J.2 Midgets
Approx. production period	Late 1931 to mid-1932	Late 1931 to late 1932	Mid-1932 to early 1934
Number produced	250	1250	380 J.1 2083 J.2
No. of cylinders	Four	Six	Four
Bore & stroke	57×83 mm	57×83 mm	57×83 mm
Capacity	847 c.c.	1271 c.c.	847 c.c.
Valve location & operation	O.h.c. driven through vertical dynamo	O.h.c. driven through vertical dynamo	O.h.c. driven through vertical dynamo
No. & type of carburetters	1 hor. SU	2 hor. SU	2 semi-d.d. SU
Power output	27 b.h.p. @ 4500 r.p.m.	37.2 b.h.p. @ 4100 r.p.m.	36 b.h.p. @ 5500 r.p.m.
Clutch & Gearbox	Dry clutch Manual 'crash' (3-sp.)	Dry clutch Manual 'crash' (4-sp.)	Dry clutch Manual 'crash' (4-sp.)
Type of suspension	½-elliptic F+R (sliding trunnion)	½-elliptic F+R (sliding trunnion)	½-elliptic F+R (sliding trunnion)
Type of road wheels	Centre-lock wire spoke	Centre-lock wire spoke	Centre-lock wire spoke
Brake type & drum diam.	8″ drum Cable-operated	8″ drum (12″ on late cars) Cable-operated	8″ drum Cable-operated
Wheelbase	Early 7′ 0″ Later 7′ 2″	7′ 10″	7′ 2″
Track	3′ 6″ F+R	3′ 6″ F+R	3′ 6″ F+R
Available coachwork	4/S and closed	F.1: 4/S & closed F.2: 2/S only F.3: 4/S & closed	J.1: 4/S & closed J.2: 2/S only

J.3 & J.4 Midgets	K-type Magnette (KA & KB engines)	K-type Magnette (KD engine)	K.3 Magnette
Late 1932 to late 1933	Late 1932 to mid-1933	Mid-1933 to early 1934	Late 1932 to late 1934
22 J.3	Believed 15 K.2	Believed 5 K.2	33 incl. prototypes
9 J.4	Possibly 71 K.1	Possibly 80 K.1	and EX. 135
Four	Six	Six	Six
57×73 mm	57×71 mm	57×83 mm	57×71 mm
746 c.c.	1087 c.c.	1271 c.c.	1087 c.c.
O.h.c. driven through vertical dynamo	O.h.c. driven through vertical dynamo	O.h.c. driven through vertical dynamo	O.h.c. driven through vertical dynamo
Single SU with various Powerplus superchargers	KA: 3 SU KB: 2 SU	2 semi-d.d. SU	Usually single SU with Powerplus (1933) or Marshall (1934) supercharger
Depending on state of tune	KA: 38.8 b.h.p. @ 5500 r.p.m. KB: 41 b.h.p. @ 5500 r.p.m.	48.5 b.h.p. @ 5500 r.p.m. 54.5 b.h.p. @ 5500 r.p.m. (2 valve timings)	Depending on state of tune
Dry clutch Manual 'crash' (4-sp.)	KA: preselector (no clutch) KB: manual 'crash' with dry clutch Both 4-sp.	Preselector 4-sp. with automatic clutch	Preselector 4-sp. without clutch
½-elliptic F+R (sliding trunnion)	½-elliptic F+R (sliding trunnion)	½-elliptic F+R (sliding trunnion)	½-elliptic F+R (sliding trunnion)
Centre-lock wire spoke	Centre-lock wire spoke	Centre-lock wire spoke	Centre-lock wire spoke
8" drum (J.3) 12" drum (J.4) Cable-operated	13" drum Cable-operated	13" drum Cable-operated	13" drum Cable-operated (twin-lever in 1934)
7' 2"	K.1: 9' 0" K.2: 7' $10\frac{3}{16}$" 4' 0" F+R	K.1: 9' 0" K.2: 7' $10\frac{3}{16}$" 4' 0" F+R	7' $10\frac{3}{16}$" 4' 0" F+R
3' 6" F+R			
2/S only (doorless on J.4)	K.1: 4/S & saloon K.2: 2/S only	K.1: saloon only K.2: 2/S only	2/S only

Model:	L-type Magna	PA & PB Midgets	NA Magnette (incl. NB & ND)
Approx. production period	Early 1933 to early 1934	Early 1934 to mid-1936	Early 1934 to late 1936
Number produced	486 L.1 90 L.2	2000 PA (less 27 conv. to PB) 526 PB (incl. 27 conv. to PB)	738
No. of cylinders	Six	Four	Six
Bore & stroke	57×71 mm	PA: 57×83 mm = 847 c.c. PB: 60×83 mm = 939 c.c.	57×83 mm
Capacity	1087 c.c.		1271 c.c.
Valve location & operation	O.h.c. driven through vertical dynamo	O.h.c. driven through vertical dynamo	O.h.c. driven through vertical dynamo
No. & type of carburetters	2 semi-d.d. SU	2 semi-d.d. SU	2 semi-d.d. SU
Power output	41 b.h.p. @ 5500 r.p.m.	PA: 34.9 b.h.p. @ 5600 r.p.m. PB: 43.3 b.h.p. @ 5500 r.p.m.	56.6 b.h.p. @ 5700 r.p.m.
Clutch & Gearbox	Dry clutch Manual 'crash' (4-sp.)	Dry clutch Manual 'crash' (4-sp.)	Dry clutch Manual 'crash' (4-sp.)
Type of suspension	$\frac{1}{2}$-elliptic F+R (sliding trunnion)	$\frac{1}{2}$-elliptic F+R (sliding trunnion)	$\frac{1}{2}$-elliptic F+R (sliding trunnion)
Type of road wheels	Centre-lock wire spoke	Centre-lock wire spoke	Centre-lock wire spoke
Brake type & drum diam.	12″ drum cable-operated	12″ drum cable-operated	12″ drum cable-operated
Wheelbase	$7' 10\frac{3}{16}''$	$7' 3\frac{5}{16}''$	$8' 0''$
Track	$3' 6''$ F+R	$3' 6''$ F+R	$3' 9''$ F+R
Available coachwork	L.1: 4/S & closed L.2: 2/S only	2/S, 4/S & 'Airline' Coupé	2/S, 4/S, 2–4/S & 'Airline' Coupé

NE Magnette	KN Magnette	Q-type Midget	R-type Midget
Late 1934	Mid-1934 to late 1935	Mid to late 1934	Mid-1935
7	201	8	10
Six	Six	Four	Four
57×83 mm	57×83 mm	57×73 mm	57×73 mm
1271 c.c.	1271 c.c.	746 c.c.	746 c.c.
O.h.c. driven through vertical dynamo	O.h.c. driven through vertical dynamo	O.h.c. driven through vertical dynamo	O.h.c. driven through dummy vertical dynamo
2 semi-d.d. SU	2 semi-d.d. SU	Single SU with Zoller super-charger	Single SU with Zoller super-charger
74 b.h.p. @ 6500 r.p.m.	56.6 b.h.p. @ 5700 r.p.m.	Depending on state of tune	Depending on state of tune
Dry clutch Manual 'crash' (4-sp.)	Dry clutch Manual 'crash' (4-sp.)	Preselector 4-sp. with overload clutch	Preselector 4-sp. with overload clutch
½-elliptic F+R (sliding trunnion)	½-elliptic F+R (sliding trunnion)	½-elliptic F+R (sliding trunnion)	Independent F+R by wishbone & torsion bar
Centre-lock wire spoke	Centre-lock wire spoke	Centre-lock wire spoke	Centre-lock wire spoke
12″ drum cable-operated	13″ drum cable-operated	12″ drum cable-operated	12″ drum (Girling) cable-operated
8′ 0″	9′ 0″	7′ 10$\frac{3}{16}$″	7′ 6½″
3′ 9″ F+R	4′ 0″ F+R	3′ 9″ F+R	3′ 10$\frac{3}{8}$″ F, 3′ 9½″ R
2/S	Saloon only	2/S only	Single-seater only

Model:	SA or 2-Litre	TA Midget	VA or 1½-Litre
Approx. production period	Early 1936 to late 1939	Mid-1936 to early 1939	Mid-1937 to late 1939
Number produced	2738	3003	2407
No. of cylinders	Six	Four	Four
Bore & stroke	Early: 69 × 102 mm	63.5 × 102 mm	69.5 × 102 mm
Capacity	= 2288 c.c. Later: 69.5 × 102 mm = 2322 c.c.	1292 c.c.	1548 c.c.
Valve location & operation	Pushrod o.h.v.	Pushrod o.h.v.	Pushrod o.h.v.
No. & type of carburetters	2 d.d. SU	2 semi-d.d. SU	2 semi-d.d. SU
Power output	75.3 b.h.p. @ 4300 r.p.m.	52.4 b.h.p. @ 5000 r.p.m.	54 b.h.p. @ 4500 r.p.m.
Clutch & Gearbox	Wet cork clutch Manual 4-sp. box, 'crash' later replaced by part-synchro	Wet clork clutch Manual 4-sp. box, part-synchro (except earliest cars)	Wet cork clutch (dry on later cars) Part-synchro 4-sp. manual gearbox
Type of suspension	½-elliptic F+R (shackled)	½-elliptic F+R (sliding trunnion)	½-elliptic F+R (shackled)
Type of road wheels	Centre-lock wire spoke	Centre-lock wire spoke	Centre-lock wire spoke
Brake type & drum diam.	Lockheed hydraulic 12″ drum	Lockheed hydraulic 9″ drum	Lockheed hydraulic 10″ drum
Wheelbase	10′ 3″	7′ 10″	9′ 0″
Track	4′ 5⅜″ F+R	3′ 9″ F+R	4′ 2″ F+R
Available coachwork	Saloon, 4/S & drophead coupé	2/S, 'Airline' coupé & drophead coupé	Saloon, 4/S & drophead coupé

VA or 6-Litre	TB Midget	TC Midget	Y-type or 1¼-Litre
ate 1938 to ate 1939	Early to late 1939	Late 1945 to late 1949	Early 1947 to late 1953
69	379	10000	6158 YA 1301 YB 877 YT
ix	Four	Four	Four
3 × 102 mm	66.5 × 90 mm	66.5 × 90 mm	66.5 × 90 mm
561 c.c.	1250 c.c.	1250 c.c.	1250 c.c.
ushrod o.h.v.	Pushrod o.h.v.	Pushrod o.h.v.	Pushrod o.h.v.
semi-d.d. SU	2 semi-d.d. SU	2 semi-d.d. SU	1 semi-d.d. SU (2 on YT)
5.5 b.h.p. @ 400 r.p.m.	54.4 b.h.p. @ 5200 r.p.m.	54.4 b.h.p. @ 5200 r.p.m.	46 b.h.p. @ 4800 r.p.m. (YT as TC)
Dry clutch Part-synchro 4-sp. manual gearbox	Dry clutch Part-synchro 4-sp. manual gearbox	Dry clutch Part-synchro 4-sp. manual gearbox	Dry clutch Part-synchro 4-sp. manual gearbox
-elliptic F+R (shackled)	½-elliptic F+R (sliding trunnion)	½-elliptic F+R (shackled)	F coil+wishbone (YB with anti-roll bar) R ½-elliptic
Centre-lock wire spoke	Centre-lock wire spoke	Centre-lock wire spoke	Bolt-on disc (smaller on YB)
Lockheed hydraulic 4" drum	Lockheed hydraulic 9" drum	Lockheed hydraulic 9" drum	Lockheed hydraulic (2LS front on YB) 9" drum
0' 3" 5⅜" F 8¼" R	7' 10" 3' 9" F+R	7' 10" 3' 9" F+R	8' 3" 3' 11⅜" F 4' 2" R
saloon, 4/S & drophead coupé	2/S & drophead coupé	2/S only	YA & YB: saloon YT: 4/S only

Model:	TD Midget (incl. TD Mk. II	TF Midget (1250 & 1500)	ZA & ZB Magnette
Approx. production period	Late 1949 to late 1953	Late 1953 to early 1955	Late 1953 to late 1958
Number produced	29664	TF. 1250: 6200 TF. 1500: 3400	ZA: 12754 ZB: 23846
No. of cylinders	Four	Four	Four
Bore & stroke	66.5 × 90 mm	66.5 × 90 mm	73.025 × 88.9 mm
Capacity	1250 c.c.	= 1250 c.c. or 72 × 90 mm = 1466 c.c.	1489 c.c.
Valve location & operation	Pushrod o.h.v.	Pushrod o.h.v.	Pushrod o.h.v.
No. & type of carburetters	2 semi-d.d. SU (larger on Mk. II)	2 semi-d.d. SU	2 semi-d.d. SU (larger on ZB)
Power output	54.4 b.h.p. @ 5200 r.p.m. (Mk. II: 57 b.h.p. @ 5500 r.p.m.)	57 b.h.p. @ 5500 r.p.m. or 63 b.h.p. @ 5000 r.p.m.	ZA: 60 b.h.p. @ 4600 r.p.m. ZB: 68.4 b.h.p. @ 5250 r.p.m.
Clutch & Gearbox	Dry clutch Part-synchro 4-sp. manual gearbox	Dry clutch Part-synchro 4-sp. manual gearbox	Dry clutch Part-synchro 4-sp. manual gearbox
Type of suspension	F coil & wishbone R ½-elliptic	F coil & wishbone R ½-elliptic	F coil & wishbone R ½-elliptic
Type of road wheels	Bolt-on disc (unperforated on early cars)	Bolt-on disc (centre-lock wire spoke optional)	Bolt-on disc
Brake type & drum diam.	Lockheed hydraulic (2 LS front) 9″ drum	Lockheed hydraulic (2 LS front) 9″ drum	Lockheed hydraulic (2 LS front) 10″ drum
Wheelbase	7′ 10″	7′ 10″	8′ 6″
Track	3′ 11⅜″ F 4′ 2″ R	3′ 11⅜″ F 4′ 2″ R (with disc wheels)	4′ 3″ F+R
Available coachwork	2/S only	2/S only	Saloon only

MGA 1500	MGA 'Twin Cam'	MGA 1600 (Mk. I & Mk. II)	Magnette Mark III
Mid-1955 to early 1959 58750	Early 1958 to early 1960 2111	Early 1959 to mid-1962 Mk I: 31501 Mk II: 8719	Early 1959 to late 1961 15676
Four 73.025 × 88.9 mm 1489 c.c.	Four 75.414 × 88.9 mm 1588 c.c.	Four Mk I: 75.414 × 88.9 mm = 1588 c.c. Mk. II: 76.2 × 88.9 mm = 1622 c.c.	Four 73.025 × 88.9 mm 1489 c.c.
Pushrod o.h.v.	Twin o.h.c. (chain-driven)	Pushrod o.h.v.	Pushrod o.h.v.
2 semi-d.d. SU	2 semi-d.d. SU	2 semi-d.d. SU	2 semi-d.d. SU
Early: 68 b.h.p. @ 5500 r.p.m. Later: 72 b.h.p. @ 5500 r.p.m.	108 b.h.p. @ 6700 r.p.m.	Mk I: 80 b.h.p. @ 5600 r.p.m. Mk II: 93 b.h.p. @ 5500 r.p.m.	66.5 b.h.p. @ 5200 r.p.m.
Dry clutch Part-synchro 4-sp. manual gearbox	Dry clutch Part-synchro 4-sp. manual gearbox	Dry clutch Part-synchro 4-sp. manual gearbox	Dry clutch Part-synchro 4-sp. manual gearbox
F coil & wishbone R $\frac{1}{2}$-elliptic	F coil & wishbone R $\frac{1}{2}$-elliptic	F coil & wishbone R $\frac{1}{2}$-elliptic	F coil & wishbone R $\frac{1}{2}$-elliptic
Bolt-on disc (centre-lock wire spoke optional)	Centre-lock perforated disc	Bolt-on disc (centre-lock wire spoke optional)	Bolt-on disc
Lockheed hydraulic (2 LS front) 10″ drum	Dunlop disc, F+R	Lockheed disc at F, drum at R	Girling hydraulic (2 LS front) 9″ drum
7′ 10″ 3′ 11$\frac{1}{2}$″ F 4′ 0$\frac{3}{4}$″ (with disc wheels)	7′ 10″ 3′ 11$\frac{29}{32}$″ F 4′ 0$\frac{7}{8}$″ R	7′ 10″ 3′ 11$\frac{1}{2}$″ F 4′ 0$\frac{3}{4}$″ R (with disc wheels)	8′ 3$\frac{3}{16}$″ 4′ 0$\frac{9}{16}$″ F 4′ 1$\frac{7}{8}$″ R
2/S & fixed head coupé	2/S & fixed head coupé	2/S & fixed head coupé	Saloon only

Model:	Midget Mk. I (GAN. I & GAN. 2)	Magnette Mark IV	MGB (Mk. I, II & III)
Approx. production period	Mid-1961 to early 1964	Late 1961 to early 1968	Late 1962 onwards
Number produced	GAN. 1: 16080 GAN. 2: 9601	13738	Over 250,000 to date
No. of cylinders	Four	Four	Four
Bore & stroke Capacity	GAN. 1: 62.9 × 76.2 mm = 948 c.c. GAN. 2: 64.58 × 83.72 mm = 1098 c.c.	76.2 × 88.9 mm 1622 c.c.	80.26 × 88.9 mm 1798 c.c.
Valve location & operation	Pushrod o.h.v.	Pushrod o.h.v.	Pushrod o.h.v.
No. & type of carburetters	2 semi-d.d. SU	2 semi-d.d. SU	2 semi-d.d. SU
Power output	GAN. 1: 46.4 @ 5500 r.p.m. GAN. 2: 55 @ 5500 r.p.m.	68 b.h.p. @ 5000 r.p.m.	95 b.h.p. @ 5400 r.p.m.
Clutch & Gearbox	Dry clutch Part-synchro 4-sp. manual gearbox	Dry clutch Part-synchro 4-sp. manual gearbox (automatic optional)	Dry clutch Part-synchro 4-sp. manual gearbox (Mk. I) All-synchro 4-sp. manual gearbox (automatic optional) on Mk. II & III
Type of suspension	F coil & wishbone R ¼-elliptic	F coil & wishbone with anti-roll bar R ½-elliptic with stabilizer	F coil & wishbone (later with anti-roll bar) R ½-elliptic
Type of road wheels	Bolt-on disc (centre-lock wire spoke optional from early 1963)	Bolt-on disc	Bolt-on disc (later 'Rostyle') (centre-lock wire spoke optional)
Brake type & drum diam.	Lockheed hydraulic, 2LS front, with 7″ drums (disc front on GAN. 2)	Girling hydraulic (2LS front) 9″ drum	Lockheed disc at F, drum at R
Wheelbase Track	6′ 8″ GAN. 1: 3′ 9¾″ F, 3′ 8¾″ R GAN. 2: 3′ 10 5/16″ F, 3′ 8¾″ R (with disc wheels)	8′ 4¼″ 4′ 2⅝″ F, 4′ 3⅜″ R	7′ 7″ 4′ 1″ F, 4′ 1¼″ R (with disc wheels or 'Rostyle')
Available coachwork	2/S only	Saloon only	2/S only & GT coupé (from late 1965)

MG 1100 (Mk. I & II) MG 1300 (Mk. I & II)	Midget Mk. II (GAN. 3)	Midget Mk. III (GAN. 4 & GAN. 5)	MGC
Late 1962 to mid-1971 1100: 116,827 1300: 26240	Early 1964 to late 1966 26601	Late 1966 onwards Over 50000 to date	Late 1967 to late 1969 2/S: 4542 GT: 4457
Four (transverse) 64.58 × 83.72 mm = 1098 c.c. or 70.63 × 81.33 mm = 1275 c.c.	Four 64.58 × 83.72 mm 1098 c.c.	Four 70.63 × 81.33 mm 1275 c.c.	Six 83.362 × 88.9 mm 2912 c.c.
Pushrod o.h.v.	Pushrod o.h.v.	Pushrod o.h.v.	Pushrod o.h.v.
2 semi-d.d. SU (single on early 1300 and with auto. transmission)	2 semi-d.d. SU	2 semi-d.d. SU	2 hor. SU
1100: 55 b.h.p. @ 5500 r.p.m. 1300: 70 b.h.p. @ 6000 r.p.m. (60 or 65 on early 1300)	59 b.h.p. @ 5750 r.p.m.	65 b.h.p. @ 6000 r.p.m.	145 b.h.p. @ 5250 r.p.m.
Front drive through dry clutch to part-synchro 4-sp. manual gearbox (all-synchro from early 1968). Automatic optional, 1967/8	Dry clutch Part-synchro 4-sp. manual gearbox	Dry clutch Part-synchro 4-sp. manual gearbox	Dry clutch All-synchro 4-sp. manual gearbox (automatic optional)
'Hydrolastic' (fluid-filled) independent, F+R	F coil & wishbone R ½-elliptic	F coil & wishbone R ½-elliptic	F torsion bar & wishbone with anti-roll bar R ½-elliptic
Bolt-on disc	Bolt-on disc (centre-lock wire spoke optional)	GAN. 4: bolt-on disc GAN. 5: 'Rostyle' bolt-on (centre-lock wire spoke optional)	Bolt-on disc (centre-lock wire spoke optional)
Lockheed disc at F, drum at R	Lockheed disc at F, drum at R	Lockheed disc at F, drum at R	Lockheed disc at F, drum at R, servo-assisted
7' 9½" 4' 3¾" F, 4' 2⅞" R	6' 8" 3' 10$\frac{5}{16}$" F, 3' 8¾" R (with disc wheels)	6' 8" 3' 10$\frac{9}{16}$" F, 3' 9" R (with 'Rostyle' wheels)	7' 7" 4' 2" F, 4' 1½" R (with disc wheels)
Saloon only (2-door & 4-door)	2/S only	2/S only	2/S & GT coupé

Appendix II

A selection of the more significant M.G. successes in races, rallies and trials, 1925–1968

Note: In the case of competition results it was thought preferable not to maintain a single standard throughout. It may be significant in the early days of the marque to record a relatively minor success that would go unnoticed later on; hence the inclusion of some lesser awards gained in the 'twenties, for example. Again, a mere class win in a major event such as Le Mans may be more meritorious than outright victory in a lesser race, so the list is not confined to victories.

The standard adopted therefore varies, and it is also influenced by the extent of M.G. works participation in competitions. Between 1930 and 1935 the M.G. Car Company participated in racing with cars designed for that purpose. These same cars continued to achieve successes occasionally until shortly after the Second World War, while works-built cars were also used effectively in trials and rallies until 1939. Subsequently, the M.G.s that took part in competitions were mostly privately owned production models, suitably modified, and the successes achieved were correspondingly less spectacular. From 1955, however, when the BMC Competitions Department was formed, M.G.s were prepared and entered for major rallies on suitable occasions, and from 1963 to 1968 the factory entered cars for selected major races. Minor successes gained during these periods of official participation are therefore omitted. So, too, are the very few achieved subsequently, as this would lend undue significance to relatively minor accomplishments.

1925
Three 1st class awards, London/Land's End Trial.
Two 1st class awards, MCC High-Speed Trial, Brooklands.

1926
1st class award, MCC High-Speed Trial, Brooklands.

1927
1st, San Martin Circuit Race, near Buenos Aires.

1929
3rd FTD, Mont des Mules Hillclimb, Monte Carlo.
Five 1st class awards, JCC High-Speed Trial, Brooklands.
Five 1st class awards, MCC High-Speed Trial, Brooklands.

1930
Class win, Mont des Mules Hillclimb, Monte Carlo.

Class win, Zbrazlav-Jiloviste Hillclimb, Czechoslovakia.
Team Prize, Double Twelve Race, Brooklands.
18 1st class awards, London/Land's End Trial.

1931
1-2-3-4-5 and Team Prize, Double Twelve Race, Brooklands.
1-2-3 and Team Prize, Saorstat Cup Race, Dublin.
1st and 3rd, Irish Grand Prix.
1st and 3rd, RAC Tourist Trophy Race, Northern Ireland.
3rd (1st in class) and Team Prize, 500 Miles Race, Brooklands.

1932
3rd, 1000 Miles Race, Brooklands.
Class win, German Grand Prix, Nürburgring.
1st, Phoenix Park Junior Race, Dublin.
2nd and 3rd, Phoenix Park Senior Race, Dublin.
3rd, RAC Tourist Trophy Race, Northern Ireland.
1st, 1-2-3 in class and Team Prize, 500 Miles Race, Brooklands.
Class win, Mont des Mules Hillclimb, Monte Carlo.
Two class wins, Shelsley Walsh Hillclimb.
Three class wins, Craigantlet Hillclimb, Belfast.

1933
1-2 in class and Team Prize, Mille Miglia, Italy.
2-3-4 (1-2-3 in class), International Trophy Race, Brooklands.
3rd, Australian Grand Prix.
Class win, Avusrennen, Germany.
Class win, Eifelrennen, Germany.
Class win, Le Mans 24 Hours Race, France.
3rd, British Empire Trophy Race, Brooklands.
2nd, Mannin Beg Race, Isle of Man.
1st, India Trophy Race, Brooklands.
1st, Relay Race, Brooklands.
1st, Phoenix Park Junior Race, Dublin.
1st, Coppa Acerbo Junior Race, Italy.
1st, Southport 100 Miles Race.
1st, 2nd and 4th, RAC Tourist Trophy Race, Northern Ireland.
1st and 2nd, 500 Miles Race, Brooklands.
FTD, Craigantlet Hillclimb, Belfast.
FTD, Mont des Mules Hillclimb, Monte Carlo.
Class wins in Freiburg and Riesengeberg Hillclimbs.

1934
1st (tie), Bol d'Or 24 Hours Race, Montlhéry, France.
2nd and 3rd, Australian Grand Prix.
Class win, International Trophy Race, Brooklands.
Class win, Avusrennen, Germany.
1-2-3-4-5, Mannin Beg Race, Isle of Man.
Class win, Eifelrennen, Germany.
1st and 3rd, Winter 100 Race, Australia.
4th (1st in class), Le Mans 24 Hours Race, France.

1st and Team Prize, British Empire Trophy Race, Brooklands.

1st, ARCA 'G.P. of America'.

3rd, Relay Race, Brooklands.

1-2-3, Coppa Acerbo Junior Race, Italy.

1st, Prix de Berne, Switzerland.

1st and 3rd, 'G.P.s de France' 1100 c.c. Race, Montlhéry, France.

1st, RAC Tourist Trophy Race, Northern Ireland.

1st, Phoenix Park Junior Race, Dublin.

3rd (1st in class), 500 Miles Race, Brooklands.

1st, Circuit of Modena, Italy.

3rd, Bray 'Round the Houses' Race, Ireland.

2nd and 3rd, County Down Trophy Race, Ireland.

2nd and 3rd, Nuffield Trophy Race, Donington Park.

Winner, 1100 c.c. Championship of Italy, 1934.

FTD and four class wins, Craigantlet Hillclimb, Belfast.

Class wins in Felsberg, Riesengeberg, Gabelbach, Shelsley Walsh, Kesselberg, Klausen, Lueckendorfer, Freiburg, Stelvio, Mont Ventoux and Vermiccino Hillclimbs.

Winner, Gloucester Cup, Colmore Trophy and Vesey Cup Trials.

35 1st class awards, London/Land's End Trial.

39 1st class awards, London/Edinburgh Trial.

1935

3rd (1st in class) and Team Prize, International Trophy Race, Brooklands.

1st, Bol d'Or 24 Hours Race, Montlhéry, France.

1-2-3-4, Australian Grand Prix.

1st, Centenary Grand Prix, Australia.

Class win, 'G.P.s de France', Montlhéry, France.

Class win, G.P. des Frontières, Belgium.

9th (1st in class), Le Mans 24 Hours Race, France.

1-2-3 in class, Eifelrennen, Germany.

1st, County Down Trophy Race, Ireland.

4th (1st in class), British Empire Trophy Race, Brooklands.

3rd, Nuffield Trophy Race, Donington Park.

2nd and Team Prize, Leinster Trophy Race, Ireland.

2nd and 3rd, Grand Prix d'Orléans, France.

4th, Albi Grand Prix, France.

2nd, Southport 100 Miles Race.

1st, 3rd and Team Prize, Phoenix Park 200 Miles Race, Ireland.

5th (1st in class), 500 Miles Race, Brooklands.

2nd (1st in class), Coupe de l'Argent Race, Montlhéry, France.

FTD, Craigantlet Hillclimb, Belfast.

Class wins in La Turbie, Stelvio, Grossglockner, Shelsley Walsh and Feldberg Hillclimbs.

Premier Award and Team Prize, Welsh Rally.

1936

1st, Australian Tourist Trophy Race.

1st, G.P. des Frontières, Belgium.

1st, Centenary 100 Miles Race, Australia.

1st in 1500 c.c. race, Circuit of Ceskobrodsky, Czechoslovakia.

1st in 1500 c.c. race, Circuit of Lochotin, Czechoslovakia.
1st, Kimberley 100 Miles Race, South Africa.
2nd (1st in class), Bol d'Or 24 Hours Race, Montlhéry, France.
2nd, County Down Trophy Race, Ireland.
1st, Limerick 'Round the Houses' Race, Ireland.
1st and 3rd, Phoenix Park 200 Miles Race, Dublin.
1st, Southport 100 Miles Race.
Two class wins, 500 Miles Race, Brooklands.
Class wins in La Turbie, Feldberg, Ratisbona, Bussaco, Santarem, Mount
   Washington and Craigantlet Hillclimbs.
Winner, MCC Trials Championship, 1936.

1937
1st and 2nd, Australian Grand Prix.
3rd, Rand 170 Miles Race, South Africa.
2nd, Rand 120 Miles Race, South Africa.
3rd (1st in class), International Trophy Race, Brooklands.
2nd, Leinster Trophy Race, Ireland.
1st, Cork Grand Prix, Ireland.
Class win, 'G.P.s de France', Montlhéry, France.
2nd and 3rd, Ulster Trophy Race, Northern Ireland.
Team Prize, Donington Park 12 Hours Race.
3rd, Phoenix Park 100 Miles Race, Dublin.
1st, Phillip Island Race, Australia.
1st, Kimberley 100 Miles Race, South Africa.
Winner, MCC Trials Championship, 1937.

1938
4th, International Trophy Race, Brooklands.
2nd (1st in class), Bol d'Or 24 Hours Race, Montlhéry, France.
1st, Limerick 'Round the Houses' Race, Ireland.
2nd, Phoenix Park Handicap Race, Dublin.
3rd, Australian Grand Prix.
1st and 2nd, Alexandria Bay Race, USA.
2nd and 3rd, South Australia Grand Prix.
1st and 3rd, South Australia 50 Miles Race.
Class win, 200 Miles Race, Brooklands.
1st, Southport President's Cup Race.
Class win, British Empire Trophy Race, Brooklands.
1st and Team Award, Derbyshire Trial.
1st, Paris/St Raphael Rally, France.
1st, Circuit of Ireland Trial.
1-2-3 in class, Scottish Rally.
1-2-3-4, New South Wales 300 Miles Trial, Australia.

1939
3rd, G.P. des Frontières, Belgium.
Class win, Bol d'Or 24 Hours Race, Montlhéry, France.
1st, Australian Grand Prix.
2nd, Leinster Trophy Race, Ireland.
2nd and 3rd, Phoenix Park Handicap Race, Dublin.

Appendix II

2nd, Coupe de la Libération Race, Paris.

1946
2nd, Coupe du Salon Race, Paris.
1-2-3, New South Wales G.P., Australia.
1st, Argentine 100 Hours Trial.

1947
6th, 7th and Fastest Lap, Rheims Cup Race, France.
5th, Lyons Cup Race, France.
1-2-3, Australian Grand Prix.
1-2-3, Prix de la Blècherette Race, Lausanne, Switzerland.
1-2-3, O'Boyle Trophy Race, Curragh, Ireland.
1st and 2nd, Ulster Trophy Handicap Race, Ballyclare, Northern Ireland.
FTD, Kilternan, Ballinascorney and Sierre/Montana Hillclimbs.
1st, Chappell Cup, Keller Cup and Colmore Trophy Trials.
1st and 2nd, Circuit of Ireland Trial.
Class win, Highland Three Days Rally.

1948
2nd, Australian Grand Prix.
1st, Berne Sports Car G.P., Switzerland.
3rd, Watkins Glen G.P., USA.
2nd and 3rd, Leinster Trophy Race, Ireland.
1st and 2nd, O'Boyle Trophy Race, Curragh, Ireland.
1-2-3 in class, Vue des Alpes Hillclimb, Switzerland.
FTD, Enniskerry and Killakee Hillclimbs.

1949
2nd, Berne Sports Car G.P., Switzerland.
1st, Leinster Trophy Race, Ireland.
1-2-3, O'Boyle Trophy Race, Curragh, Ireland.
2nd, Fairfield Memorial Trophy Race, South Africa.
2nd in class, Spa/Francorchamps 24 Hours Race, Belgium.
3rd in class, Lisbon Rally, Portugal.
1st and 2nd in class and Coupe des Dames, Alpine Trial.
Team Prize, Circuit of Ireland Trial.

1950
2nd and 3rd, Leinster Trophy Race, Ireland.
1st and 3rd, O'Boyle Trophy Race, Curragh, Ireland.
2nd in class, Le Mans 24 Hours Race, France.
1-2-3 in class, RAC Tourist Trophy Race, Northern Ireland.
2-3-4 in class, Production Car Race, Silverstone.
3rd, Champion Trophy Race, Dundrod, Northern Ireland.
1st and 3rd, Van Riebeck Trophy Race, South Africa.
1st and 3rd, Fairfield Memorial Trophy Race, South Africa.
1st and 3rd, Westhampton Races, USA.
2nd and 3rd, Palm Springs Sports Car Race, USA.
1st and 2nd in class, Palm Beach Races, USA.
Class win and Team Award, Alpine Trial.
1st and 3rd, Palm Beach '1300' Rally.

1951
3rd, Australian Jubilee Grand Prix.
3rd, Champion Trophy Race, Dundrod, Northern Ireland.
Class win, Production Car Race, Silverstone.
3rd and Team Prize, Leinster Trophy Handicap Race, Ireland.
3rd, Leinster Trophy Scratch Race, Ireland.
2nd and 3rd in class, British Empire Trophy Race, Isle of Man.
Class win, San Diego Road Race, USA.
1st, Interlaken Rally, Switzerland.
2nd, Rallye des Neiges, France.
3rd (1st in class), Paris/St Raphael Rally, France.
1st, Circuit of Ireland Trial.
1-2-3 in class, Team Prize and Coupe des Dames, Isle of Wight Rally.
Two class wins and Team Prize, Scottish Rally.
2nd and two class wins, Morecambe Rally.
1st and 3rd in class, RAC Rally of Great Britain.
3rd in class, Alpine Trial.
1st, Lakeland '300' Rally, USA.
1st, *Daily Express* Rally.

1952
1st, Helsingland Sports Car Race, Sweden.
Team Prize, Sebring 12 Hours Race, USA.
Class win, Production Car Race, Silverstone.
1st, Ulster Trophy 1300 c.c. Race, Dundrod, Northern Ireland.
2nd and 3rd, Leinster Trophy Handicap Race, Ireland.
1-2-3-4, Johore Production Car Race, Malaya.
3rd, O'Boyle Trophy Race, Curragh, Ireland.
1-2-3, Edenvale Sports Car Race, Canada.
1st and Team Award, Circuit of Ireland Trial.
3rd (1st in class), Tulip Rally, Holland.
1st, Circuit of Munster Rally, Ireland.
1st, Falkirk Rally, Scotland.
1-2-3 in class and Team Award, *Daily Express* Rally.

1953
2-3-4 in class, Sebring 12 Hours Race, USA.
Class win, Sam Collier Memorial Trophy Race, USA.
2nd and 3rd, Australian Grand Prix.
1st and 3rd in class, Production Car Race, Silverstone.
3rd in class, British Empire Trophy Race, Isle of Man.
2nd and 3rd, Omaha National Sports Car Race, USA.
2nd and 3rd, Delaware Valley Trophy Race, USA.
1st and 2nd, Winter Handicap Race, South Africa.
1-2-3 in class, Johore Production Car Race, Malaya.
Class win, RAC Tourist Trophy Race, Northern Ireland.
1-2-3 in class, RAC Rally of Great Britain.
1st, Falkirk Rally, Scotland.
3rd in class, Team Award and Coupe des Dames, Circuit of Ireland Trial.
Class win, Tulip Rally, Holland.
Class win and Team Award, Morecambe Rally.

1st and two class wins, Great American Mountain Rally, USA.
1st, Canyon Rally, Canada.
Class win, Rally to the Midnight Sun, Sweden.
3rd in class, Evian/Mont Blanc Rally, France.
1-2-3 in two classes and Team Award, *Daily Express* Rally.

1954
1st, False Bay Production Car Race, South Africa.
Class win, Mount Druitt 24 Hours Race, Australia.
Class win, Production Car Race, Silverstone.
Class win, Westhampton Production Car Race, USA.
1st, Leinster Trophy Handicap Race, Ireland.
2nd, Australian Grand Prix.
1-2-3 in class, Bogota Sports Car Race, Colombia.
2nd and 3rd and Team Award, Circuit of Ireland Trial.
Class win, RAC Rally of Great Britain.
1st and 2nd in class, British Redex Rally.

1955
1-2-3 in class, Production Car Race, Silverstone.
2nd and 3rd, Settlers' Handicap Race, South Africa.
2nd, Van Riebeck Trophy Race, South Africa.
1-2-3 in class and Team Prize, Scottish Rally.
Two class wins, RAC Rally of Great Britain.
1st and Team Award, MCC Hastings Rally.

1956
Team Prize, Sebring 12 Hours Race, USA.
1st, Cape Grand Prix, South Africa.
Winner, *Autosport* Production Sports Car Championship.
1-2-3 in class, RAC Rally of Great Britain.
Coupe des Dames, Lyons/Charbonnières Rally, France.
Team Award, Circuit of Ireland Trial.
2nd in class and Coupe des Dames, Scottish Rally.
1-2-3 in class, Geneva Rally, Switzerland.
3rd in category and Coupe des Dames, Alpine Trial.
Winner, Ladies' European Rally Championship, 1956.

1957
1st and 2nd in class and Team Prize, Sebring 12 Hours Race, USA.
2nd and 3rd in class, Mille Miglia, Italy.
2nd, Leinster Trophy Handicap Race, Ireland.
3rd, Settlers' Handicap Race, South Africa.
Coupe des Dames, Lyons/Charbonnières Rally, France.
Coupe des Dames, Liège/Rome/Liège Rally.
Winner, Ladies' European Rally Championship, 1957.

1958
3rd, *Autosport* Three Hours Race, Snetterton.
3rd in class, RAC Tourist Trophy Race, Goodwood.
Class win, BRSCC Saloon Car Racing Championship.

1959
2nd and 3rd in class, Sebring 12 Hours Race, USA.
1-2-3-4 in class, Grand Touring Race, Silverstone.
2nd and 3rd on Index, Pietermaritzburg Six Hours Race, South Africa.
3rd, Rand Nine Hours Race, South Africa.
Class win, *Autosport* Production Sports Car Championship.
3rd in class, Circuit of Ireland Trial.
2nd and 3rd in class, Acropolis Rally, Greece.

1960
3rd in class, Sebring 12 Hours Race, USA.
Class win, Le Mans 24 Hours Race, France.
2nd and 3rd, Phoenix Park Handicap Race, Dublin.
3rd, *Autosport* Three Hours Race, Snetterton.
3rd in class, RAC Tourist Trophy Race, Goodwood.
Class win, *Autosport* Production Sports Car Championship.
3rd in class, Circuit of Ireland Trial.
2nd in class, Rallye Deutschland, Germany.

1961
1st and 2nd in class, Sebring 12 Hours Race, USA.
1st and 2nd in class, RAC Rally of Great Britain.

1962
Two class wins, Monte Carlo Rally.
Class win, Tulip Rally, Holland.
Class win, Brands Hatch Six Hours Race.
Class win, Bad Homburg Rally, Germany.
Class win, Dunlop Hillclimb, Singapore.

1963
Class win, Monte Carlo Rally.
Six class wins, Riverside Sports Car Races, USA.
Class win, Le Mans 24 Hours Race, France.
1st and 2nd in class, Grand Touring Race, Silverstone.
3rd, Leinster Trophy Race, Ireland.
2nd and 3rd in class, Nürburgring 1000 Kilometres Race, Germany.
3rd (1st in class), *Autosport* Production Sports Car Championship.

1964
1st in Grand Touring Category, Monte Carlo Rally.
3rd in class, Sebring 12 Hours Race, USA.
Motor Trophy, Le Mans 24 Hours Race, France.
1st, Warwick Farm Sports Car Race, NSW, Australia.
1st and 2nd in class, Nürburgring 1000 Kilometres Race, Germany.
Class win, Grand Touring Race, Silverstone.
1st and 2nd in class, Austrian Alpine Rally.

1965
1st and 2nd in class, Sebring 12 Hours Race, USA.
2nd in class, Targa Florio, Sicily.
1st and 1-2-3 in class, Brands Hatch 1000 Miles Race.
2nd in class, Le Mans 24 Hours Race, France.

Appendix II

1-2-3-4-5, Kingsway Trophy Race, Phoenix Park, Dublin.
4th (1st in class), Bridgehampton 500 Miles Race, USA.
1st, Austrian Gold Cup Rally.
2nd in class (Midget), GT Constructors' Championship, 1965.
3rd in class (MGB), GT Constructors' Championship, 1965.

1966
3rd in GT Category (1st in class), Sebring 12 Hours Race, USA.
1st in GT Category (1st and 2nd in class), Targa Florio, Sicily.
3rd and two class wins, Brands Hatch 500 Miles Race.
1st in GT Category (1st in class), Spa 1000 Kilometres Race, Belgium.
3rd in GT Category, Circuit of Mugello Race, Italy.
1st, 84 Hours Marathon, Nürburgring, Germany.
Class win, Surfers Paradise 12 Hours Race, Queensland, Australia.
2nd and 3rd in class, Montlhéry 1000 Kilometres Race, France.
Winner, Scottish National Speed Championship, 1966.
Winner, Class 'G' Championship of the USA, 1966.
Class win, Circuit of Ireland Trial.
2nd in class, Austrian Alpine Rally.

1967
3rd in Prototype and GT Categories, Sebring 12 Hours Race, USA.
3rd in class, Targa Florio, Sicily.
Class win, Monza 1000 Kilometres Race, Italy.
Class win, Spa Sports Car G.P., Belgium.
Winner, Amasco Racing Championship, 1967.
1st, Berglandfahrt Rally, Austria.
1st, Rallye de Styrie Orientale, Austria.
Class win, London Rally.

1968
1st in Sports, 3rd in Prototype Category, Sebring 12 Hours Race, USA.
2nd in Sports Category, Targa Florio, Sicily.
Class win, 84 Hours Marathon, Nürburgring, Germany.

Appendix III
International Class Records established by M.G., 1930–1959

Note: The figures listed are international class records recognized by the FIA or its predecessor, the AIACR; the many local national class records established simultaneously with international class records—often forty or more in one record attempt—are not listed. Nor are the enormous number of circuit lap records, sprint and hillclimb records established in different capacity classes over many courses throughout the world.

Date	Place	Driver(s)	Car	Class	Records attained
Dec. 1930	Montlhéry	Eyston	EX.120 (u/s)	750 c.c.	3 up to 87.3 m.p.h.
Feb. 1931	Montlhéry	Eyston	EX.120 (s/c)	750 c.c.	5 up to 97.07 m.p.h.
Feb. 1931	Montlhéry	Eyston	EX.120 (s/c)	750 c.c.	4 up to 103.13 m.p.h.
Mar. 1931	Brooklands	Eyston	EX.120 (s/c)	750 c.c.	2 up to 97.09 m.p.h.
Sept. 1931	Montlhéry	Eyston	EX.120 (s/c)	750 c.c.	1 at 101.1 m.p.h.
Sept. 1931	Montlhéry	Eldridge	EX.127 (s/c)	750 c.c.	1 at 110.28 m.p.h.
Feb. 1932	Pendine	Eyston	EX.127 (s/c)	750 c.c.	1 at 118.39 m.p.h.
Nov. 1932	Brooklands	Hall	Midget (s/c)	750 c.c.	2 up to 74.74 m.p.h.
Dec. 1932	Montlhéry	Eyston	EX.127 (s/c)	750 c.c.	2 up to 120.56 m.p.h.
Dec. 1932	Montlhéry	Eyston, Denly & Wisdom	s/c J.3 & EX.127 (s/c)	750 c.c.	All remaining Class 'H' records.
Sept. 1933	Brooklands	Eyston	EX.127 (s/c)	750 c.c.	3 up to 106.72 m.p.h.
Oct. 1933	Montlhéry	Eyston, Wisdom, Denly & Yallop	L.2 Magna (u/s)	1100 c.c.	Various incl. 2000 m. at 80.49 m.p.h.
Oct./Nov. 1933	Montlhéry	Denly	EX.127 (s/c)	750 c.c.	11 up to 128.63 m.p.h.
Mar. 1934	Brooklands	Horton	s/c K.3 s/seater	1100 c.c.	6 incl. 117.03 miles in 1 hour
May 1934	Brooklands	Horton	s/c C-type s/seater	750 c.c.	6 up to 111.74 m.p.h.
July 1934	Brooklands	Horton	s/c K.3 s/seater	1100 c.c.	1 at 83.2 m.p.h.
Aug. 1934	Brooklands	Everitt	s/c Q-type	750 c.c.	2 up to 79.88 m.p.h.
Oct. 1934	Brooklands	Everitt	s/c Q-type	750 c.c.	2 up to 85.59 m.p.h.
Oct. 1934	Montlhéry	Eyston	EX.135 (s/c)	1100 c.c.	12 up to 128.69 m.p.h.
Dec. 1934	Montlhéry	Maillard-Brune & Druck	s/c Q-type	750 c.c.	Various up to 24 hrs at 76.30 m.p.h.
May 1935	Gyon	Kohlrausch	EX.127 (s/c)	750 c.c.	4 up to 130.51 m.p.h.
Oct. 1936	Frankfurt	Kohlrausch	EX.127 (s/c)	750 c.c.	3 up to 140.6 m.p.h.

Date	Place	Driver(s)	Car	Class	Records attained
Dec. 1936	Montlhéry	Hertzberger	s/c K.3	1100 c.c.	3 up to 109.74 m.p.h.
June 1937	Frankfurt	Gardner	ex-Horton s/c K.3 s/seater	1100 c.c.	2 up to 142.63 m.p.h.
June 1937	Montlhéry	Gardner	ex-Horton s/c K.3 s/seater	1100 c.c.	5 up to 130.52 m.p.h.
Oct. 1937	Frankfurt	Gardner	ex-Horton s/c K.3 s/seater	1100 c.c.	4 up to 148.8 m.p.h.
Nov. 1938	Frankfurt	Gardner	Gardner-M.G. s/c	1100 c.c.	2 up to 187.62 m.p.h.
May 1939	Dessau	Gardner	Gardner-M.G. s/c	1100 c.c.	3 up to 203.5 m.p.h.
June 1939	Dessau	Gardner	Gardner-M.G. s/c	1500 c.c.	3 up to 204.2 m.p.h.
Oct. 1946	Jabbeke	Gardner	Gardner-M.G. s/c	750 c.c.	3 up to 159.151 m.p.h.
July 1947	Jabbeke	Gardner	Gardner-M.G. s/c	500 c.c.	4 up to 118.061 m.p.h
Sept. 1949	Jabbeke	Gardner	Gardner-M.G. s/c	500 c.c.	3 up to 154.86 m.p.h.
July 1950	Jabbeke	Gardner	Gardner-M.G. s/c	350 c.c.	3 up to 121.09 m.p.h.
Aug. 1951	Utah	Gardner	Gardner-M.G. with s/c TD engine	1500 c.c.	6 up to 137.4 m.p.h.
Aug. 1952	Utah	Gardner	Gardner-M.G. with s/c TD engine	1500 c.c.	2 up to 189.5 m.p.h.
Aug. 1954	Utah	Eyston & Miles	EX.179 with u/s TF engine	1500 c.c.	8 up to 153.69 m.p.h.
Aug. 1956	Utah	Miles & Lockett	EX.179 with prototype Twin Cam engine (u/s)	1500 c.c.	16 up to 170.15 m.p.h.
Aug. 1957	Utah	Ash & Wisdom	EX.179 with prototype Sprite/Midget engine (u/s)	1100 c.c.	3 incl. 12 hours at 118.13 m.p.h.
Aug. 1957	Utah	Ash & Hill (P.)	As above but s/c	1100 c.c.	6 up to 143.47 m.p.h.
Aug. 1957	Utah	Moss	EX.181 with prototype Twin Cam engine (s/c)	1500 c.c.	5 up to 245.64 m.p.h.
Sept. 1959	Utah	Wisdom, Ehrman & Leavens	EX.219 with Sprite/Midget engine (s/c)	1100 c.c.	15 up to 146.95 m.p.h.
Sept. 1959	Utah	Hill (P.)	EX.181 with enlarged Twin Cam engine (s/c)	2000 c.c.	6 up to 254.91 m.p.h.

Appendix IVa

Total Annual Production of M.G.s, 1923–1939 inclusive

NOTES

1. Pre-1927 production figures have been estimated, as has the total for 1939.
2. As far as possible, annual totals have been drawn up by calendar (not financial) year.
3. There are no reliable figures on record for pre-war M.G. exports.
4. The total number of M.G.s built before the opening of the Abingdon factory in late 1929 is approximately 2000.
5. The grand total of M.G. production pre-war is approximately 22,500.

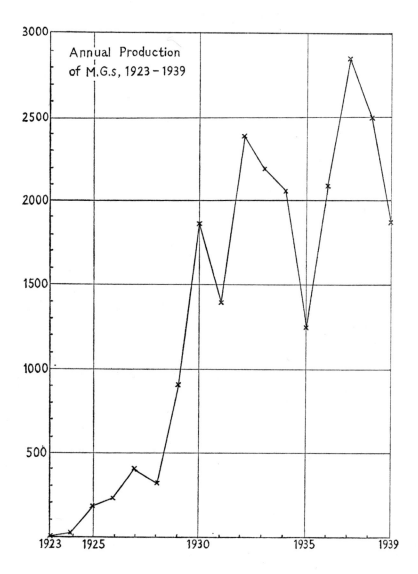

Annual Production
of M.G.s, 1923 – 1939

Appendix IVb

Total Annual Production and Exports of Abingdon-built M.G.s, 1945–1971 inclusive

NOTES

1. All totals have been drawn up by calendar (not financial) year.

2. M.G.s built elsewhere in the BMC or BLMC organization have not been included. From 1959 to 1971 inclusive, 172,481 M.G. saloons were built outside Abingdon. The number of these cars exported is not known.

3. These graphs do not represent the total number of *cars* built at or exported from Abingdon at certain periods. From 1949 to 1958 inclusive, 19,834 Rileys were also built at Abingdon. From 1960 to 1964 inclusive, 20,014 Morris Travellers and vans were built there. From 1957 to 1970 inclusive, 179,159 Austin-Healeys were built at Abingdon, followed by a further 1,022 cars built under the name of Austin Sprite in the first half of 1971. The transfer of Austin-Healey production to Abingdon in 1957 partly explains the subsequent fall in M.G. output; in 1959 and 1960, for example, the M.G. factory built appreciably more Austin-Healeys than M.G.s, and in the following two years approximately equal quantities of the two marques were produced at Abingdon.

4. M.G. production for the financial year 1970/71 constituted a new record, but a strike at a component-supplying factory caused a seven-week loss of production later on, and correspondingly reduced the total for the calendar year 1971.

5. The grand total of M.G.s built at Abingdon, 1945–1971 inclusive, is 582,609. Of these cars, 459,565 have been exported.

6. The grand total of sports cars built at Abingdon over the same period is 721,854. Of these, 610,683 have been exported, 463,379 of them to the U.S.A.

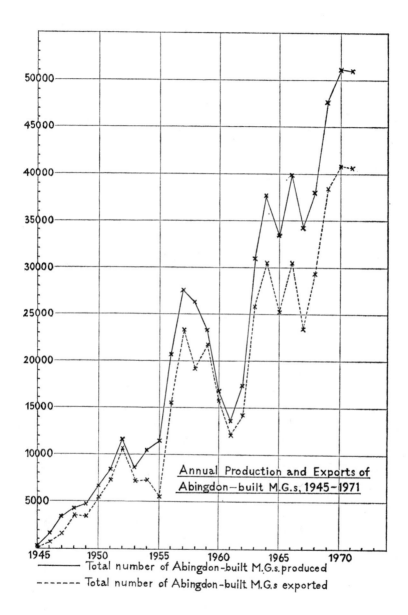

Annual Production and Exports of
Abingdon—built M.G.s, 1945—1971

———— Total number of Abingdon-built M.G.s produced

------- Total number of Abingdon-built M.G.s exported

Index

Index

Index

Index

Index